AMERICAN

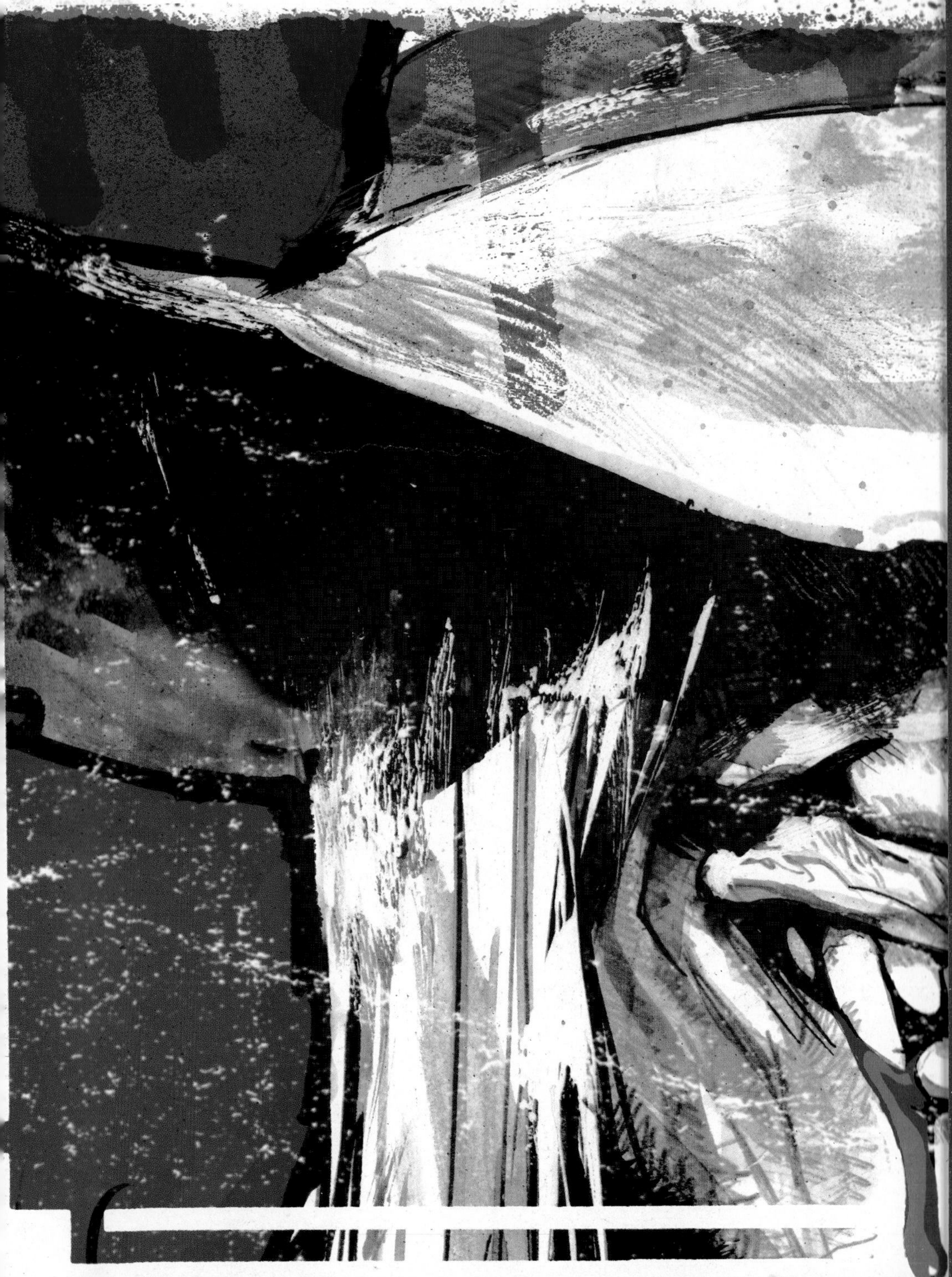

American Vampire

VAMPIRE

Scott Snyder Stephen King Writers
Rafael Albuquerque Artist
Dave McCaig Colorist
Steve Wands Letterer
American Vampire created by Scott Snyder

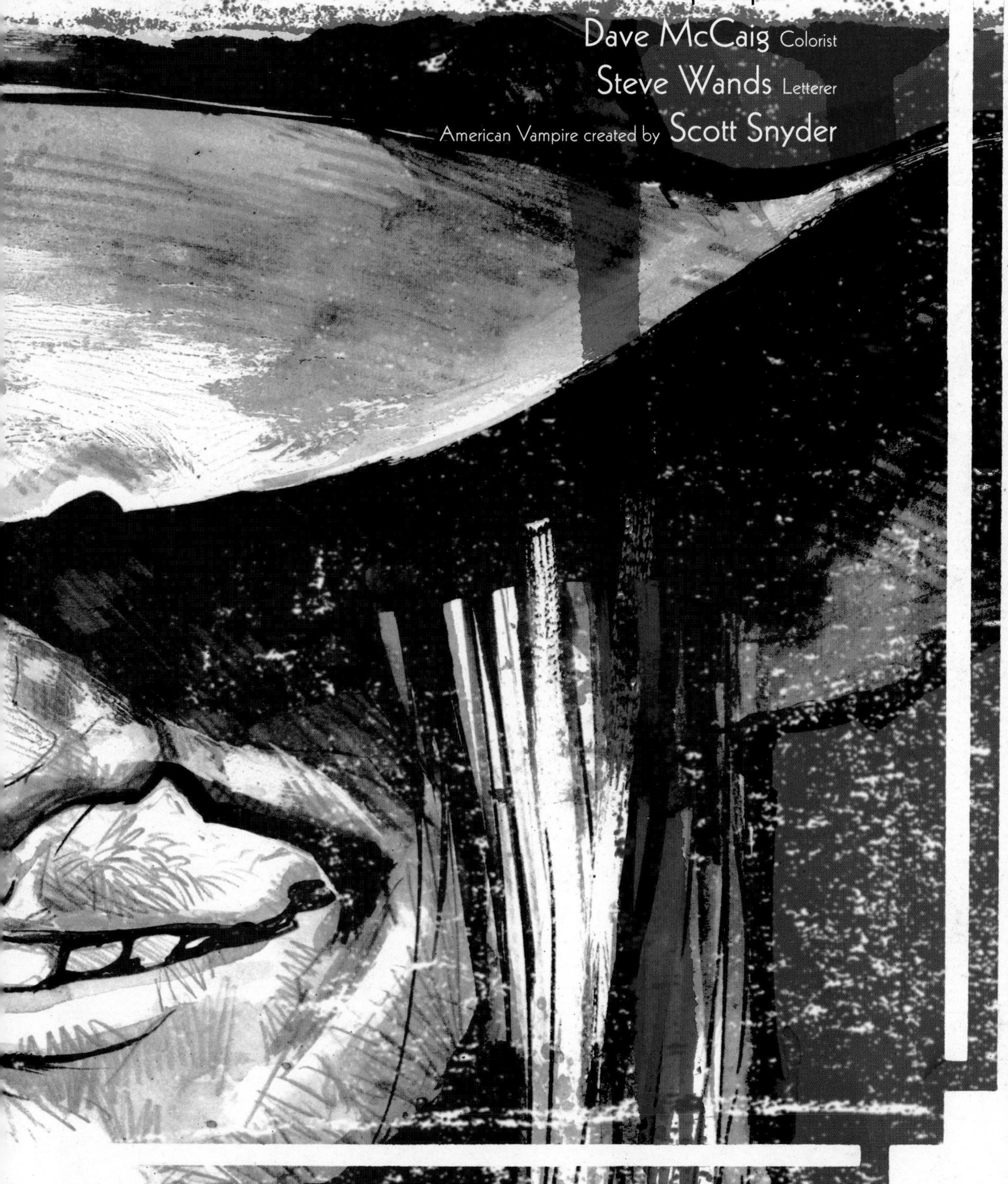

AMERICAN VAMPIRE.
Published by DC Comics. Cover, text and compilation Copyright ©
2010 Scott Snyder and Stephen King. All Rights Reserved.

Originally published in single magazine form as AMERICAN
VAMPIRE 1-5 Copyright © 2010 Scott Snyder and Stephen King.
All Rights Reserved. VERTIGO and all characters, their distinctive
likenesses, and related elements featured in this publication are
trademarks of DC Comics. The stories, characters and incidents
featured in this publication are entirely fictional. DC Comics does not
read or accept unsolicited submissions of ideas, stories or artwork.

DC Comics, 1700 Broadway, New York, NY 10019
A Warner Bros. Entertainment Company.
Printed by RR Donnelley,
Salem, VA, USA. 09/01/10 First Printing.
ISBN: 978-1-4012-2830-9
SC ISBN: 978-1-4012-2974-0

SUCK ON THIS

By

Stephen King

Here's what vampires shouldn't be: pallid detectives who drink Bloody Marys and only work at night; lovelorn southern gentlemen; anorexic teenage girls; boy-toys with big dewy eyes.

What should they be?

Killers, honey. Stone killers who never get enough of that tasty Type-A. Bad boys and girls. Hunters. In other words, Midnight America. Red, white and blue, accent on the red. Those vamps got hijacked by a lot of soft-focus romance. That's why I was so excited when Scott Snyder—a writer I knew from his excellent book of short stories, *Voodoo Heart*—mentioned to me in an email that he was in talks with the folks at Vertigo about doing a vampire comic series. His take was unique, his enthusiasm infectious.

His ambition for the continuing story of Skinner Sweet (and his victims) was awesome: nothing more or less than to trace the emergence of America through the immortal eyes of a new kind of vampire, one that can walk in the sun. I saw the potential for some terrific stories, and I also liked the resonance of the thing. There's a subtext here that whispers powerful messages about boundless American energy and that energy's darker side: a grasping, stop-at-nothing hunger for money and power.

Scott wanted a blurb.

I asked him if I could write a story instead. In fact, I wanted to light a blowtorch and burn one in, incise it like a big ole scary tattoo.

I ended up writing the Skinner Sweet origin story, and nobody is happier about that than I am. If you like it, don't thank me; I wrote it from Scott's detailed outline, adding bells and whistles here and there but never straying too far from his narrative line. Why fuck with genius?

If you don't like it, you can blame the fact that I'm new to this kind of storytelling. (Of course, if you don't like it, why the heck are you even here???) I've been a lifelong comics reader—cut my teeth on Plastic Man and Combat Casey—but in the last fifteen years or so, the medium has grown up. I owe great thanks to Mark Doyle, who edits AMVAMP. It was Mark who eased me in, sending me scripts for most excellent comix like NORTHLANDERS and SCALPED. I learned as much from these as I could (and re-read all of my son Joe Hill's *Locke & Key* stories), then listened humbly when I was instructed on some of the new rules (thought balloons, I discovered, are now passé).

It was Mark and Scott who (with great tact) corrected my layouts when they went wrong. And this, most of all: it was the remarkable Rafael Albuquerque who brought our words and descriptions to vibrant, scary life. I can't thank him enough. As a guy who can't even draw stick figures, I am in awe. Seeing those panels grow from rough sketches to finished art has been the most rewarding thing to happen in my creative life for quite some time. I can do story, and I can do dialogue, but the spell Rafa's art casts adds a whole new dimension to those things.

In the end, though, it's all about giving back the teeth that the current "sweetie-vamp" craze has, by and large, stolen from the bloodsuckers. It's about making them *scary* again. Thanks, you guys, for letting me be a part of that. Skinner Sweet really sucks, and man, that's a good thing.

Stephen King

May, 2010

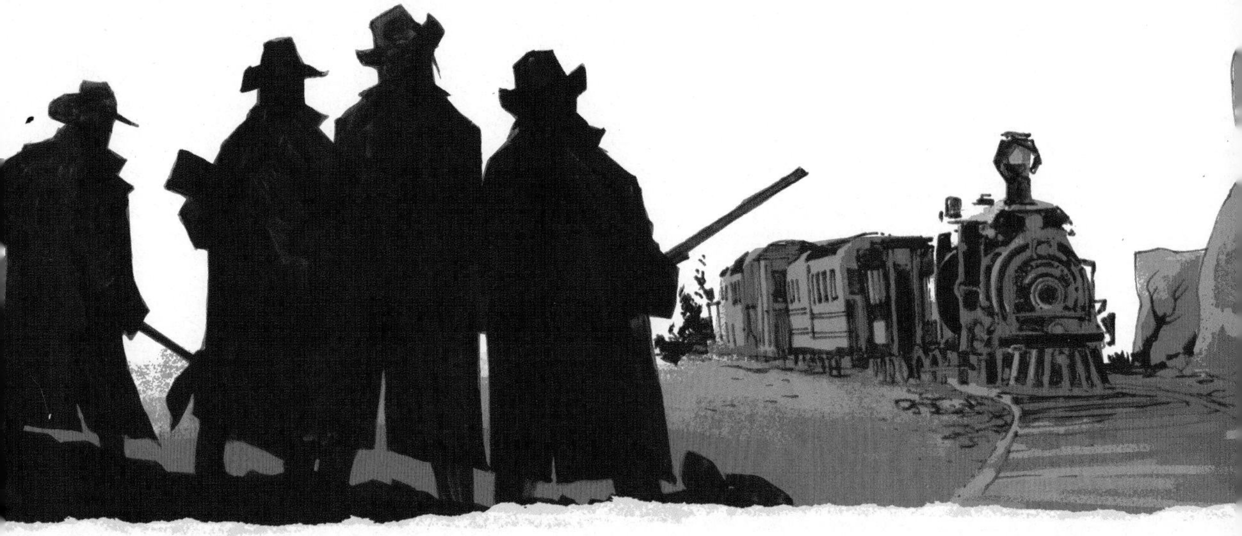

Chapter One

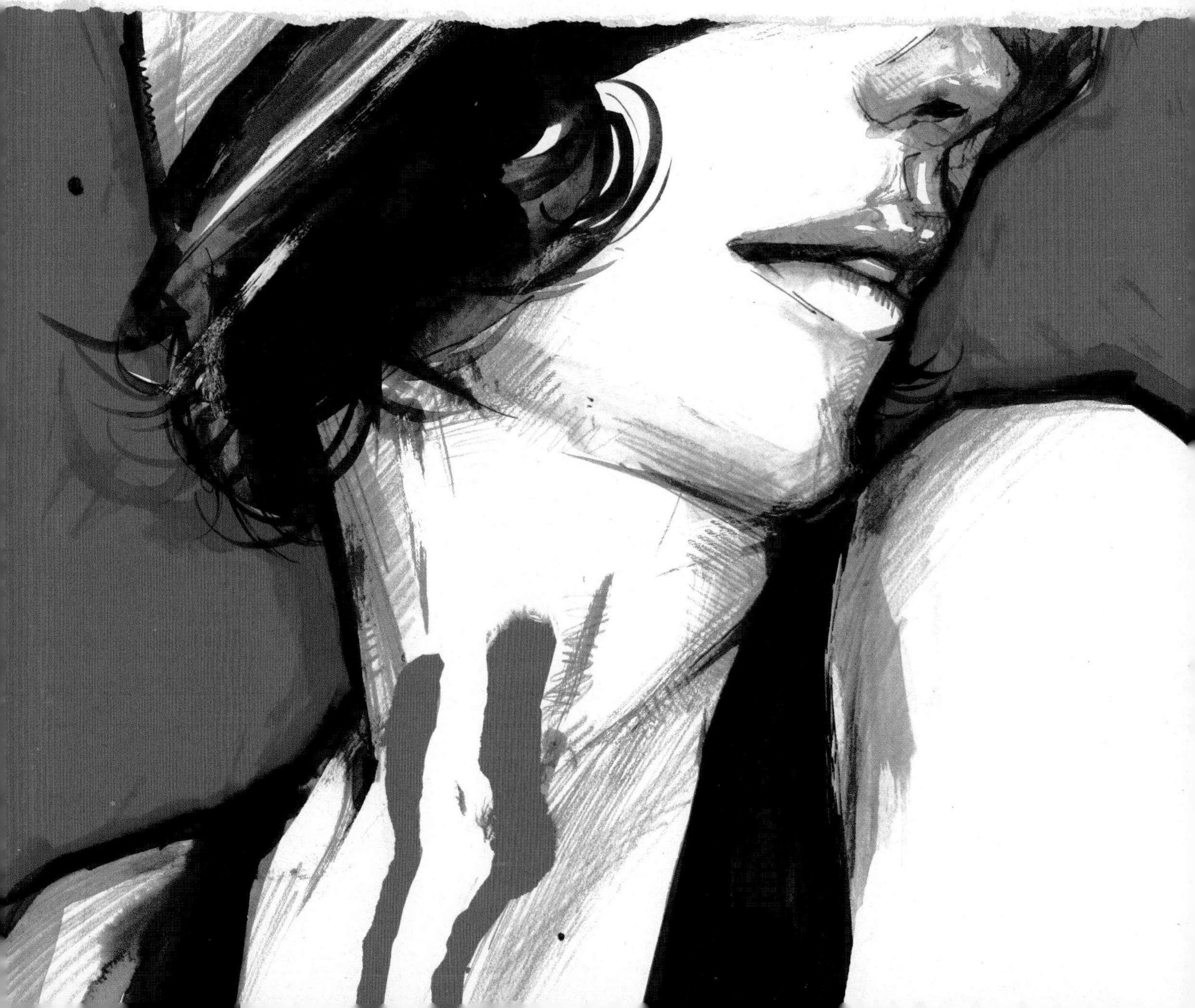

Big Break
Scott Snyder Writer

⟨❦⟩

Bad Blood
Stephen King Writer

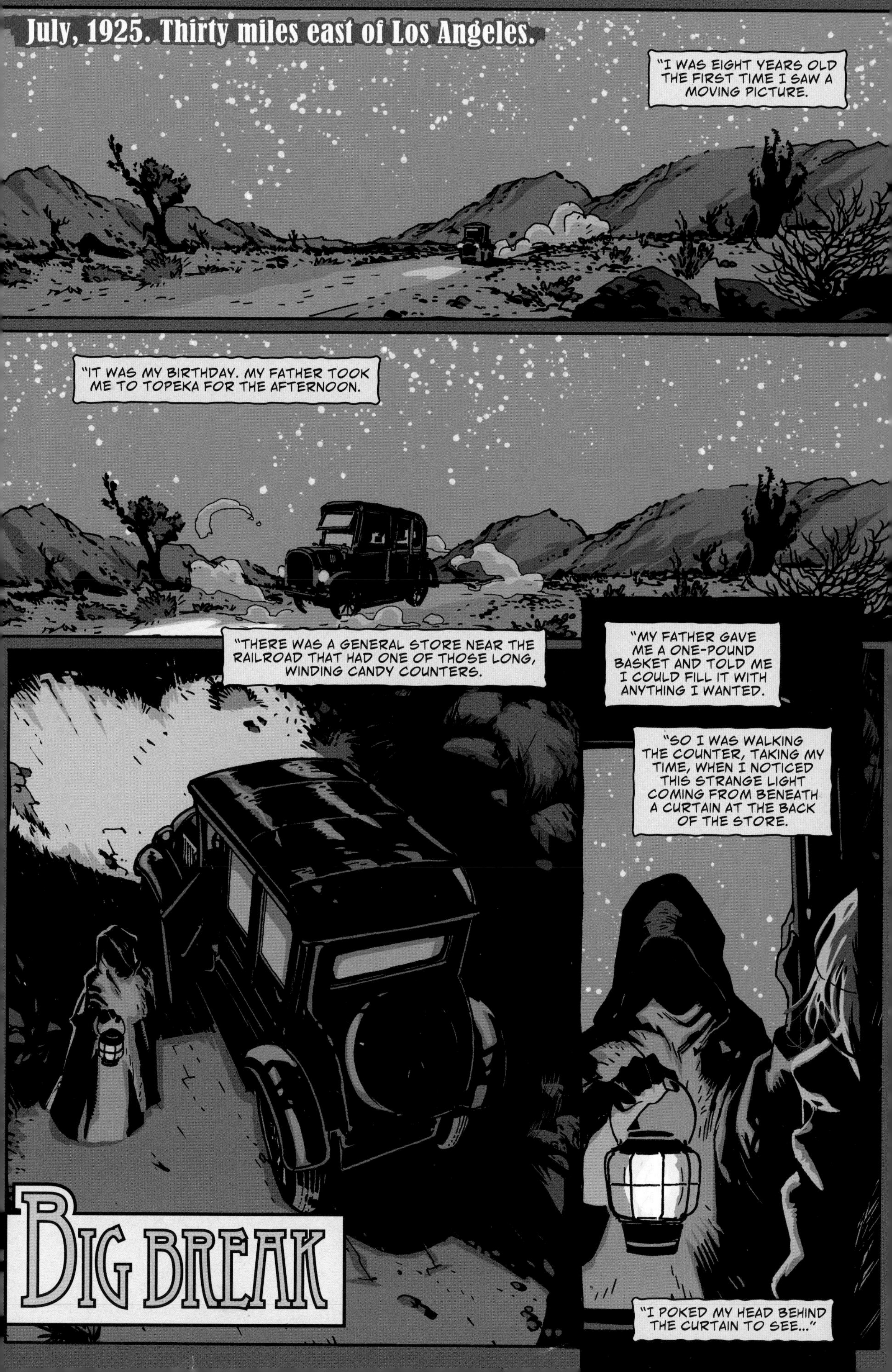
July, 1925. Thirty miles east of Los Angeles.
"I WAS EIGHT YEARS OLD THE FIRST TIME I SAW A MOVING PICTURE.
"IT WAS MY BIRTHDAY. MY FATHER TOOK ME TO TOPEKA FOR THE AFTERNOON.
"THERE WAS A GENERAL STORE NEAR THE RAILROAD THAT HAD ONE OF THOSE LONG, WINDING CANDY COUNTERS.
"MY FATHER GAVE ME A ONE-POUND BASKET AND TOLD ME I COULD FILL IT WITH ANYTHING I WANTED.
"SO I WAS WALKING THE COUNTER, TAKING MY TIME, WHEN I NOTICED THIS STRANGE LIGHT COMING FROM BENEATH A CURTAIN AT THE BACK OF THE STORE.
BIG BREAK
"I POKED MY HEAD BEHIND THE CURTAIN TO SEE..."

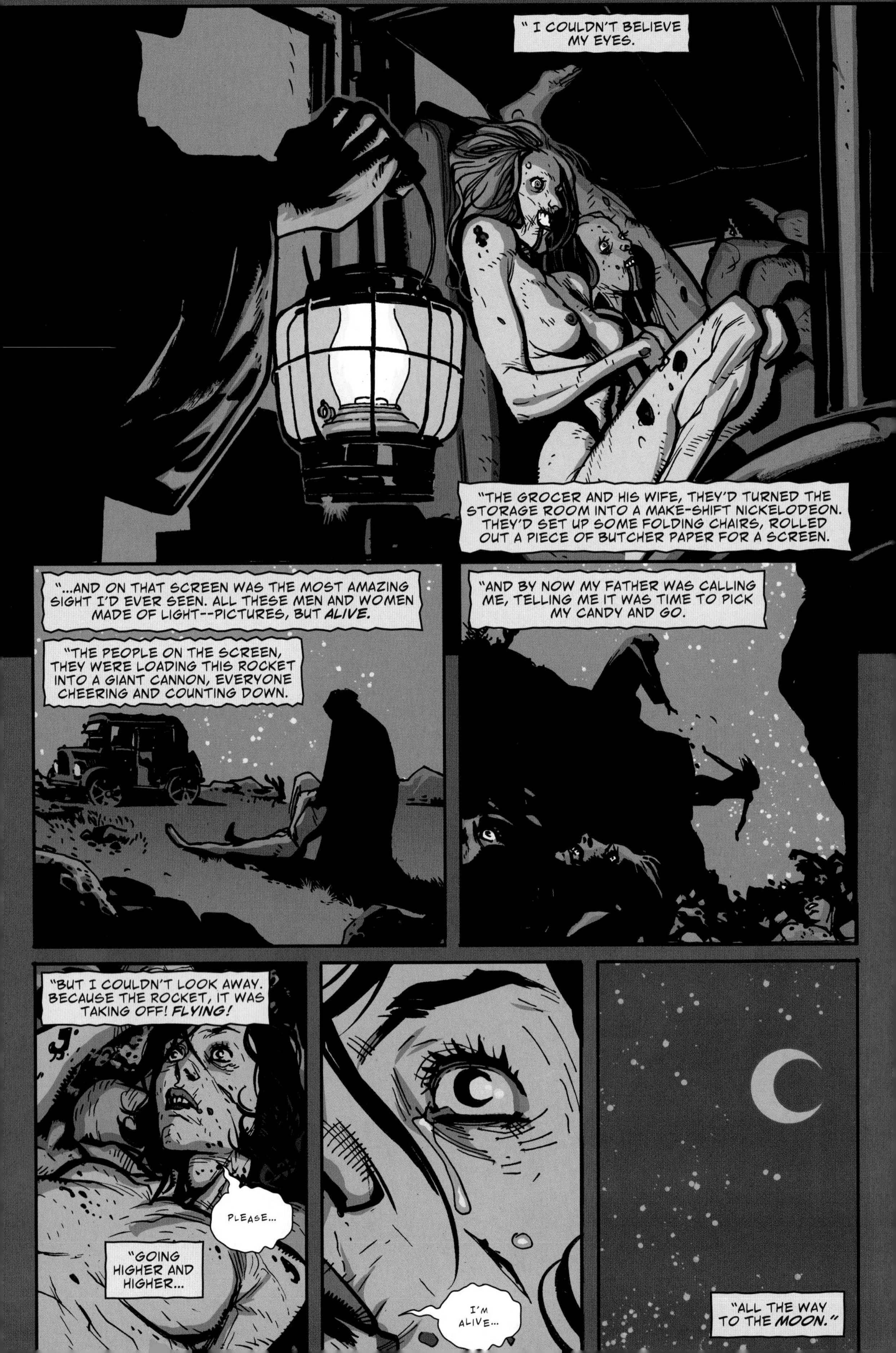
" I COULDN'T BELIEVE MY EYES.
"THE GROCER AND HIS WIFE, THEY'D TURNED THE STORAGE ROOM INTO A MAKE-SHIFT NICKELODEON. THEY'D SET UP SOME FOLDING CHAIRS, ROLLED OUT A PIECE OF BUTCHER PAPER FOR A SCREEN.
"...AND ON THAT SCREEN WAS THE MOST AMAZING SIGHT I'D EVER SEEN. ALL THESE MEN AND WOMEN MADE OF LIGHT--PICTURES, BUT ALIVE.
"THE PEOPLE ON THE SCREEN, THEY WERE LOADING THIS ROCKET INTO A GIANT CANNON, EVERYONE CHEERING AND COUNTING DOWN.
"AND BY NOW MY FATHER WAS CALLING ME, TELLING ME IT WAS TIME TO PICK MY CANDY AND GO.
"BUT I COULDN'T LOOK AWAY. BECAUSE THE ROCKET, IT WAS TAKING OFF! FLYING!
PLEASE...
"GOING HIGHER AND HIGHER...
I'M ALIVE...
"ALL THE WAY TO THE MOON."

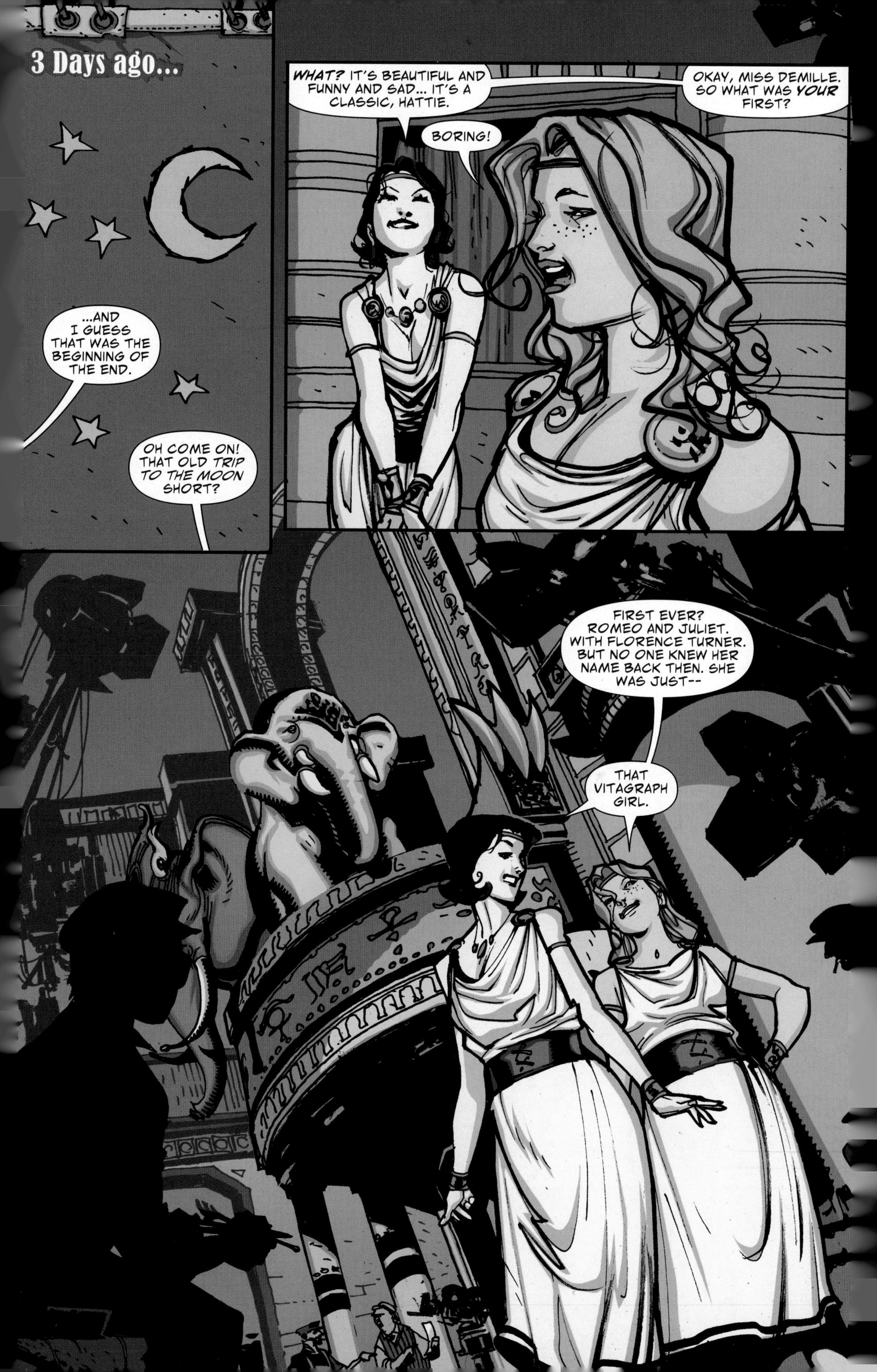
3 Days ago...
...AND I GUESS THAT WAS THE BEGINNING OF THE END.
OH COME ON! THAT OLD TRIP TO THE MOON SHORT?
WHAT? IT'S BEAUTIFUL AND FUNNY AND SAD... IT'S A CLASSIC, HATTIE.
BORING!
OKAY, MISS DEMILLE. SO WHAT WAS YOUR FIRST?
FIRST EVER? ROMEO AND JULIET. WITH FLORENCE TURNER. BUT NO ONE KNEW HER NAME BACK THEN. SHE WAS JUST--
THAT VITAGRAPH GIRL.

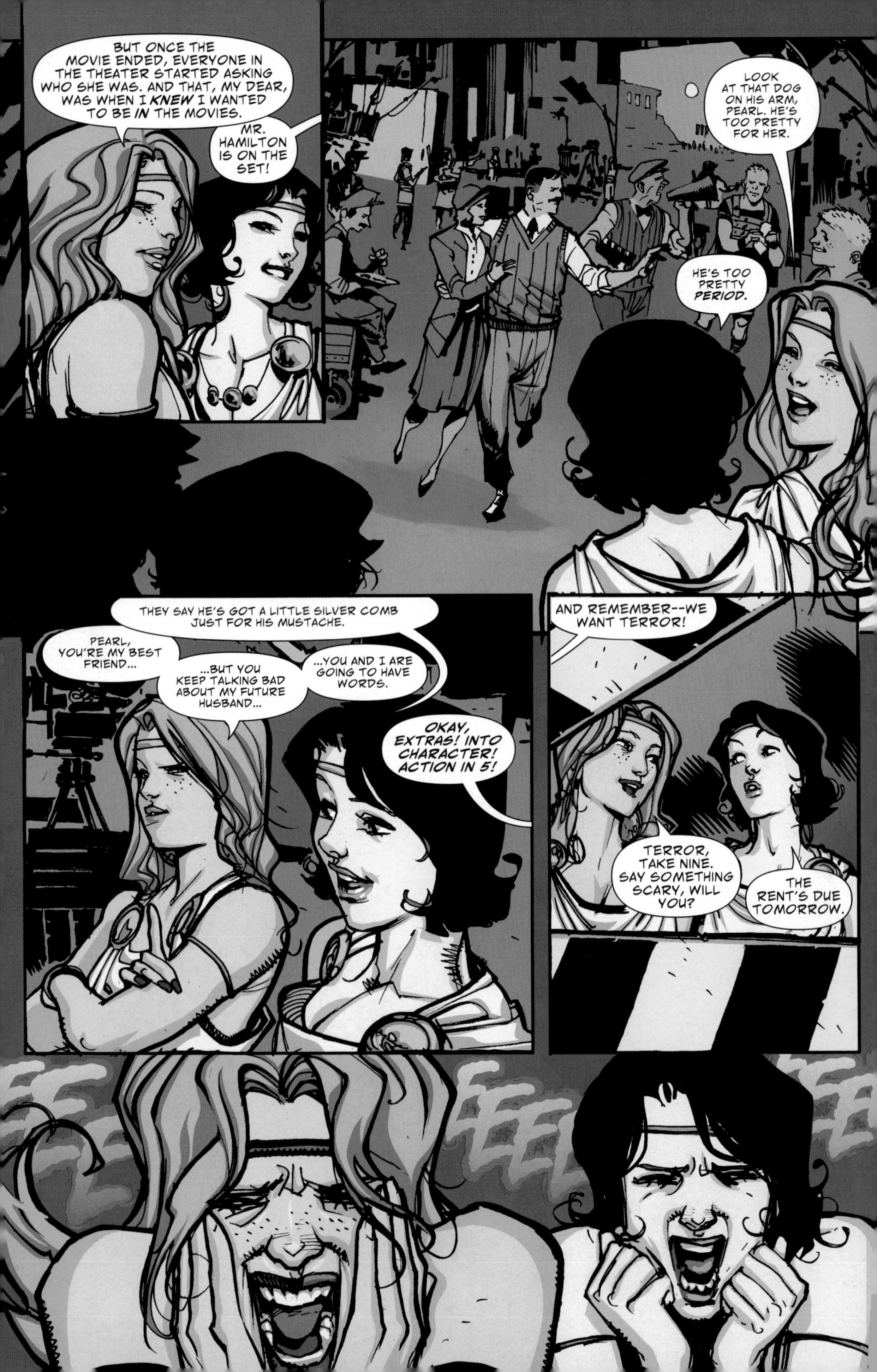
BUT ONCE THE MOVIE ENDED, EVERYONE IN THE THEATER STARTED ASKING WHO SHE WAS. AND THAT, MY DEAR, WAS WHEN I KNEW I WANTED TO BE IN THE MOVIES.
MR. HAMILTON IS ON THE SET!
LOOK AT THAT DOG ON HIS ARM, PEARL. HE'S TOO PRETTY FOR HER.
HE'S TOO PRETTY PERIOD.
THEY SAY HE'S GOT A LITTLE SILVER COMB JUST FOR HIS MUSTACHE.
PEARL, YOU'RE MY BEST FRIEND...
...BUT YOU KEEP TALKING BAD ABOUT MY FUTURE HUSBAND...
...YOU AND I ARE GOING TO HAVE WORDS.
OKAY, EXTRAS! INTO CHARACTER! ACTION IN 5!
AND REMEMBER--WE WANT TERROR!
TERROR, TAKE NINE. SAY SOMETHING SCARY, WILL YOU?
THE RENT'S DUE TOMORROW.

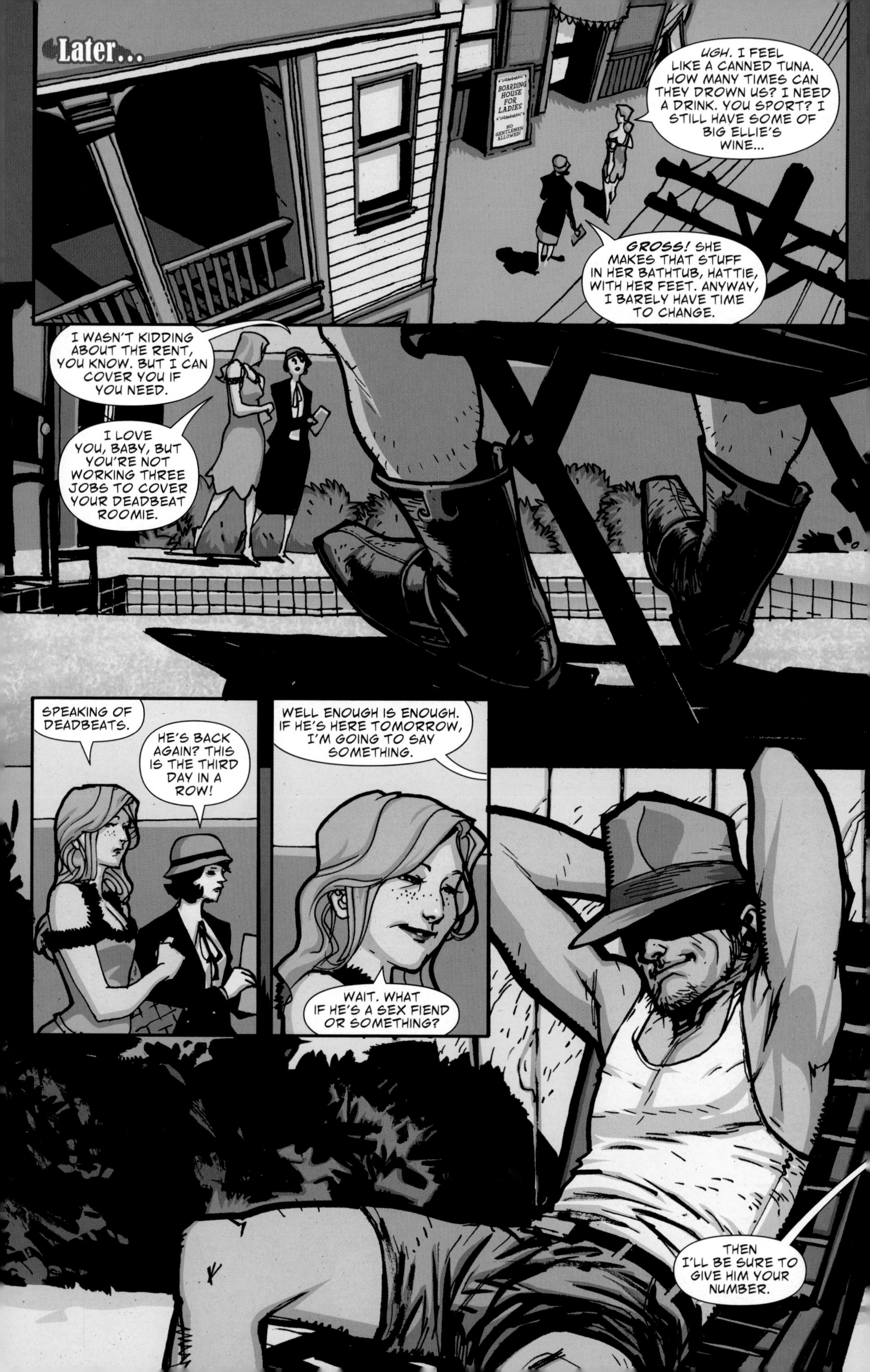
Later...
BOARDING HOUSE FOR LADIES
NO GENTLEMEN ALLOWED!
UGH. I FEEL LIKE A CANNED TUNA. HOW MANY TIMES CAN THEY DROWN US? I NEED A DRINK. YOU SPORT? I STILL HAVE SOME OF BIG ELLIE'S WINE...
GROSS! SHE MAKES THAT STUFF IN HER BATHTUB, HATTIE, WITH HER FEET. ANYWAY, I BARELY HAVE TIME TO CHANGE.
I WASN'T KIDDING ABOUT THE RENT, YOU KNOW. BUT I CAN COVER YOU IF YOU NEED.
I LOVE YOU, BABY, BUT YOU'RE NOT WORKING THREE JOBS TO COVER YOUR DEADBEAT ROOMIE.
SPEAKING OF DEADBEATS.
HE'S BACK AGAIN? THIS IS THE THIRD DAY IN A ROW!
WELL ENOUGH IS ENOUGH. IF HE'S HERE TOMORROW, I'M GOING TO SAY SOMETHING.
WAIT. WHAT IF HE'S A SEX FIEND OR SOMETHING?
THEN I'LL BE SURE TO GIVE HIM YOUR NUMBER.

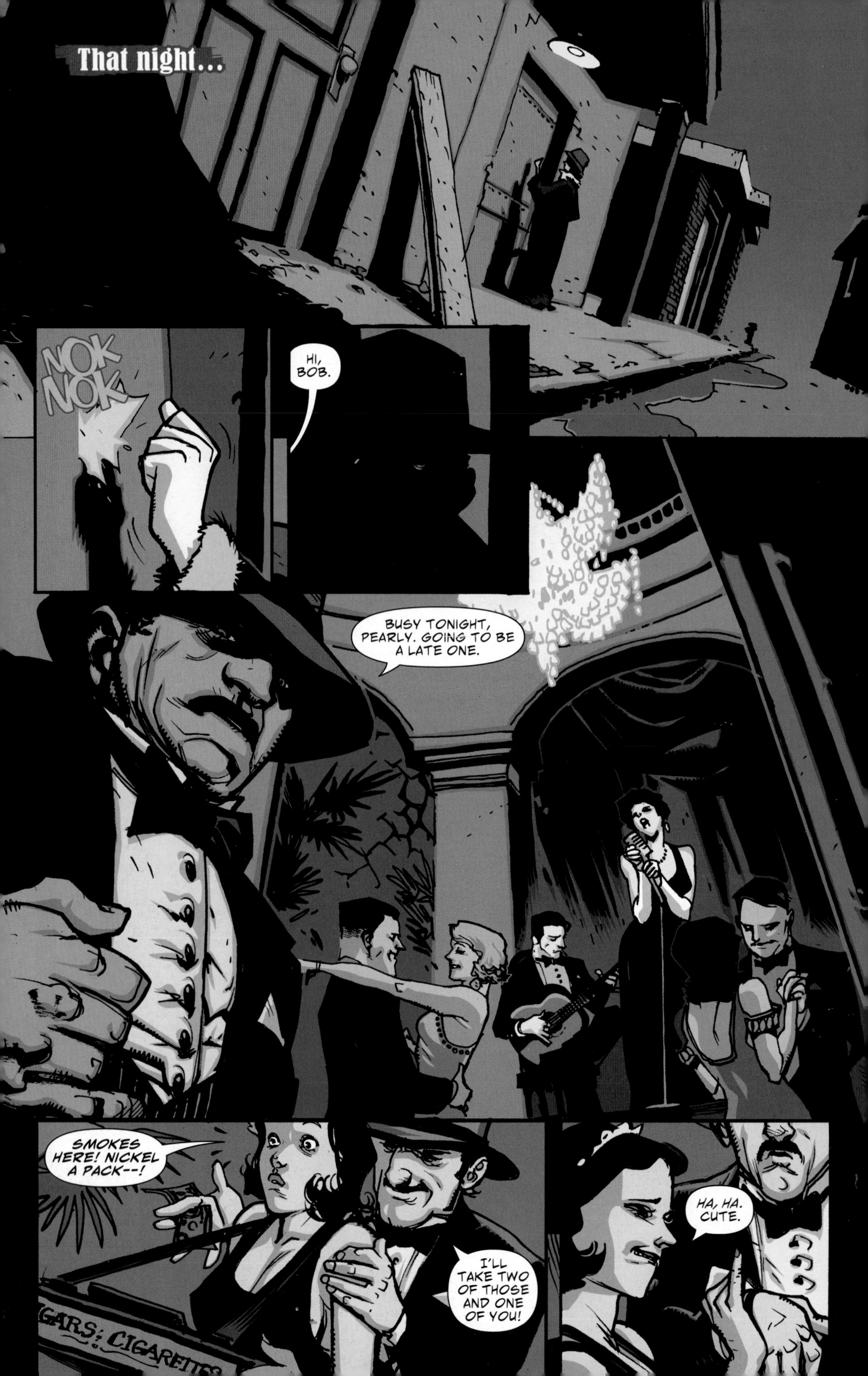
That night...
NOK NOK
HI, BOB.
BUSY TONIGHT, PEARLY. GOING TO BE A LATE ONE.
SMOKES HERE! NICKEL A PACK--!
I'LL TAKE TWO OF THOSE AND ONE OF YOU!
HA, HA. CUTE.
CIGARS: CIGARETTES

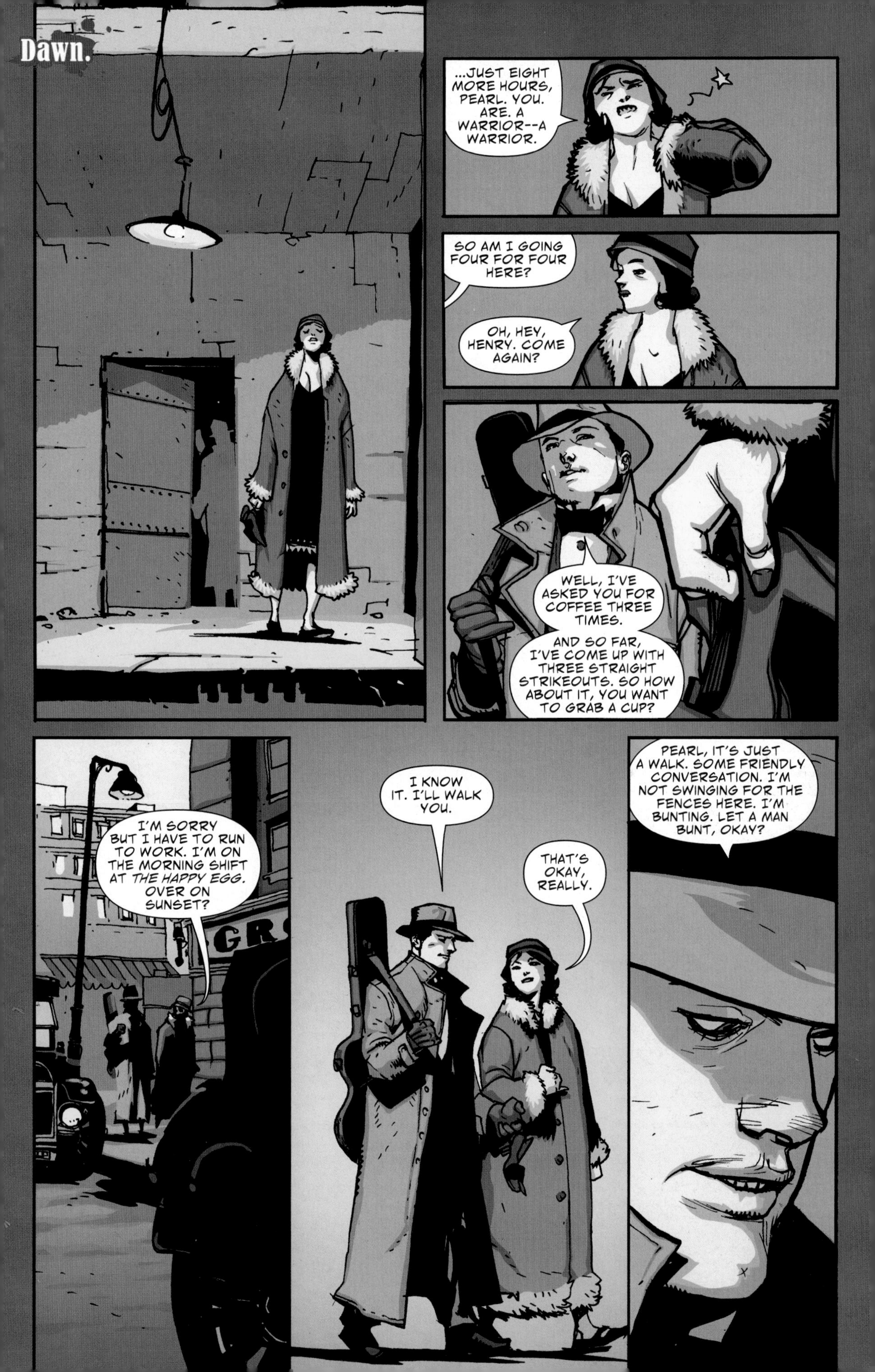
Dawn.
...JUST EIGHT MORE HOURS, PEARL. YOU. ARE. A WARRIOR--A WARRIOR.
SO AM I GOING FOUR FOR FOUR HERE?
OH, HEY, HENRY. COME AGAIN?
WELL, I'VE ASKED YOU FOR COFFEE THREE TIMES.
AND SO FAR, I'VE COME UP WITH THREE STRAIGHT STRIKEOUTS. SO HOW ABOUT IT, YOU WANT TO GRAB A CUP?
I'M SORRY BUT I HAVE TO RUN TO WORK. I'M ON THE MORNING SHIFT AT *THE HAPPY EGG.* OVER ON SUNSET?
I KNOW IT. I'LL WALK YOU.
THAT'S OKAY, REALLY.
PEARL, IT'S JUST A WALK. SOME FRIENDLY CONVERSATION. I'M NOT SWINGING FOR THE FENCES HERE. I'M BUNTING. LET A MAN BUNT, OKAY?

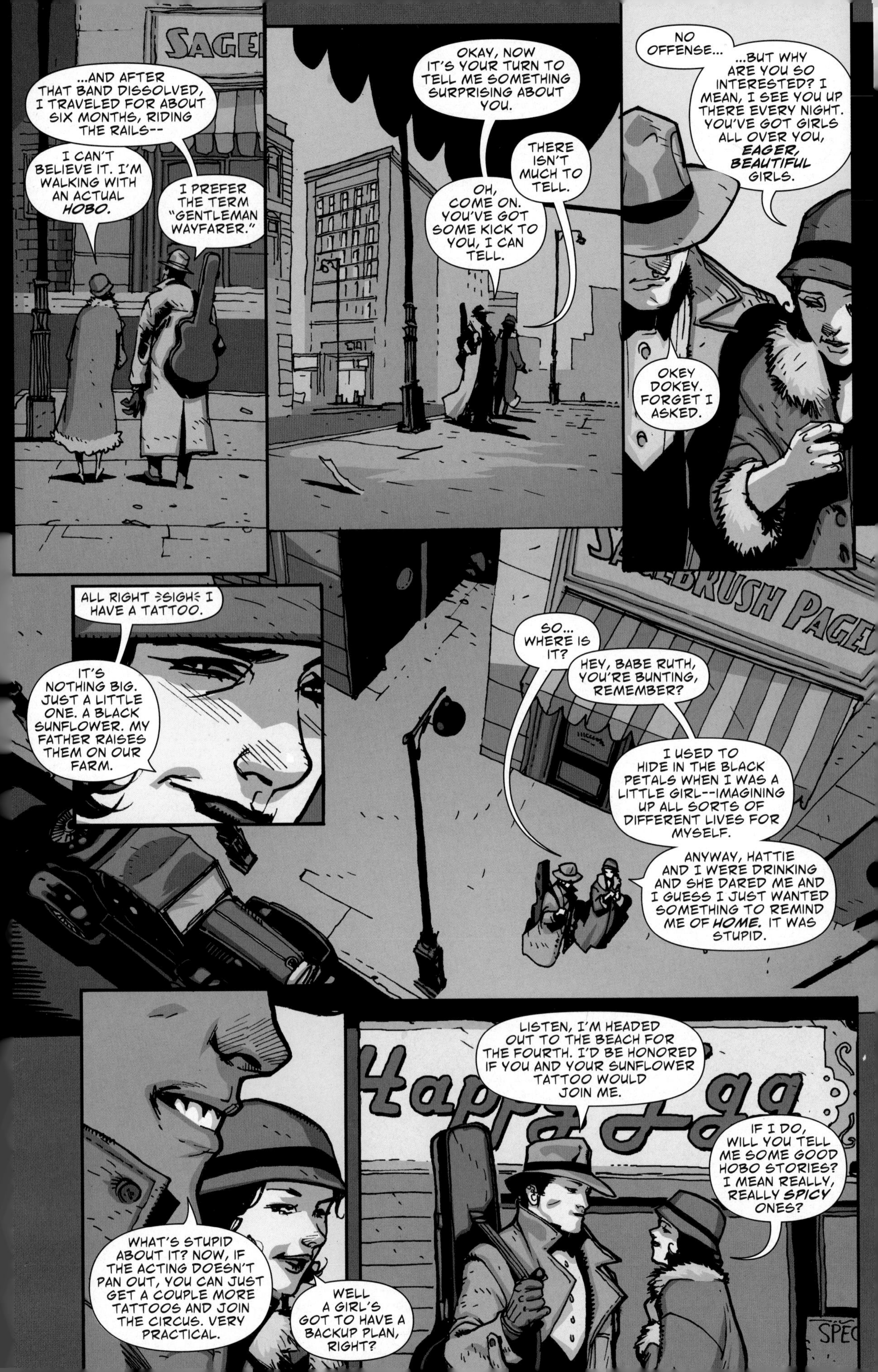
SAGE
...AND AFTER THAT BAND DISSOLVED, I TRAVELED FOR ABOUT SIX MONTHS, RIDING THE RAILS--
I CAN'T BELIEVE IT. I'M WALKING WITH AN ACTUAL HOBO.
I PREFER THE TERM "GENTLEMAN WAYFARER."
OKAY, NOW IT'S YOUR TURN TO TELL ME SOMETHING SURPRISING ABOUT YOU.
THERE ISN'T MUCH TO TELL.
OH, COME ON. YOU'VE GOT SOME KICK TO YOU, I CAN TELL.
NO OFFENSE...
...BUT WHY ARE YOU SO INTERESTED? I MEAN, I SEE YOU UP THERE EVERY NIGHT. YOU'VE GOT GIRLS ALL OVER YOU, EAGER, BEAUTIFUL GIRLS.
OKEY DOKEY. FORGET I ASKED.
ALL RIGHT *SIGH* I HAVE A TATTOO.
IT'S NOTHING BIG. JUST A LITTLE ONE. A BLACK SUNFLOWER. MY FATHER RAISES THEM ON OUR FARM.
SAGEBRUSH PAGES
SO... WHERE IS IT?
HEY, BABE RUTH, YOU'RE BUNTING, REMEMBER?
I USED TO HIDE IN THE BLACK PETALS WHEN I WAS A LITTLE GIRL--IMAGINING UP ALL SORTS OF DIFFERENT LIVES FOR MYSELF.
ANYWAY, HATTIE AND I WERE DRINKING AND SHE DARED ME AND I GUESS I JUST WANTED SOMETHING TO REMIND ME OF HOME. IT WAS STUPID.
WHAT'S STUPID ABOUT IT? NOW, IF THE ACTING DOESN'T PAN OUT, YOU CAN JUST GET A COUPLE MORE TATTOOS AND JOIN THE CIRCUS. VERY PRACTICAL.
WELL A GIRL'S GOT TO HAVE A BACKUP PLAN, RIGHT?
LISTEN, I'M HEADED OUT TO THE BEACH FOR THE FOURTH. I'D BE HONORED IF YOU AND YOUR SUNFLOWER TATTOO WOULD JOIN ME.
IF I DO, WILL YOU TELL ME SOME GOOD HOBO STORIES? I MEAN REALLY, REALLY SPICY ONES?

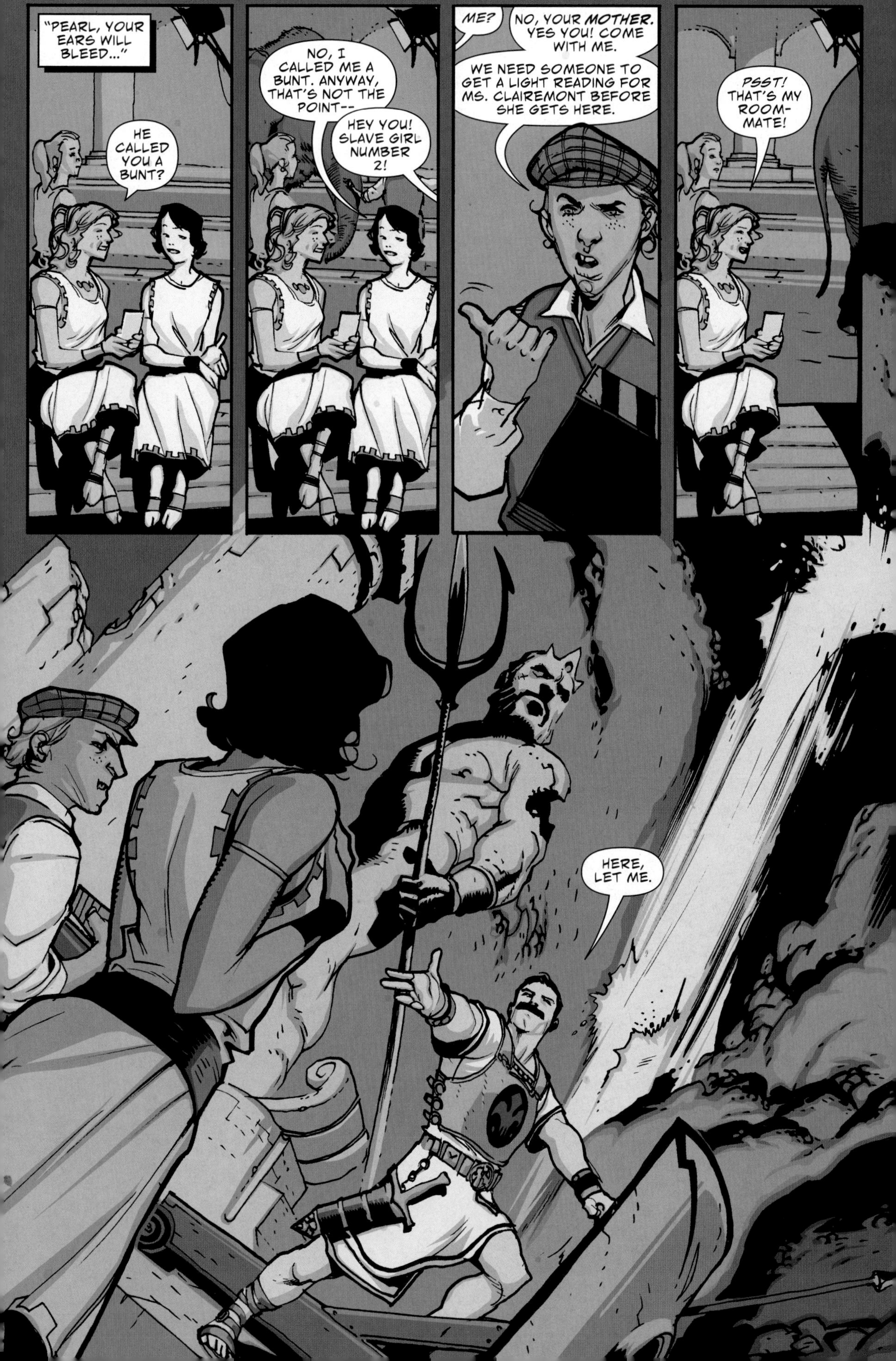

"PEARL, YOUR EARS WILL BLEED..."
HE CALLED YOU A BUNT?
NO, I CALLED ME A BUNT. ANYWAY, THAT'S NOT THE POINT--
HEY YOU! SLAVE GIRL NUMBER 2!
ME?
NO, YOUR *MOTHER*. YES YOU! COME WITH ME.
WE NEED SOMEONE TO GET A LIGHT READING FOR MS. CLAIREMONT BEFORE SHE GETS HERE.
PSST! THAT'S MY ROOM-MATE!
HERE, LET ME.

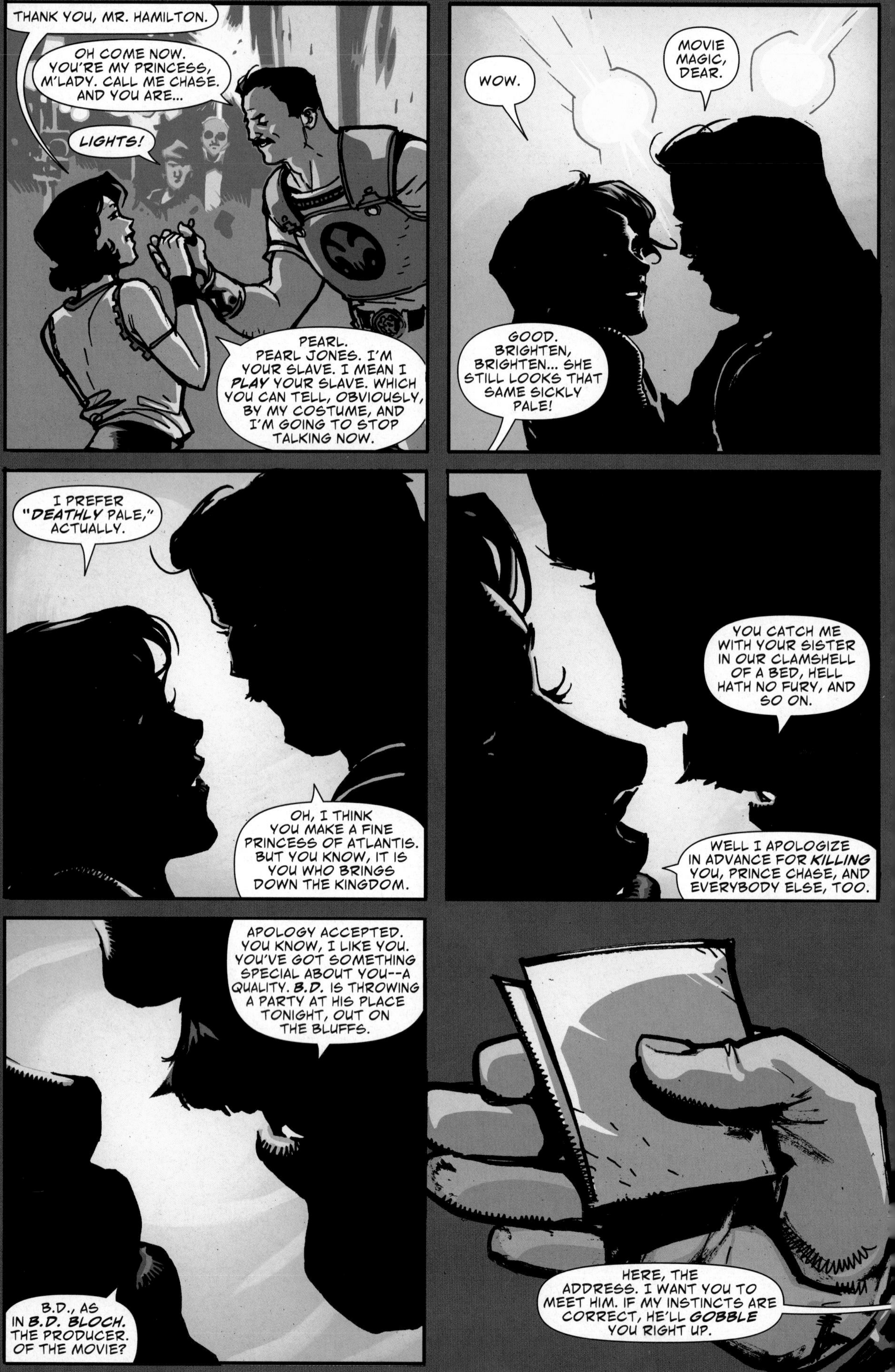

THANK YOU, MR. HAMILTON.
OH COME NOW. YOU'RE MY PRINCESS, M'LADY. CALL ME CHASE. AND YOU ARE...
LIGHTS!
PEARL. PEARL JONES. I'M YOUR SLAVE. I MEAN I PLAY YOUR SLAVE. WHICH YOU CAN TELL, OBVIOUSLY, BY MY COSTUME, AND I'M GOING TO STOP TALKING NOW.
WOW.
MOVIE MAGIC, DEAR.
GOOD. BRIGHTEN, BRIGHTEN... SHE STILL LOOKS THAT SAME SICKLY PALE!
I PREFER "DEATHLY PALE," ACTUALLY.
OH, I THINK YOU MAKE A FINE PRINCESS OF ATLANTIS. BUT YOU KNOW, IT IS YOU WHO BRINGS DOWN THE KINGDOM.
YOU CATCH ME WITH YOUR SISTER IN OUR CLAMSHELL OF A BED, HELL HATH NO FURY, AND SO ON.
WELL I APOLOGIZE IN ADVANCE FOR KILLING YOU, PRINCE CHASE, AND EVERYBODY ELSE, TOO.
APOLOGY ACCEPTED. YOU KNOW, I LIKE YOU. YOU'VE GOT SOMETHING SPECIAL ABOUT YOU--A QUALITY. B.D. IS THROWING A PARTY AT HIS PLACE TONIGHT, OUT ON THE BLUFFS.
B.D., AS IN B.D. BLOCH. THE PRODUCER. OF THE MOVIE?
HERE, THE ADDRESS. I WANT YOU TO MEET HIM. IF MY INSTINCTS ARE CORRECT, HE'LL GOBBLE YOU RIGHT UP.

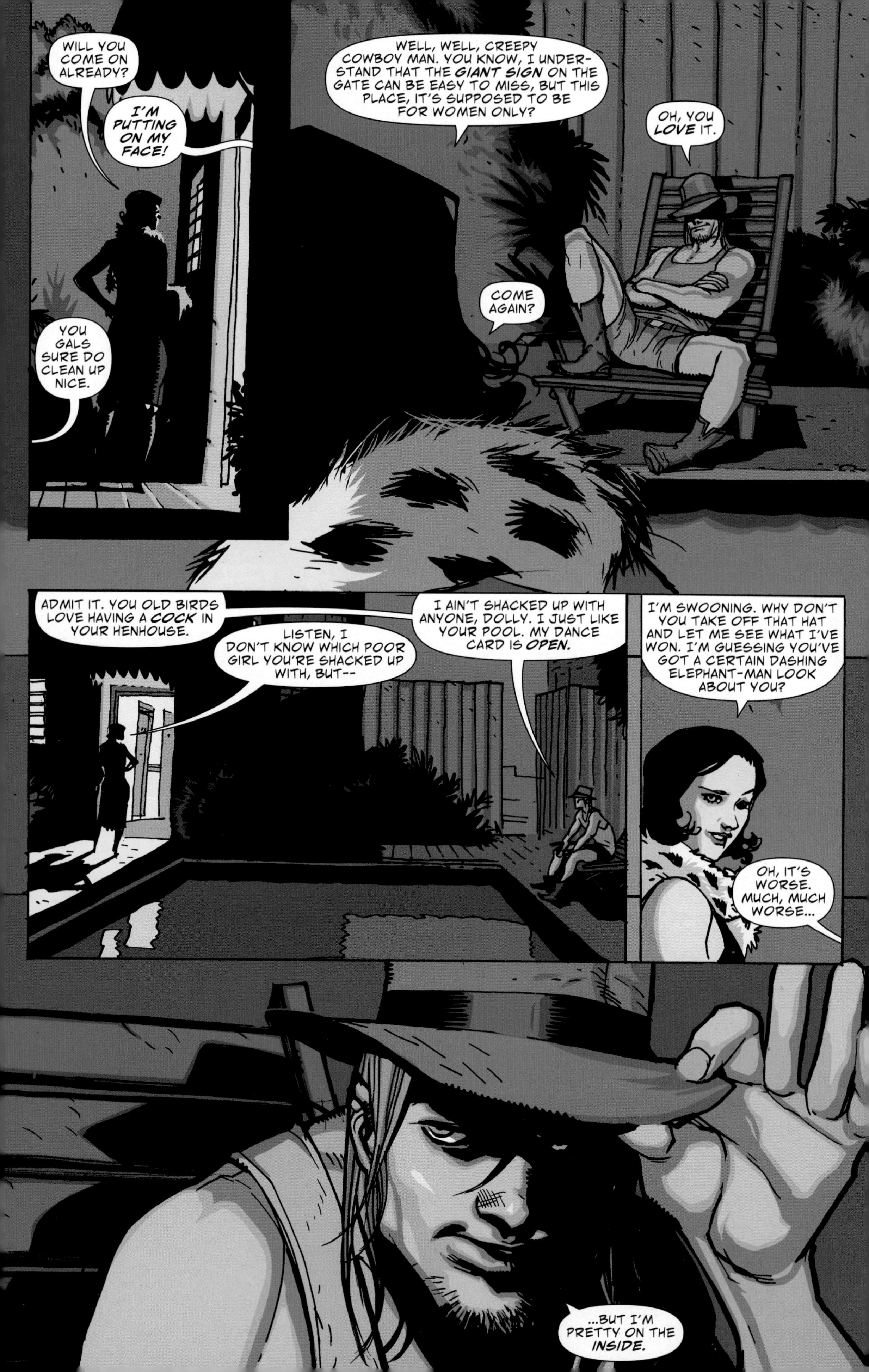
WILL YOU COME ON ALREADY?
I'M PUTTING ON MY FACE!
WELL, WELL, CREEPY COWBOY MAN. YOU KNOW, I UNDERSTAND THAT THE GIANT SIGN ON THE GATE CAN BE EASY TO MISS, BUT THIS PLACE, IT'S SUPPOSED TO BE FOR WOMEN ONLY?
OH, YOU LOVE IT.
COME AGAIN?
YOU GALS SURE DO CLEAN UP NICE.
ADMIT IT. YOU OLD BIRDS LOVE HAVING A COCK IN YOUR HENHOUSE.
LISTEN, I DON'T KNOW WHICH POOR GIRL YOU'RE SHACKED UP WITH, BUT--
I AIN'T SHACKED UP WITH ANYONE, DOLLY. I JUST LIKE YOUR POOL. MY DANCE CARD IS OPEN.
I'M SWOONING. WHY DON'T YOU TAKE OFF THAT HAT AND LET ME SEE WHAT I'VE WON. I'M GUESSING YOU'VE GOT A CERTAIN DASHING ELEPHANT-MAN LOOK ABOUT YOU?
OH, IT'S WORSE. MUCH, MUCH WORSE...
...BUT I'M PRETTY ON THE INSIDE.

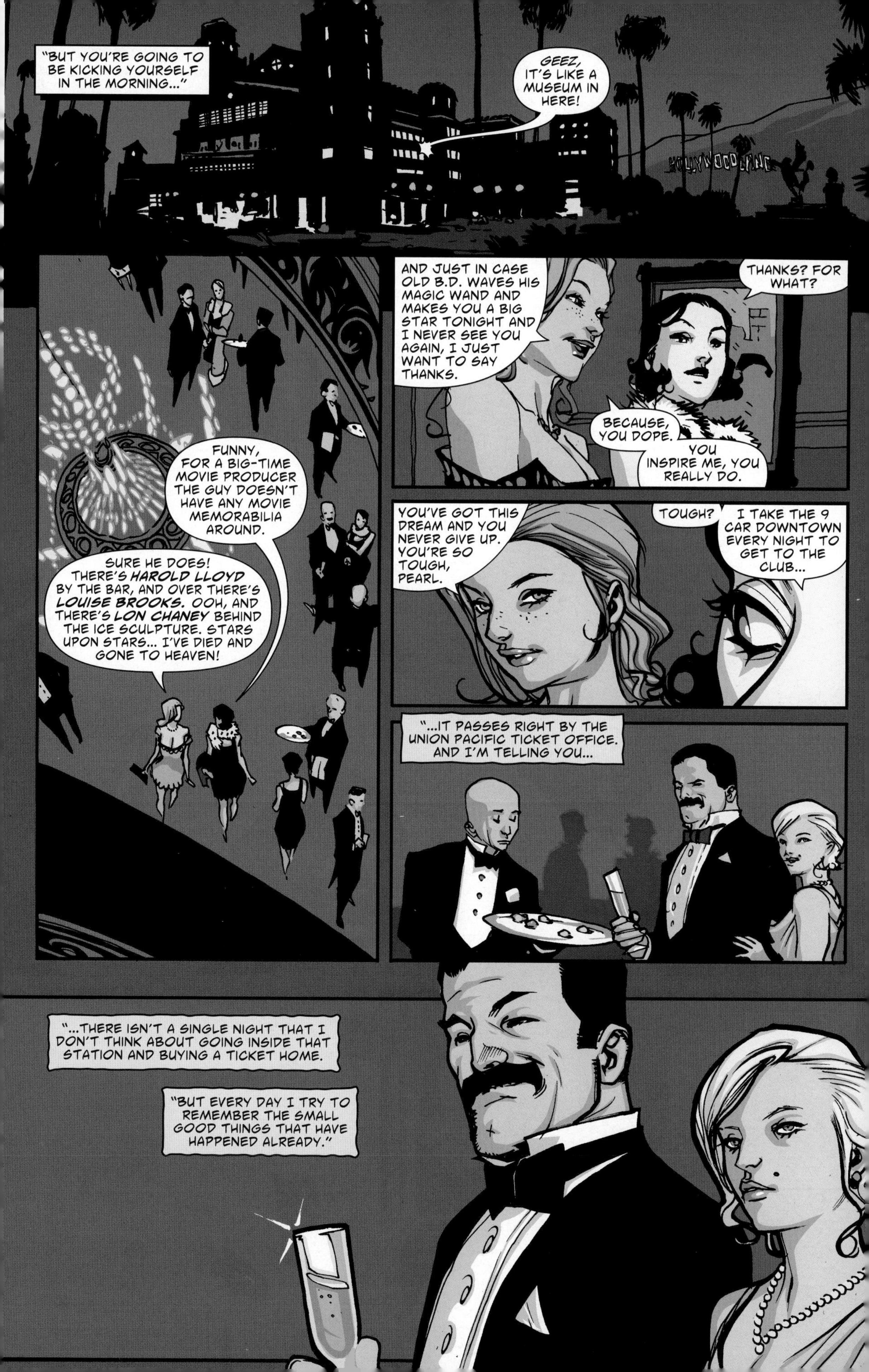
"BUT YOU'RE GOING TO BE KICKING YOURSELF IN THE MORNING..."
GEEZ, IT'S LIKE A MUSEUM IN HERE!
FUNNY, FOR A BIG-TIME MOVIE PRODUCER THE GUY DOESN'T HAVE ANY MOVIE MEMORABILIA AROUND.
SURE HE DOES! THERE'S HAROLD LLOYD BY THE BAR, AND OVER THERE'S LOUISE BROOKS. OOH, AND THERE'S LON CHANEY BEHIND THE ICE SCULPTURE. STARS UPON STARS... I'VE DIED AND GONE TO HEAVEN!
AND JUST IN CASE OLD B.D. WAVES HIS MAGIC WAND AND MAKES YOU A BIG STAR TONIGHT AND I NEVER SEE YOU AGAIN, I JUST WANT TO SAY THANKS.
THANKS? FOR WHAT?
BECAUSE, YOU DOPE.
YOU INSPIRE ME, YOU REALLY DO.
YOU'VE GOT THIS DREAM AND YOU NEVER GIVE UP. YOU'RE SO TOUGH, PEARL.
TOUGH?
I TAKE THE 9 CAR DOWNTOWN EVERY NIGHT TO GET TO THE CLUB...
"...IT PASSES RIGHT BY THE UNION PACIFIC TICKET OFFICE. AND I'M TELLING YOU...
"...THERE ISN'T A SINGLE NIGHT THAT I DON'T THINK ABOUT GOING INSIDE THAT STATION AND BUYING A TICKET HOME.
"BUT EVERY DAY I TRY TO REMEMBER THE SMALL GOOD THINGS THAT HAVE HAPPENED ALREADY."

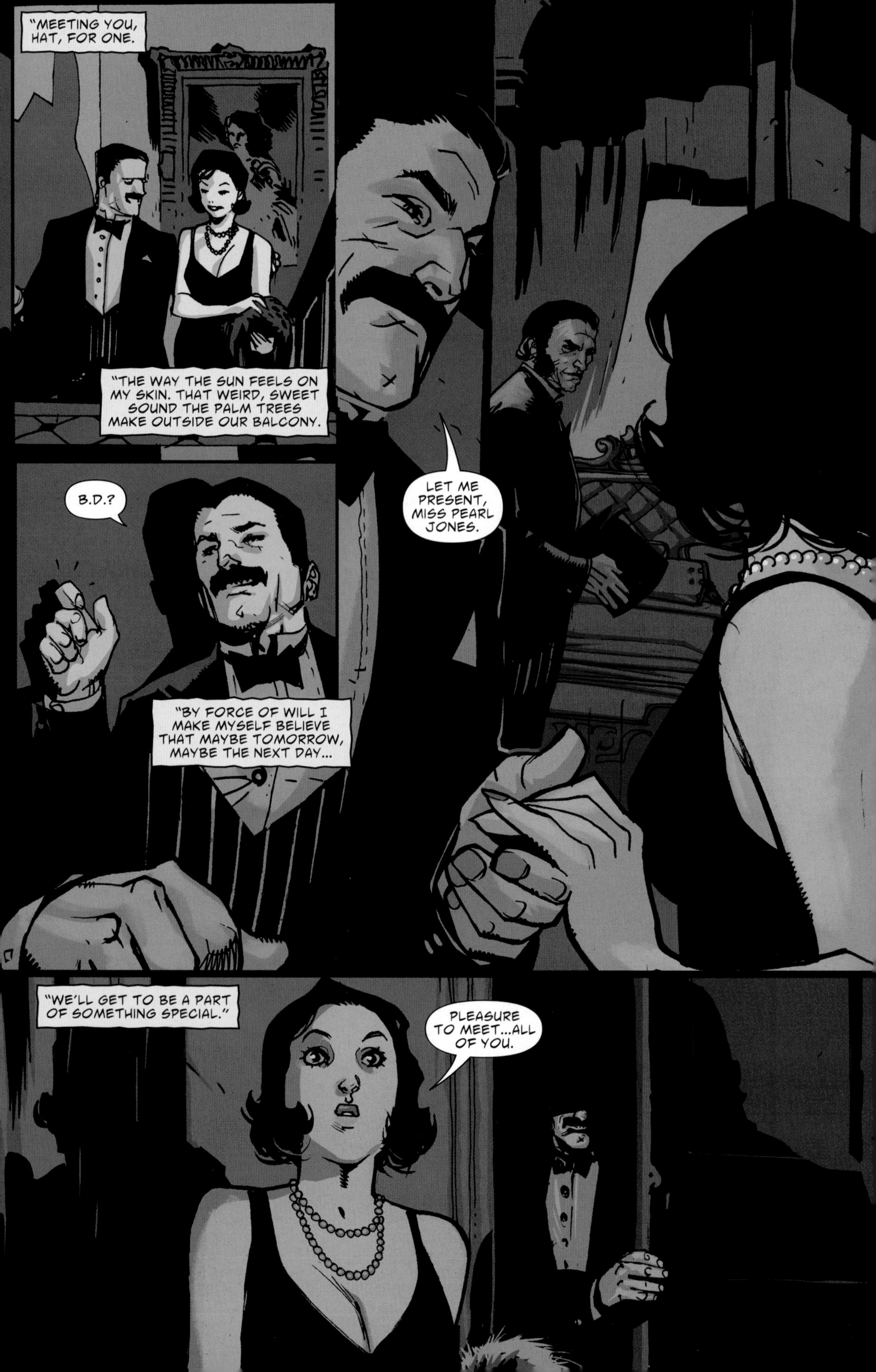
"MEETING YOU, HAT, FOR ONE.
"THE WAY THE SUN FEELS ON MY SKIN. THAT WEIRD, SWEET SOUND THE PALM TREES MAKE OUTSIDE OUR BALCONY.
B.D.?
"BY FORCE OF WILL I MAKE MYSELF BELIEVE THAT MAYBE TOMORROW, MAYBE THE NEXT DAY...
LET ME PRESENT, MISS PEARL JONES.
"WE'LL GET TO BE A PART OF SOMETHING SPECIAL."
PLEASURE TO MEET...ALL OF YOU.

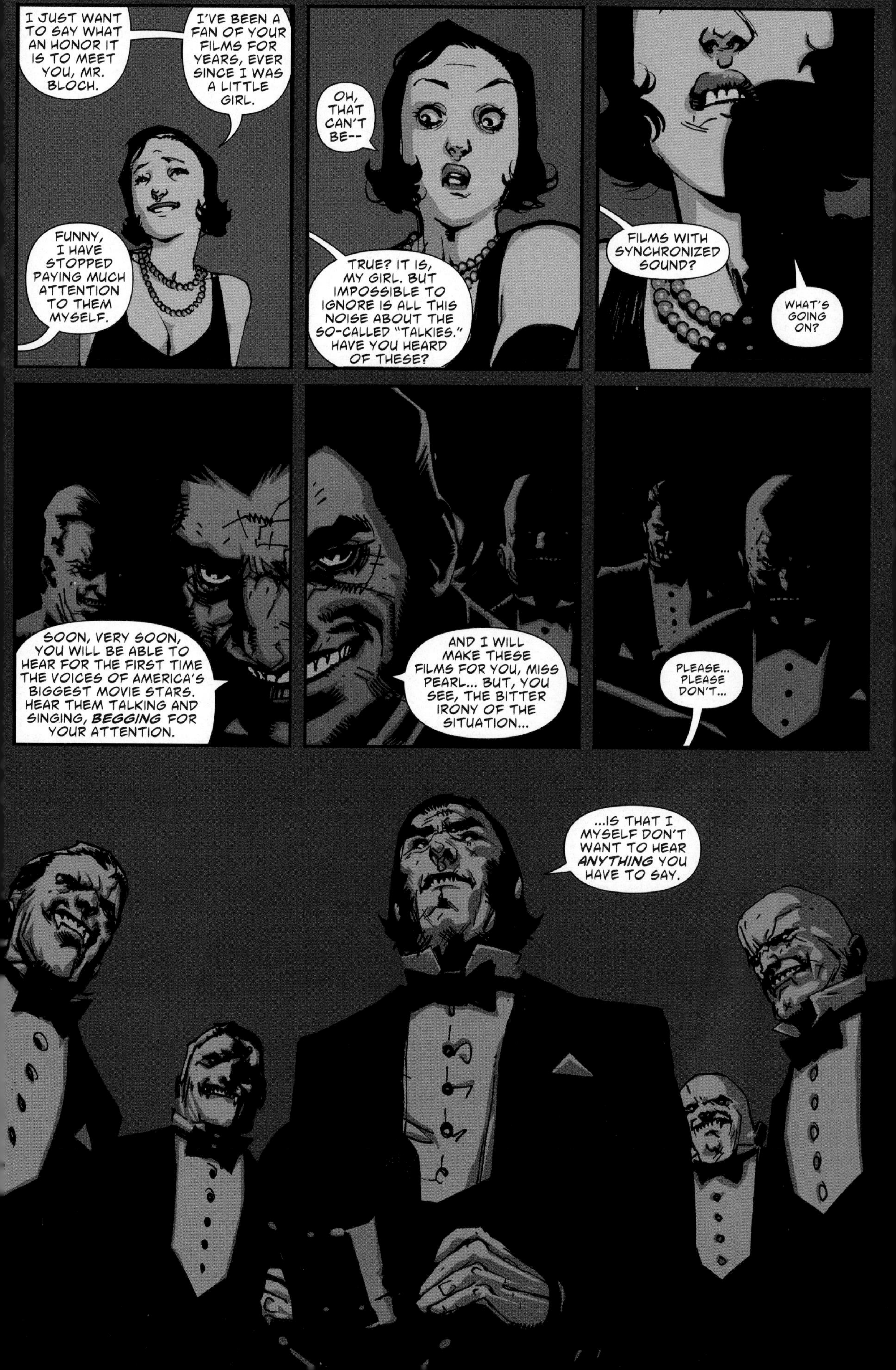
I JUST WANT TO SAY WHAT AN HONOR IT IS TO MEET YOU, MR. BLOCH.
I'VE BEEN A FAN OF YOUR FILMS FOR YEARS, EVER SINCE I WAS A LITTLE GIRL.
FUNNY, I HAVE STOPPED PAYING MUCH ATTENTION TO THEM MYSELF.
OH, THAT CAN'T BE--
TRUE? IT IS, MY GIRL. BUT IMPOSSIBLE TO IGNORE IS ALL THIS NOISE ABOUT THE SO-CALLED "TALKIES." HAVE YOU HEARD OF THESE?
FILMS WITH SYNCHRONIZED SOUND?
WHAT'S GOING ON?
SOON, VERY SOON, YOU WILL BE ABLE TO HEAR FOR THE FIRST TIME THE VOICES OF AMERICA'S BIGGEST MOVIE STARS. HEAR THEM TALKING AND SINGING, *BEGGING* FOR YOUR ATTENTION.
AND I WILL MAKE THESE FILMS FOR YOU, MISS PEARL... BUT, YOU SEE, THE BITTER IRONY OF THE SITUATION...
PLEASE... PLEASE DON'T...
...IS THAT I MYSELF DON'T WANT TO HEAR *ANYTHING* YOU HAVE TO SAY.

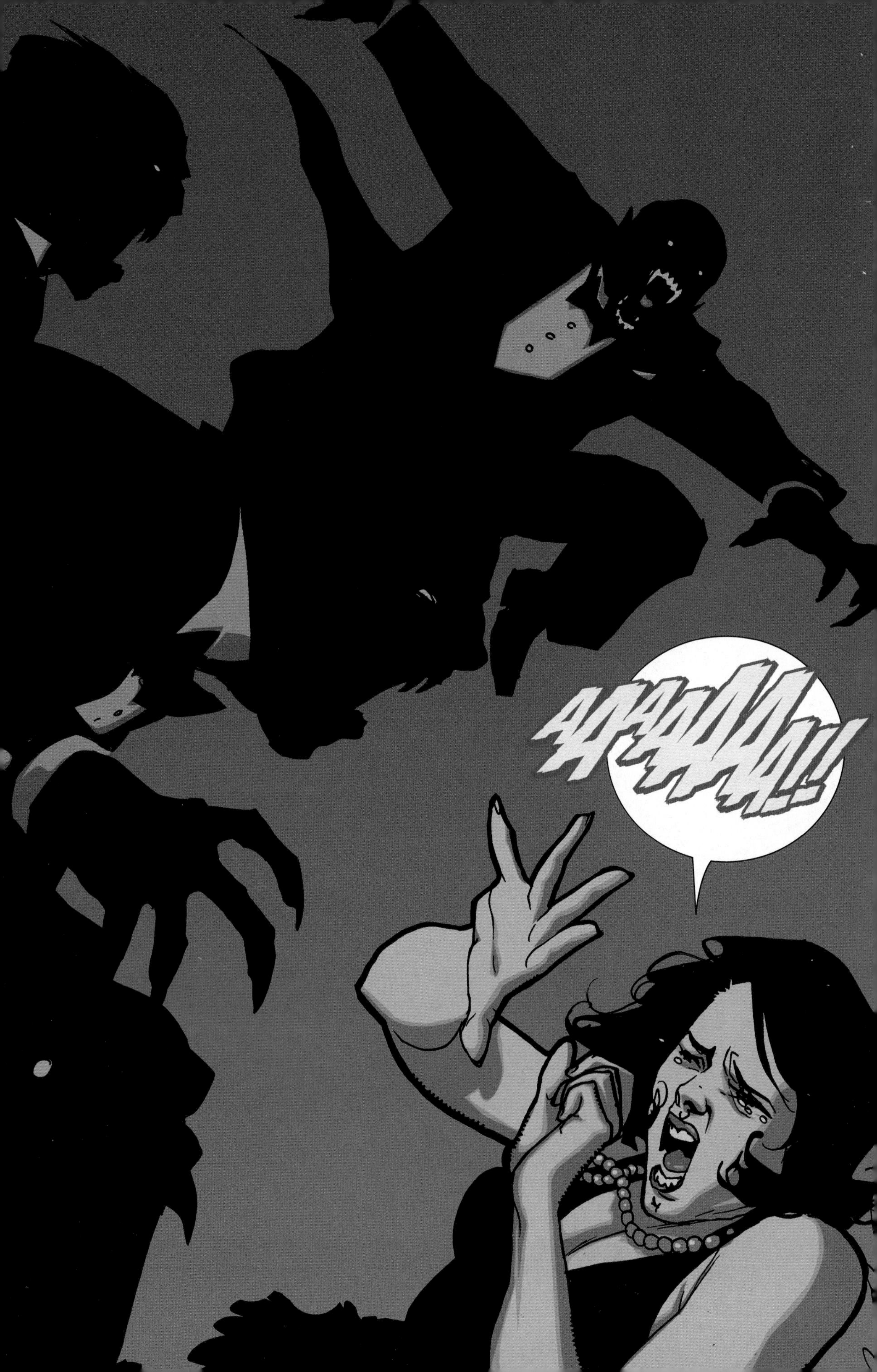
AAAAAAH!!

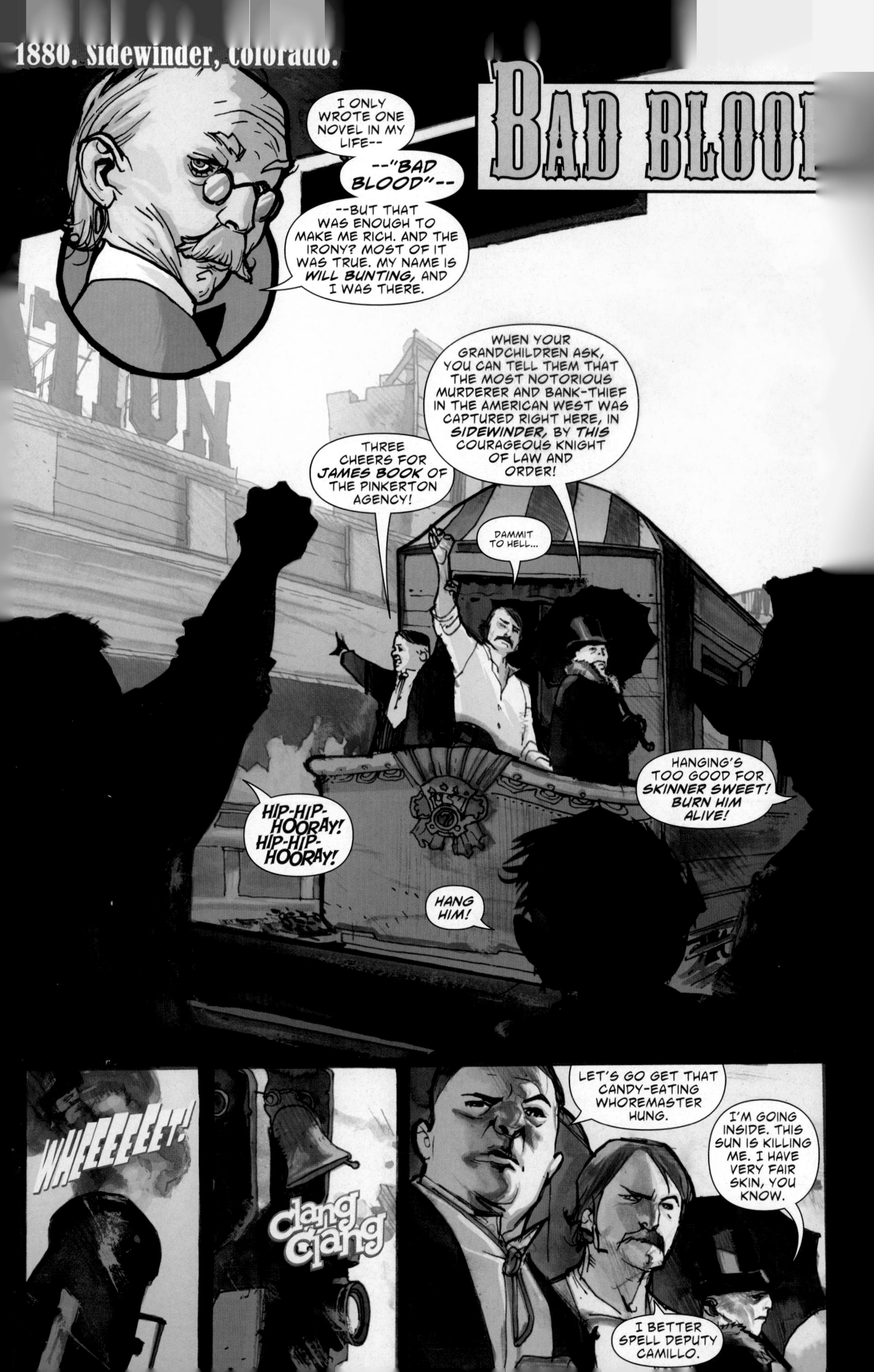
1880. Sidewinder, Colorado.
BAD BLOOD
I ONLY WROTE ONE NOVEL IN MY LIFE--
--"BAD BLOOD"--
--BUT THAT WAS ENOUGH TO MAKE ME RICH. AND THE IRONY? MOST OF IT WAS TRUE. MY NAME IS WILL BUNTING, AND I WAS THERE.
WHEN YOUR GRANDCHILDREN ASK, YOU CAN TELL THEM THAT THE MOST NOTORIOUS MURDERER AND BANK-THIEF IN THE AMERICAN WEST WAS CAPTURED RIGHT HERE, IN SIDEWINDER, BY THIS COURAGEOUS KNIGHT OF LAW AND ORDER!
THREE CHEERS FOR JAMES BOOK OF THE PINKERTON AGENCY!
DAMMIT TO HELL...
HANGING'S TOO GOOD FOR SKINNER SWEET! BURN HIM ALIVE!
HIP-HIP-HOORAY! HIP-HIP-HOORAY!
HANG HIM!
WHEEEEEEET!
clang clang
LET'S GO GET THAT CANDY-EATING WHOREMASTER HUNG.
I'M GOING INSIDE. THIS SUN IS KILLING ME. I HAVE VERY FAIR SKIN, YOU KNOW.
I BETTER SPELL DEPUTY CAMILLO.

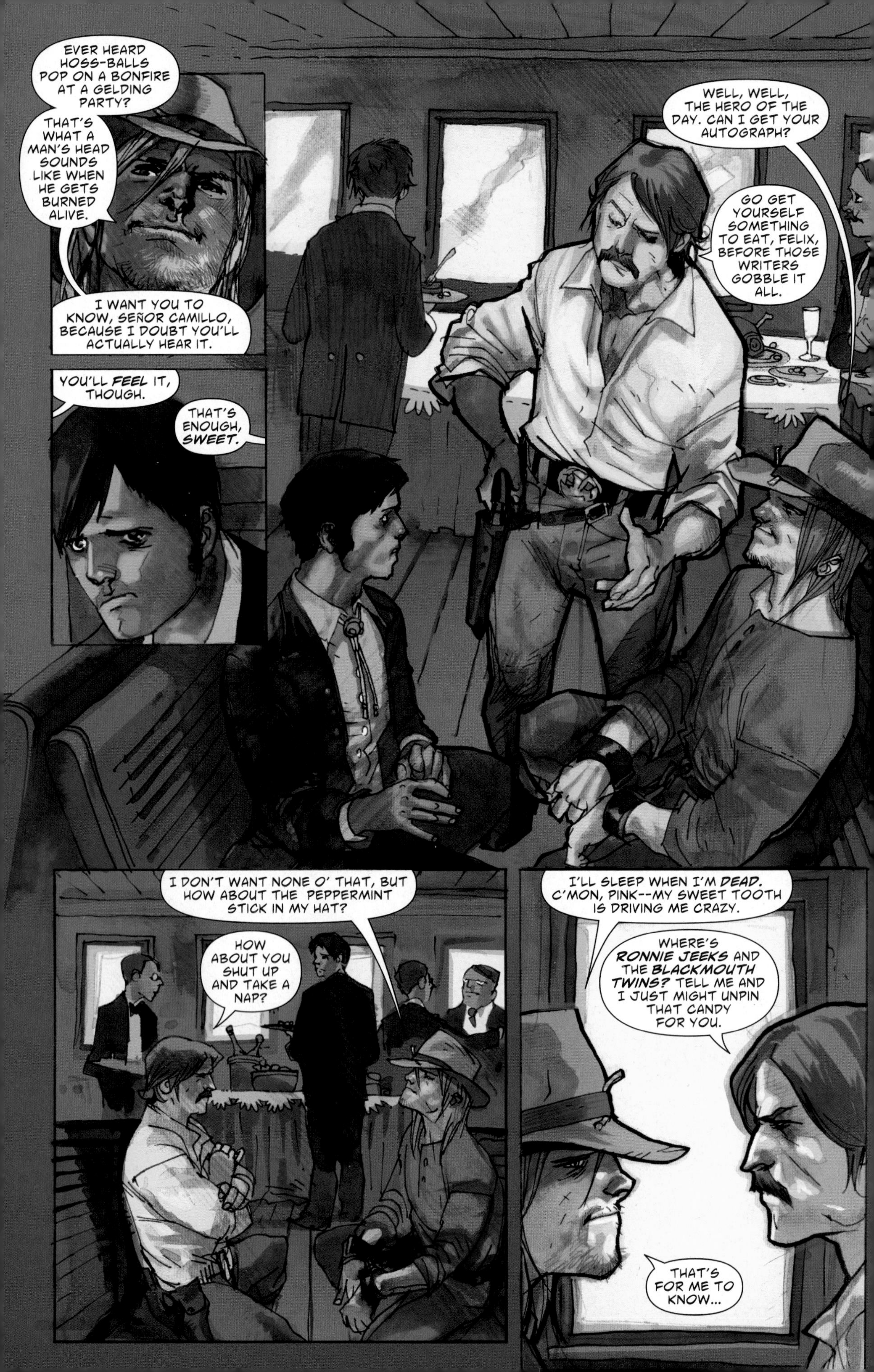
EVER HEARD HOSS-BALLS POP ON A BONFIRE AT A GELDING PARTY?
THAT'S WHAT A MAN'S HEAD SOUNDS LIKE WHEN HE GETS BURNED ALIVE.
I WANT YOU TO KNOW, SEÑOR CAMILLO, BECAUSE I DOUBT YOU'LL ACTUALLY HEAR IT.
WELL, WELL, THE HERO OF THE DAY. CAN I GET YOUR AUTOGRAPH?
GO GET YOURSELF SOMETHING TO EAT, FELIX, BEFORE THOSE WRITERS GOBBLE IT ALL.
YOU'LL *FEEL* IT, THOUGH.
THAT'S ENOUGH, *SWEET.*
I DON'T WANT NONE O' THAT, BUT HOW ABOUT THE PEPPERMINT STICK IN MY HAT?
HOW ABOUT YOU SHUT UP AND TAKE A NAP?
I'LL SLEEP WHEN I'M *DEAD.* C'MON, PINK--MY SWEET TOOTH IS DRIVING ME CRAZY.
WHERE'S *RONNIE JEEKS* AND THE *BLACKMOUTH TWINS?* TELL ME AND I JUST MIGHT UNPIN THAT CANDY FOR YOU.
THAT'S FOR ME TO KNOW...

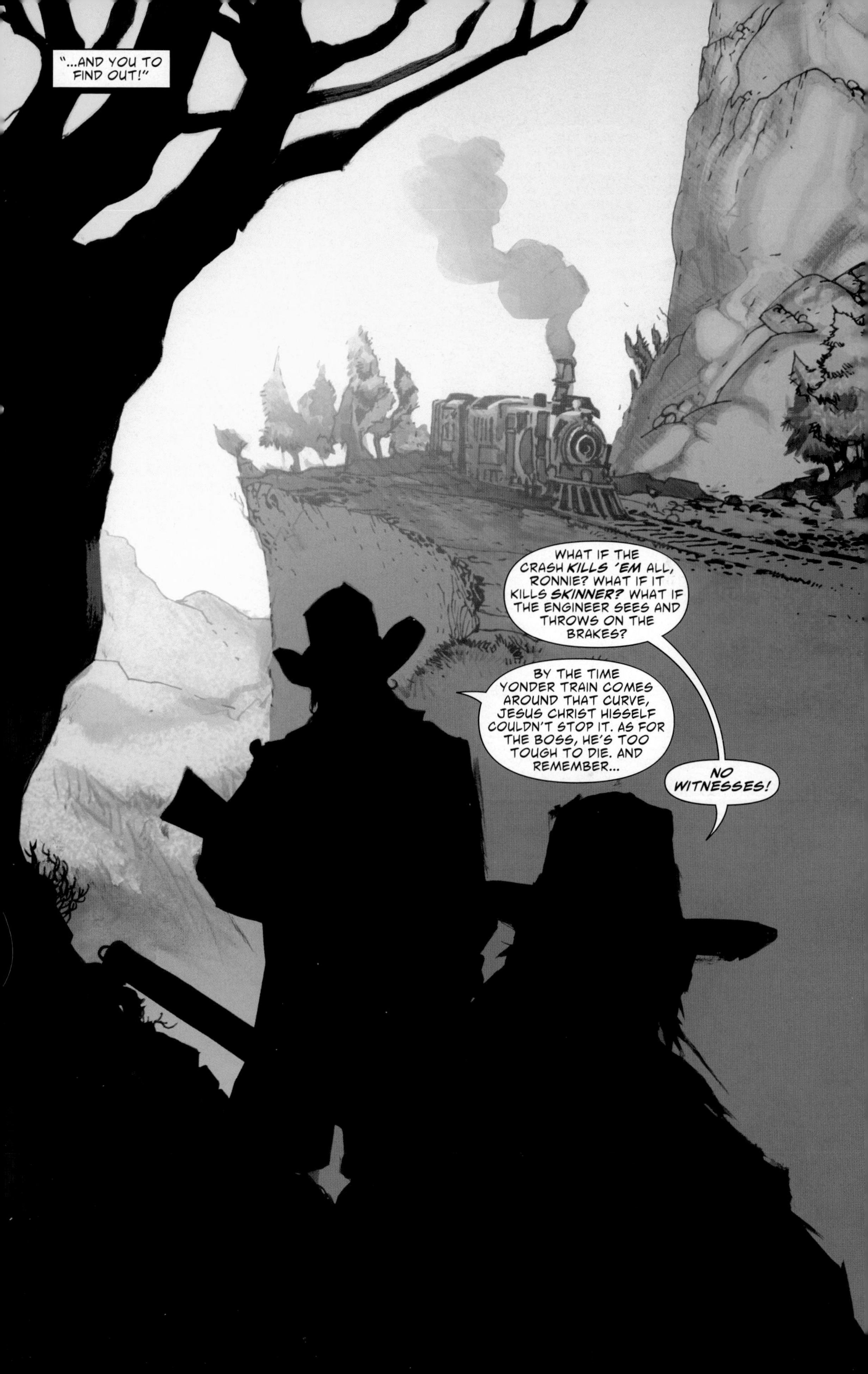
"...AND YOU TO FIND OUT!"
WHAT IF THE CRASH KILLS 'EM ALL, RONNIE? WHAT IF IT KILLS SKINNER? WHAT IF THE ENGINEER SEES AND THROWS ON THE BRAKES?
BY THE TIME YONDER TRAIN COMES AROUND THAT CURVE, JESUS CHRIST HISSELF COULDN'T STOP IT. AS FOR THE BOSS, HE'S TOO TOUGH TO DIE. AND REMEMBER...
NO WITNESSES!

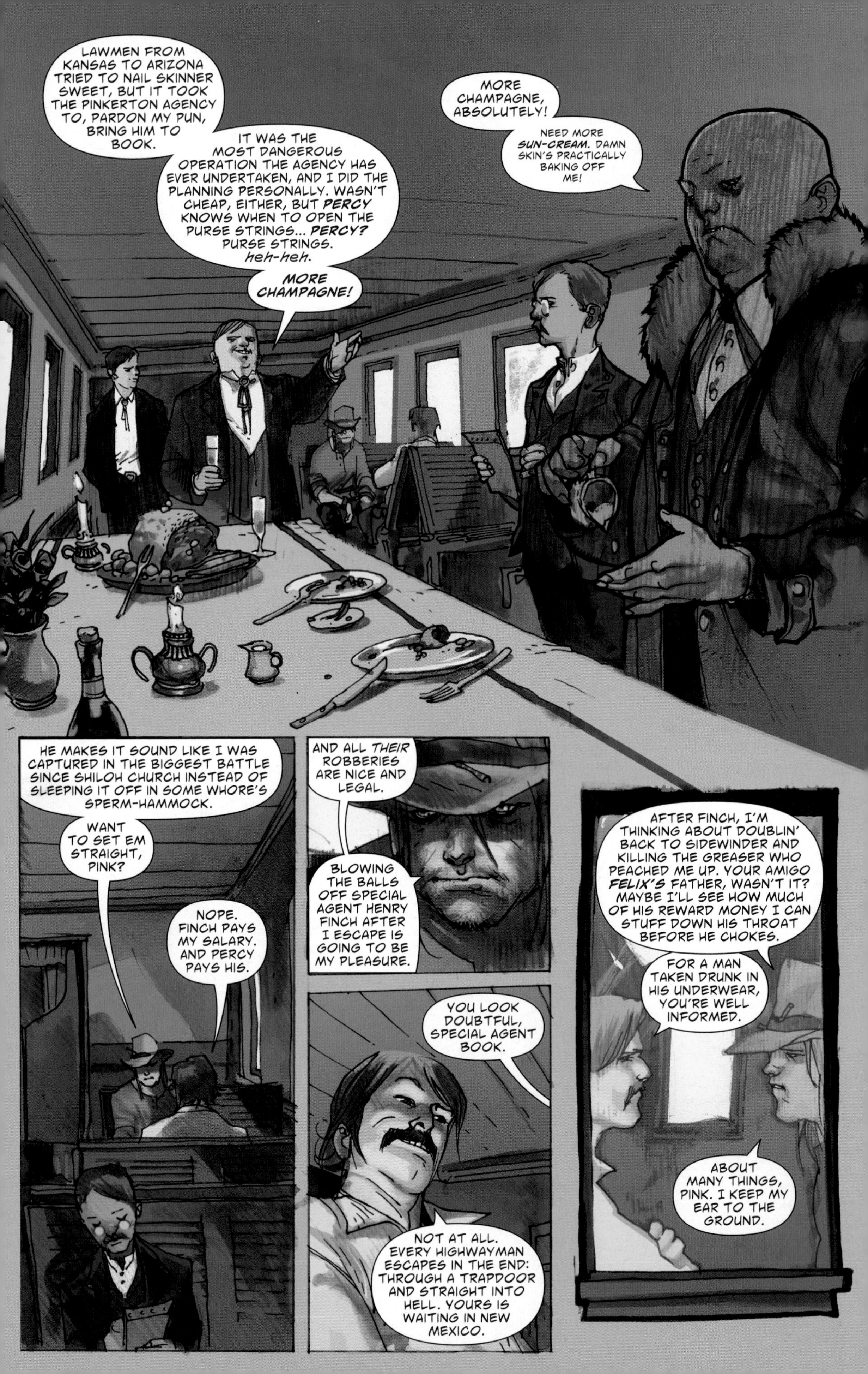
LAWMEN FROM KANSAS TO ARIZONA TRIED TO NAIL SKINNER SWEET, BUT IT TOOK THE PINKERTON AGENCY TO, PARDON MY PUN, BRING HIM TO BOOK.
IT WAS THE MOST DANGEROUS OPERATION THE AGENCY HAS EVER UNDERTAKEN, AND I DID THE PLANNING PERSONALLY. WASN'T CHEAP, EITHER, BUT *PERCY* KNOWS WHEN TO OPEN THE PURSE STRINGS... *PERCY?* PURSE STRINGS. *heh-heh.*
MORE CHAMPAGNE!
MORE CHAMPAGNE, ABSOLUTELY!
NEED MORE *SUN-CREAM.* DAMN SKIN'S PRACTICALLY BAKING OFF ME!
HE MAKES IT SOUND LIKE I WAS CAPTURED IN THE BIGGEST BATTLE SINCE SHILOH CHURCH INSTEAD OF SLEEPING IT OFF IN SOME WHORE'S SPERM-HAMMOCK.
WANT TO SET EM STRAIGHT, PINK?
NOPE. FINCH PAYS MY SALARY. AND PERCY PAYS HIS.
AND ALL *THEIR* ROBBERIES ARE NICE AND LEGAL.
BLOWING THE BALLS OFF SPECIAL AGENT HENRY FINCH AFTER I ESCAPE IS GOING TO BE MY PLEASURE.
YOU LOOK DOUBTFUL, SPECIAL AGENT BOOK.
NOT AT ALL. EVERY HIGHWAYMAN ESCAPES IN THE END: THROUGH A TRAPDOOR AND STRAIGHT INTO HELL. YOURS IS WAITING IN NEW MEXICO.
AFTER FINCH, I'M THINKING ABOUT DOUBLIN' BACK TO SIDEWINDER AND KILLING THE GREASER WHO PEACHED ME UP. YOUR AMIGO *FELIX'S* FATHER, WASN'T IT? MAYBE I'LL SEE HOW MUCH OF HIS REWARD MONEY I CAN STUFF DOWN HIS THROAT BEFORE HE CHOKES.
FOR A MAN TAKEN DRUNK IN HIS UNDERWEAR, YOU'RE WELL INFORMED.
ABOUT MANY THINGS, PINK. I KEEP MY EAR TO THE GROUND.

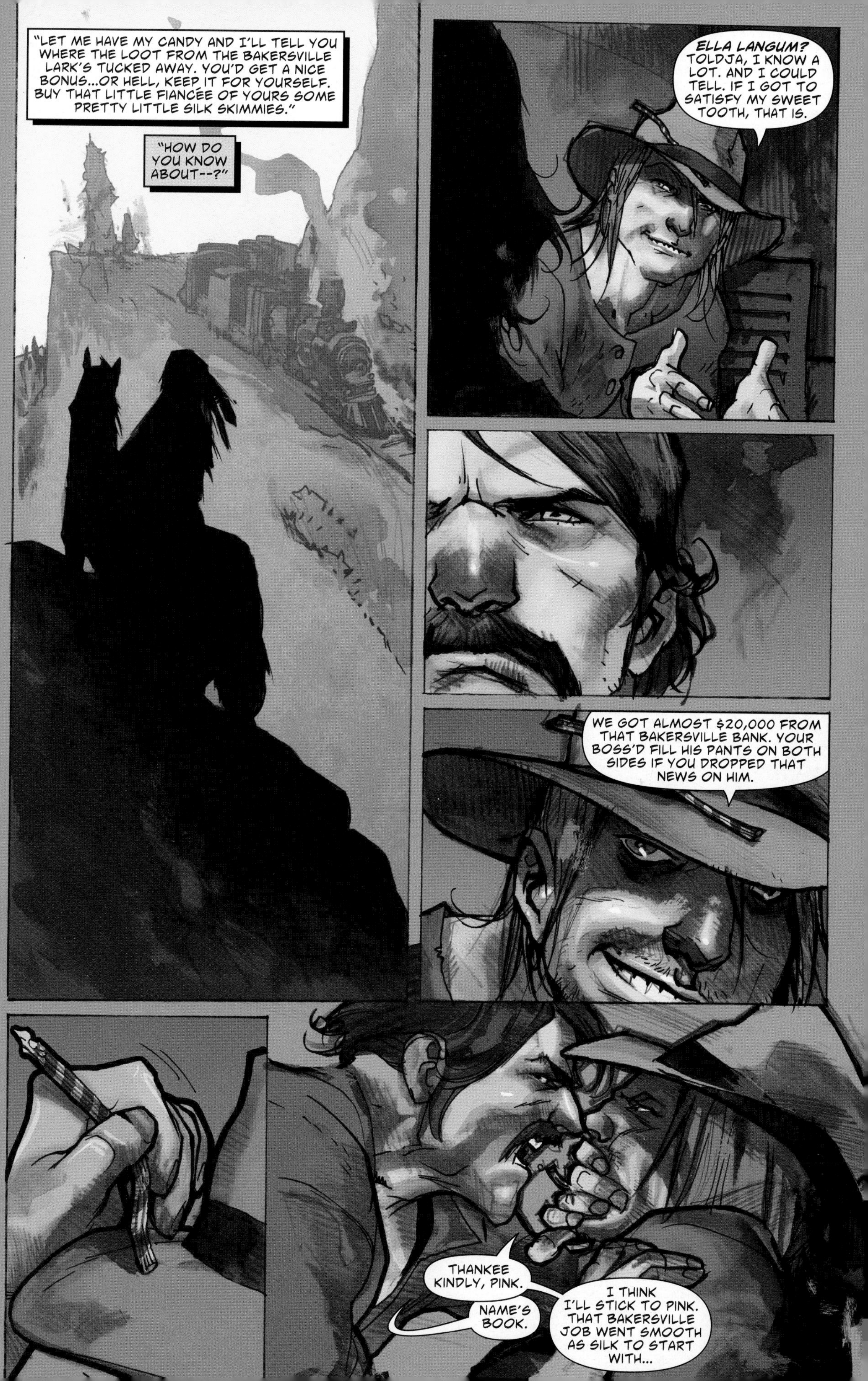
"LET ME HAVE MY CANDY AND I'LL TELL YOU WHERE THE LOOT FROM THE BAKERSVILLE LARK'S TUCKED AWAY. YOU'D GET A NICE BONUS...OR HELL, KEEP IT FOR YOURSELF. BUY THAT LITTLE FIANCÉE OF YOURS SOME PRETTY LITTLE SILK SKIMMIES."
"HOW DO YOU KNOW ABOUT--?"
ELLA LANGUM? TOLDJA, I KNOW A LOT. AND I COULD TELL. IF I GOT TO SATISFY MY SWEET TOOTH, THAT IS.
WE GOT ALMOST $20,000 FROM THAT BAKERSVILLE BANK. YOUR BOSS'D FILL HIS PANTS ON BOTH SIDES IF YOU DROPPED THAT NEWS ON HIM.
THANKEE KINDLY, PINK.
NAME'S BOOK.
I THINK I'LL STICK TO PINK. THAT BAKERSVILLE JOB WENT SMOOTH AS SILK TO START WITH...

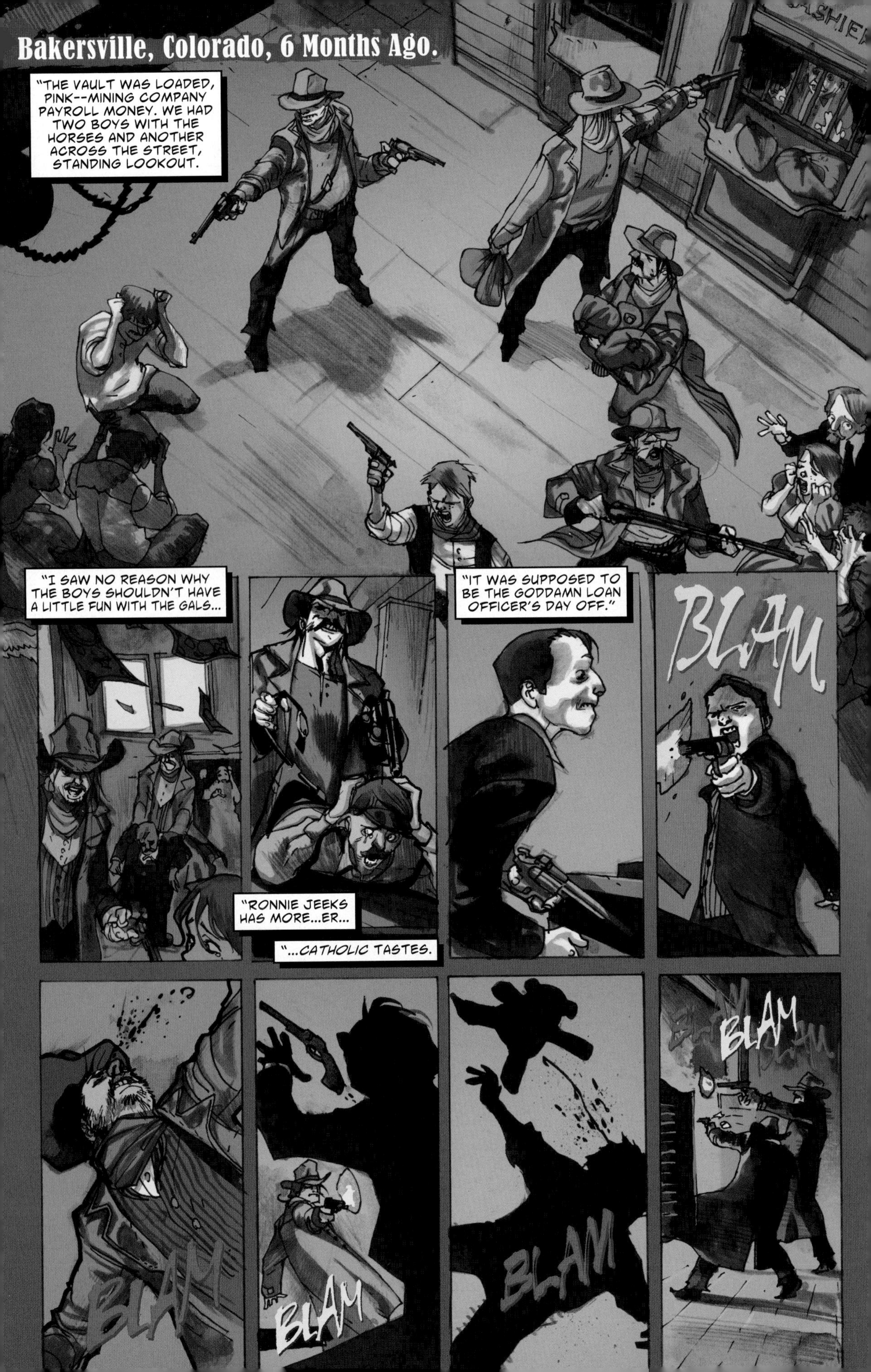

Bakersville, Colorado, 6 Months Ago.
"THE VAULT WAS LOADED, PINK--MINING COMPANY PAYROLL MONEY. WE HAD TWO BOYS WITH THE HORSES AND ANOTHER ACROSS THE STREET, STANDING LOOKOUT.
"I SAW NO REASON WHY THE BOYS SHOULDN'T HAVE A LITTLE FUN WITH THE GALS...
"RONNIE JEEKS HAS MORE...ER...
"...CATHOLIC TASTES.
"IT WAS SUPPOSED TO BE THE GODDAMN LOAN OFFICER'S DAY OFF."
BLAM
BLAM
BLAM
BLAM
BLAM

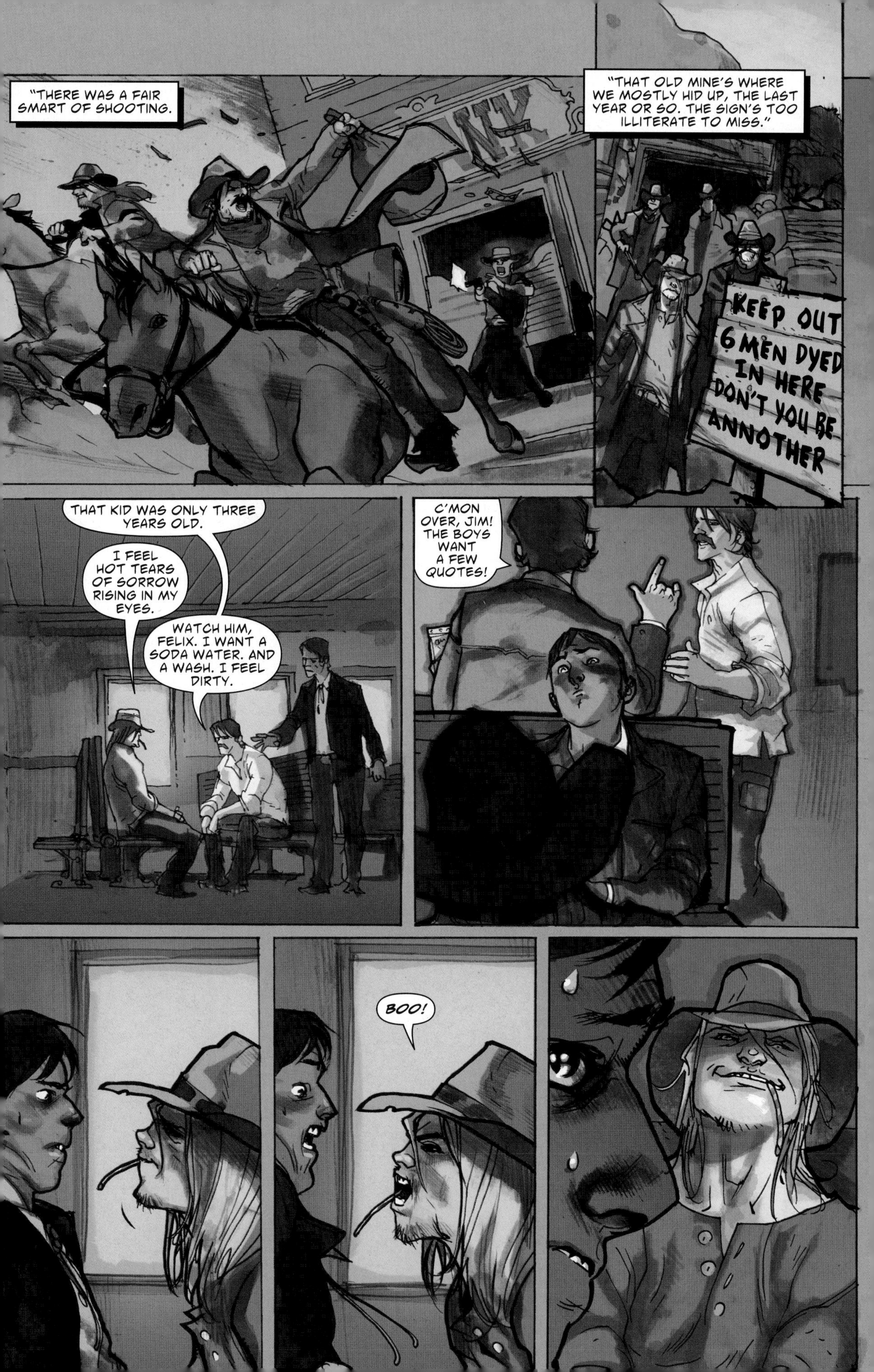
"THERE WAS A FAIR SMART OF SHOOTING.
"THAT OLD MINE'S WHERE WE MOSTLY HID UP, THE LAST YEAR OR SO. THE SIGN'S TOO ILLITERATE TO MISS."
KEEP OUT 6 MEN DYED IN HERE DON'T YOU BE ANNOTHER
THAT KID WAS ONLY THREE YEARS OLD.
I FEEL HOT TEARS OF SORROW RISING IN MY EYES.
WATCH HIM, FELIX. I WANT A SODA WATER. AND A WASH. I FEEL DIRTY.
C'MON OVER, JIM! THE BOYS WANT A FEW QUOTES!
BOO!

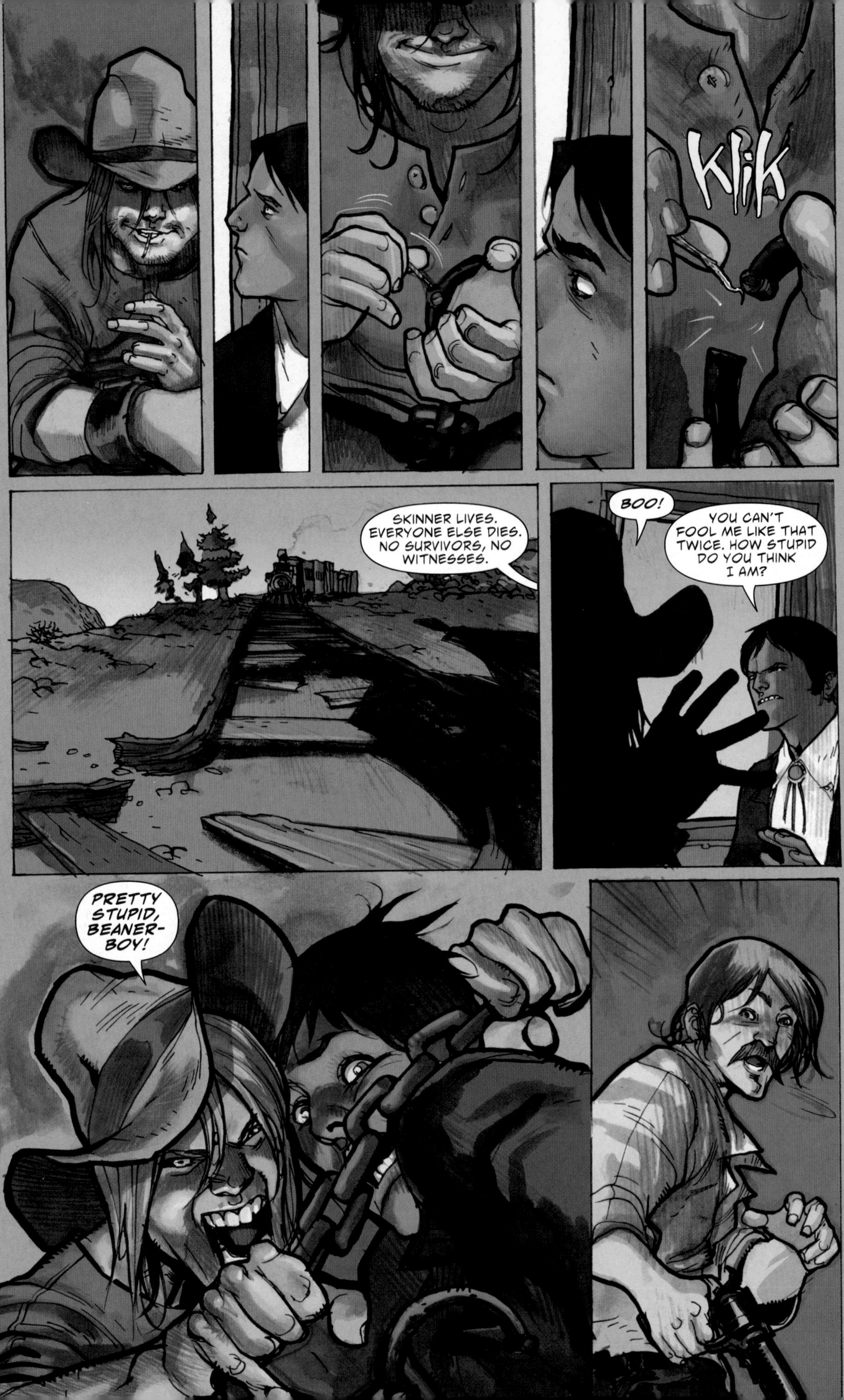
KLIK
SKINNER LIVES. EVERYONE ELSE DIES. NO SURVIVORS, NO WITNESSES.
BOO!
YOU CAN'T FOOL ME LIKE THAT TWICE. HOW STUPID DO YOU THINK I AM?
PRETTY STUPID, BEANER-BOY!

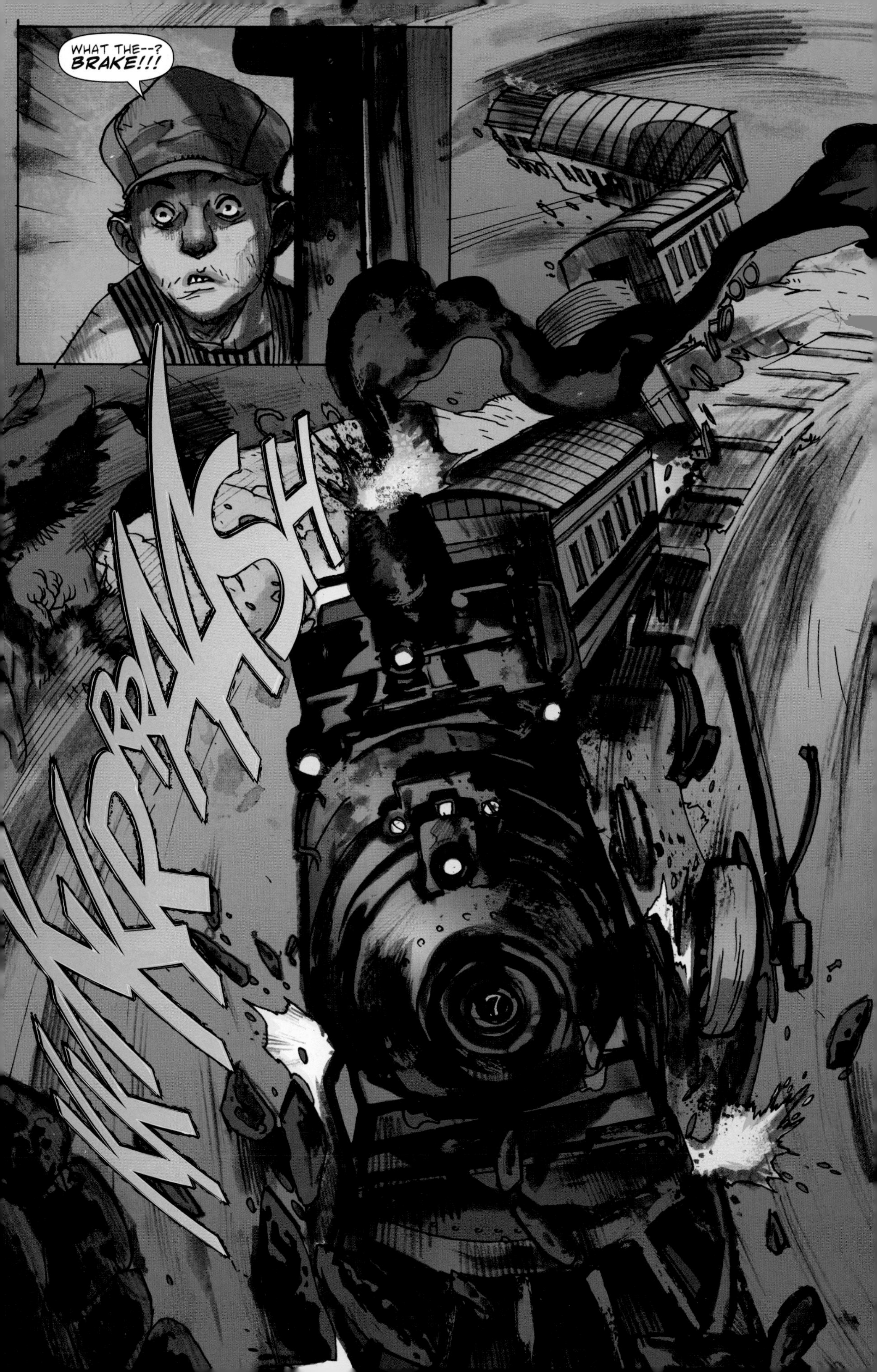
WHAT THE--? BRAKE!!!
WHHRRAASH

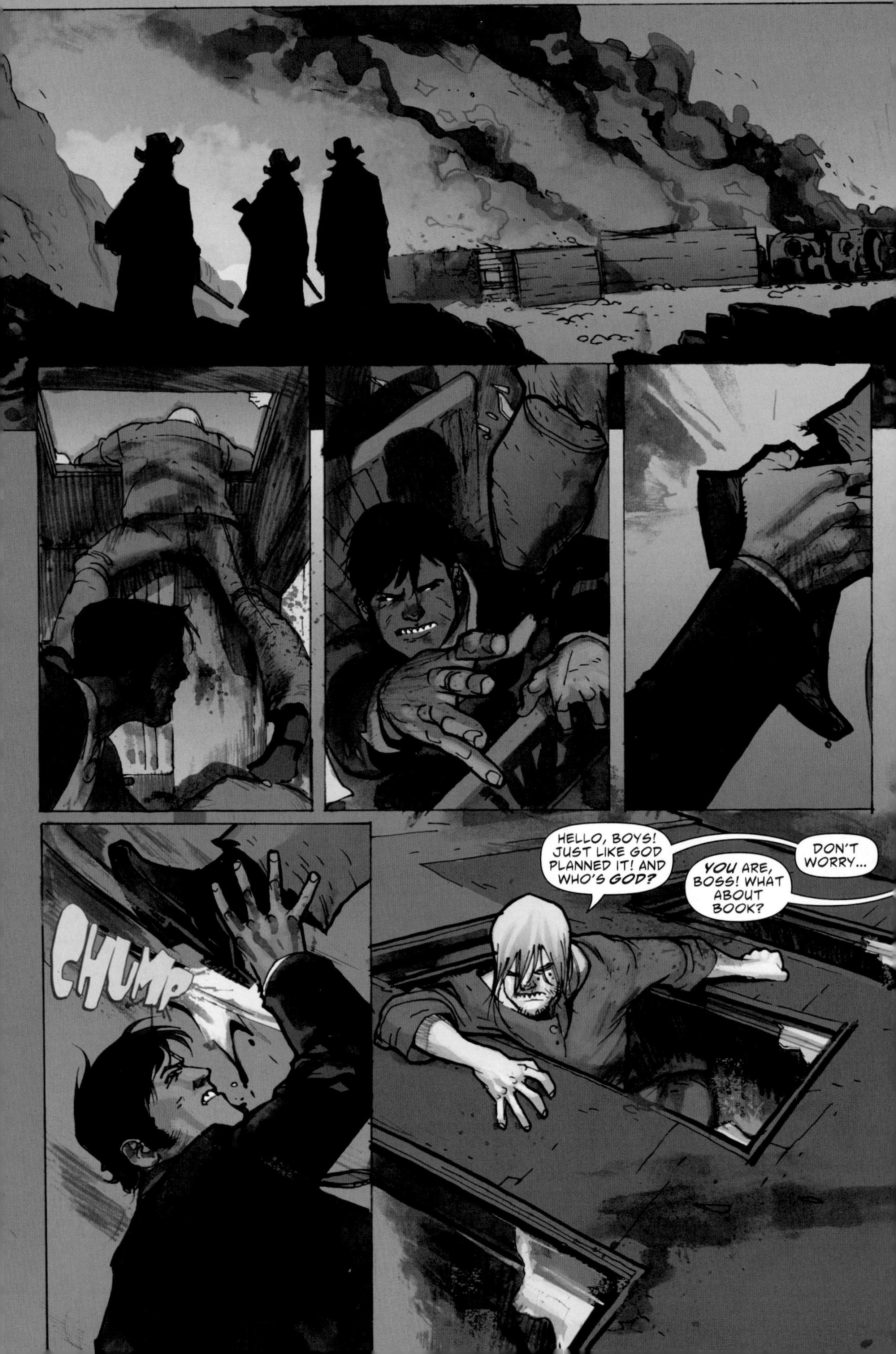
CHUMP
HELLO, BOYS! JUST LIKE GOD PLANNED IT! AND WHO'S GOD?
YOU ARE, BOSS! WHAT ABOUT BOOK?
DON'T WORRY...

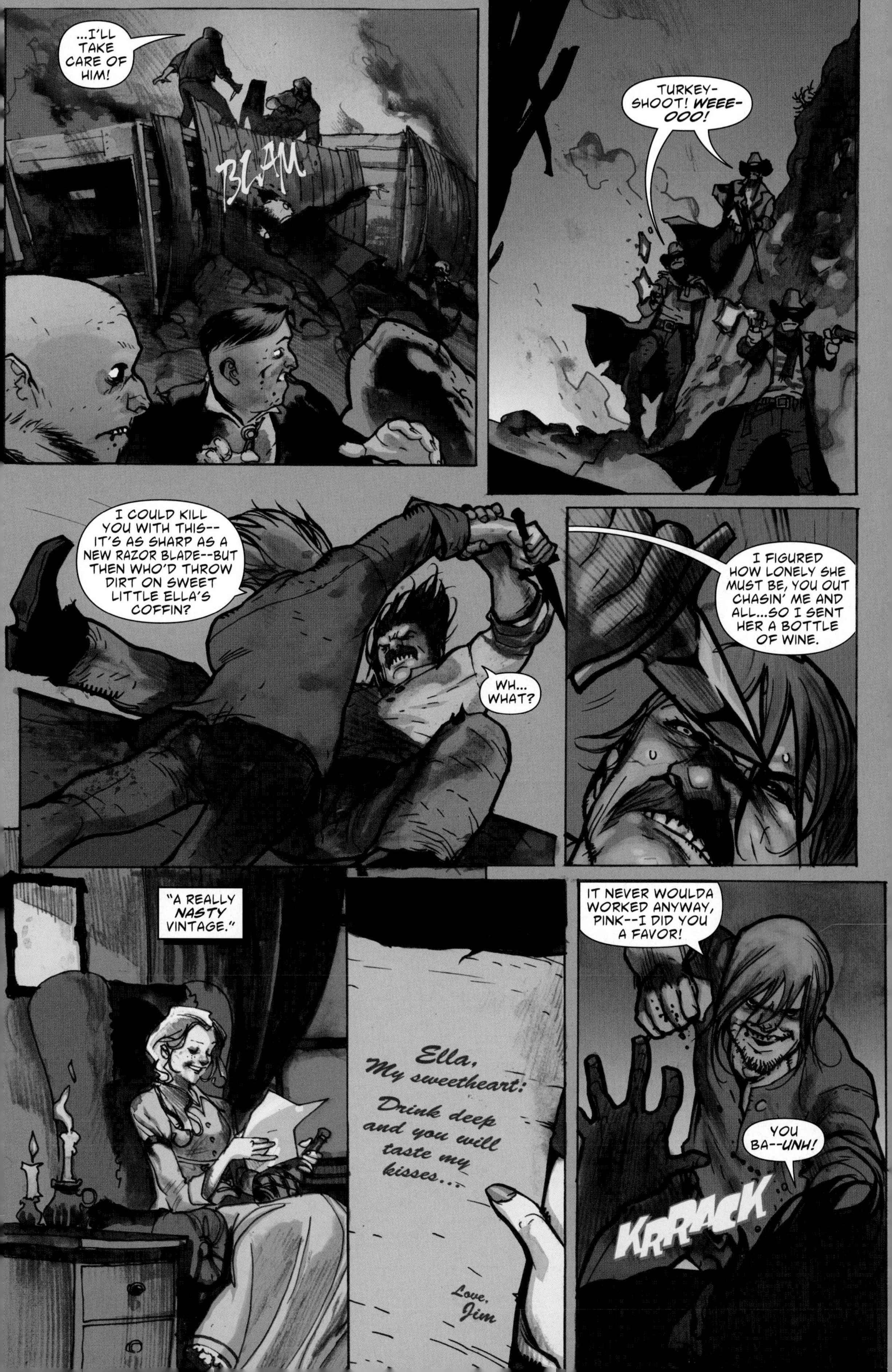
...I'LL TAKE CARE OF HIM!
BLAM
TURKEY-SHOOT! WEEE-OOO!
I COULD KILL YOU WITH THIS--IT'S AS SHARP AS A NEW RAZOR BLADE--BUT THEN WHO'D THROW DIRT ON SWEET LITTLE ELLA'S COFFIN?
WH... WHAT?
I FIGURED HOW LONELY SHE MUST BE, YOU OUT CHASIN' ME AND ALL...SO I SENT HER A BOTTLE OF WINE.
"A REALLY NASTY VINTAGE."
Ella, My sweetheart: Drink deep and you will taste my kisses...
Love, Jim
IT NEVER WOULDA WORKED ANYWAY, PINK--I DID YOU A FAVOR!
YOU BA--UNH!
KRRACK

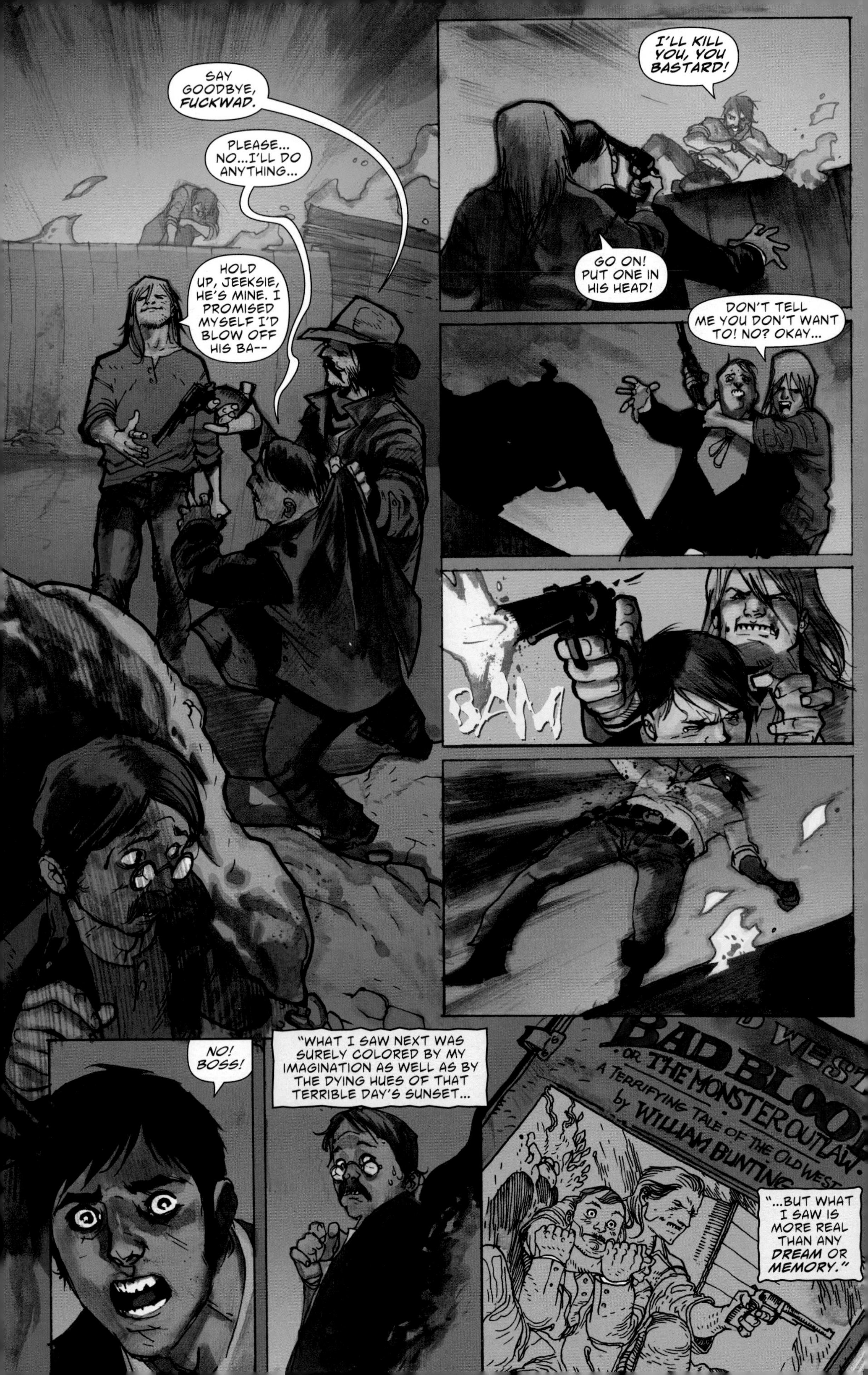
SAY GOODBYE, *FUCKWAD.*
PLEASE... NO...I'LL DO ANYTHING...
HOLD UP, JEEKSIE, HE'S MINE. I PROMISED MYSELF I'D BLOW OFF HIS BA--
I'LL KILL YOU, YOU BASTARD!
GO ON! PUT ONE IN HIS HEAD!
DON'T TELL ME YOU DON'T WANT TO! NO? OKAY...
BAM
NO! BOSS!
"WHAT I SAW NEXT WAS SURELY COLORED BY MY IMAGINATION AS WELL AS BY THE DYING HUES OF THAT TERRIBLE DAY'S SUNSET...
BAD BLOOD
OR THE MONSTER OUTLAW
A TERRIFYING TALE OF THE OLD WEST
by WILLIAM BUNTING
"...BUT WHAT I SAW IS MORE REAL THAN ANY *DREAM OR MEMORY.*"

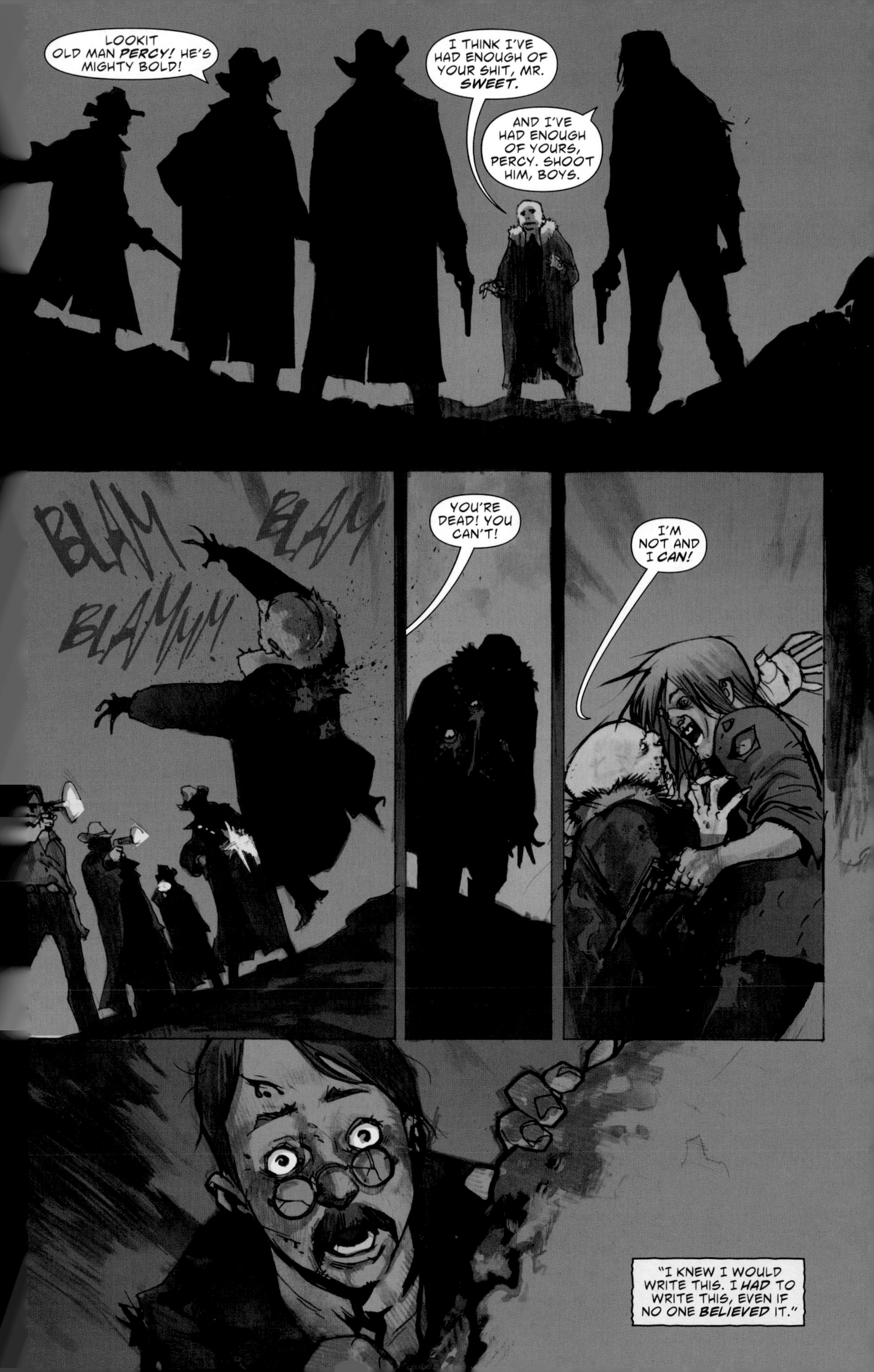
LOOKIT OLD MAN PERCY! HE'S MIGHTY BOLD!
I THINK I'VE HAD ENOUGH OF YOUR SHIT, MR. SWEET.
AND I'VE HAD ENOUGH OF YOURS, PERCY. SHOOT HIM, BOYS.
BLAM
BLAM
BLAMMM!
YOU'RE DEAD! YOU CAN'T!
I'M NOT AND I CAN!
"I KNEW I WOULD WRITE THIS. I HAD TO WRITE THIS, EVEN IF NO ONE BELIEVED IT."

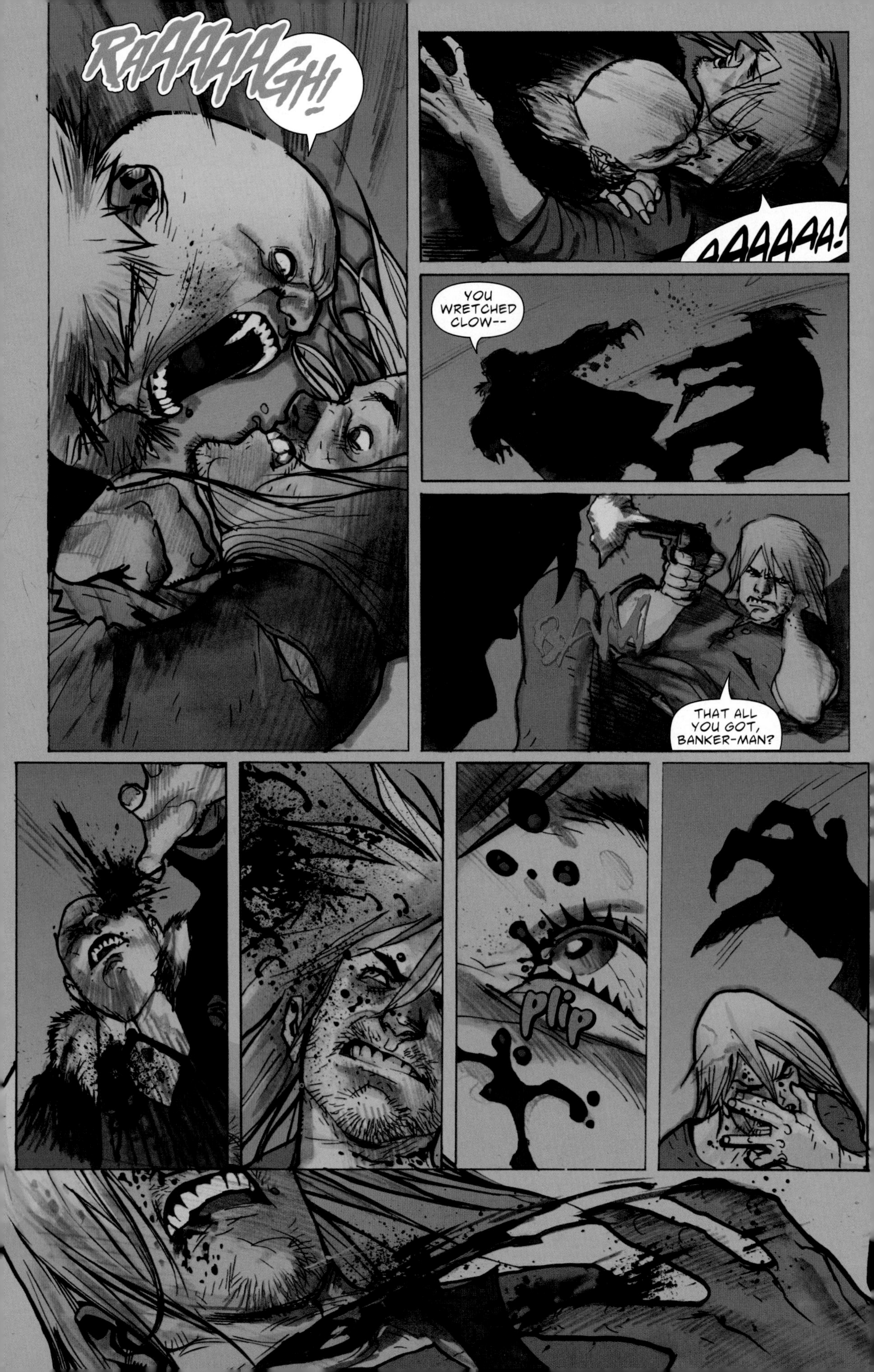
RAAAAAAGH!
AAAAAA!
YOU WRETCHED CLOW--
THAT ALL YOU GOT, BANKER-MAN?
plip

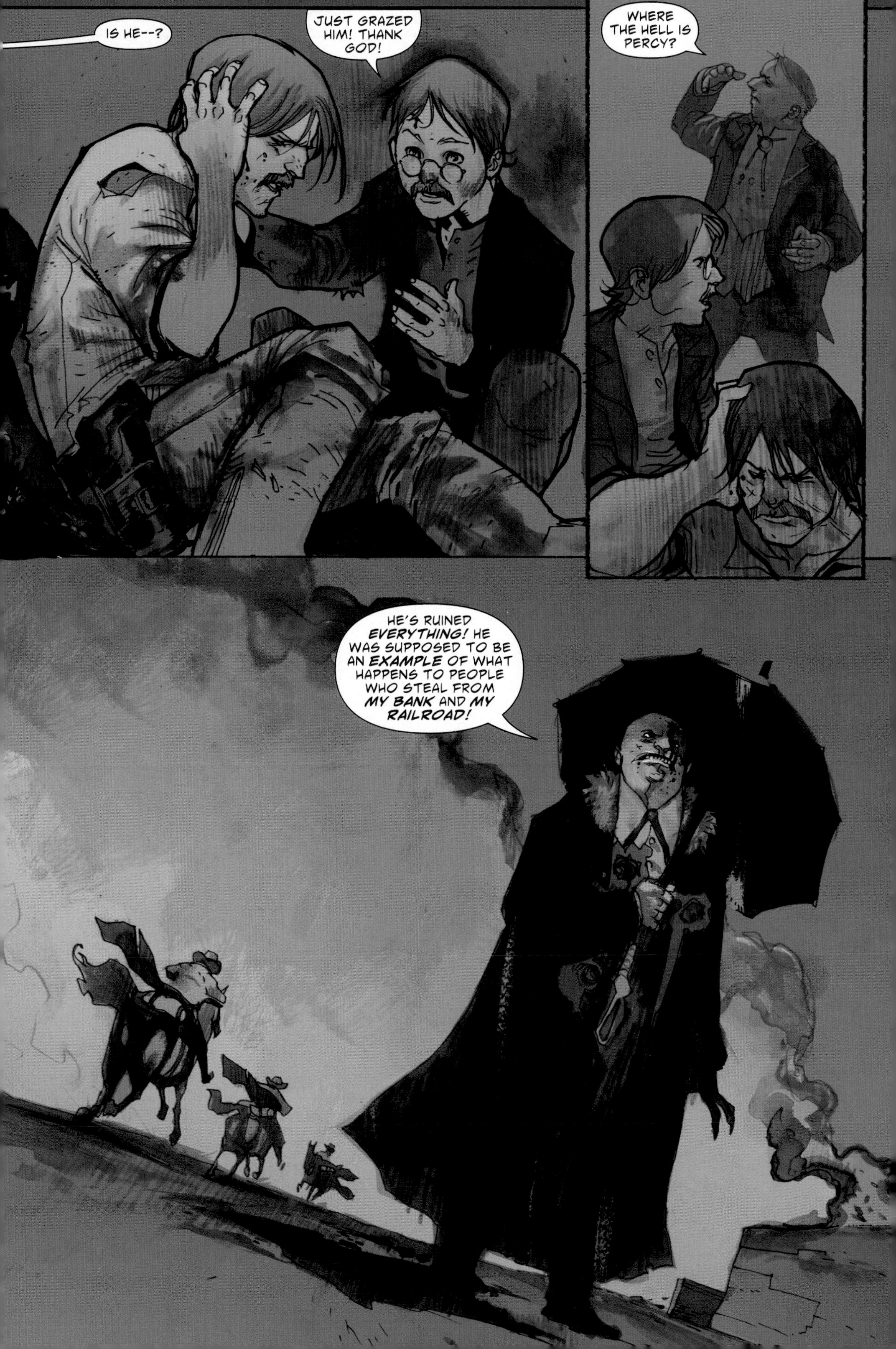
IS HE--?
JUST GRAZED HIM! THANK GOD!
WHERE THE HELL IS PERCY?
HE'S RUINED *EVERYTHING!* HE WAS SUPPOSED TO BE AN *EXAMPLE* OF WHAT HAPPENS TO PEOPLE WHO STEAL FROM *MY BANK* AND *MY RAILROAD!*

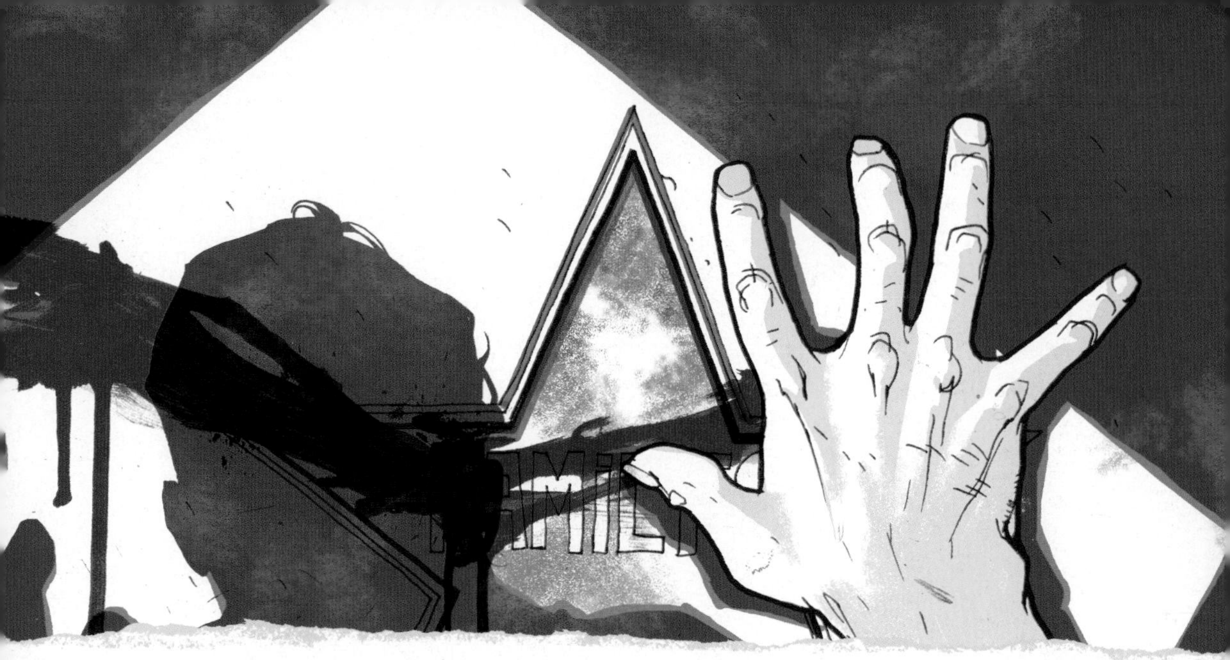

Chapter Two

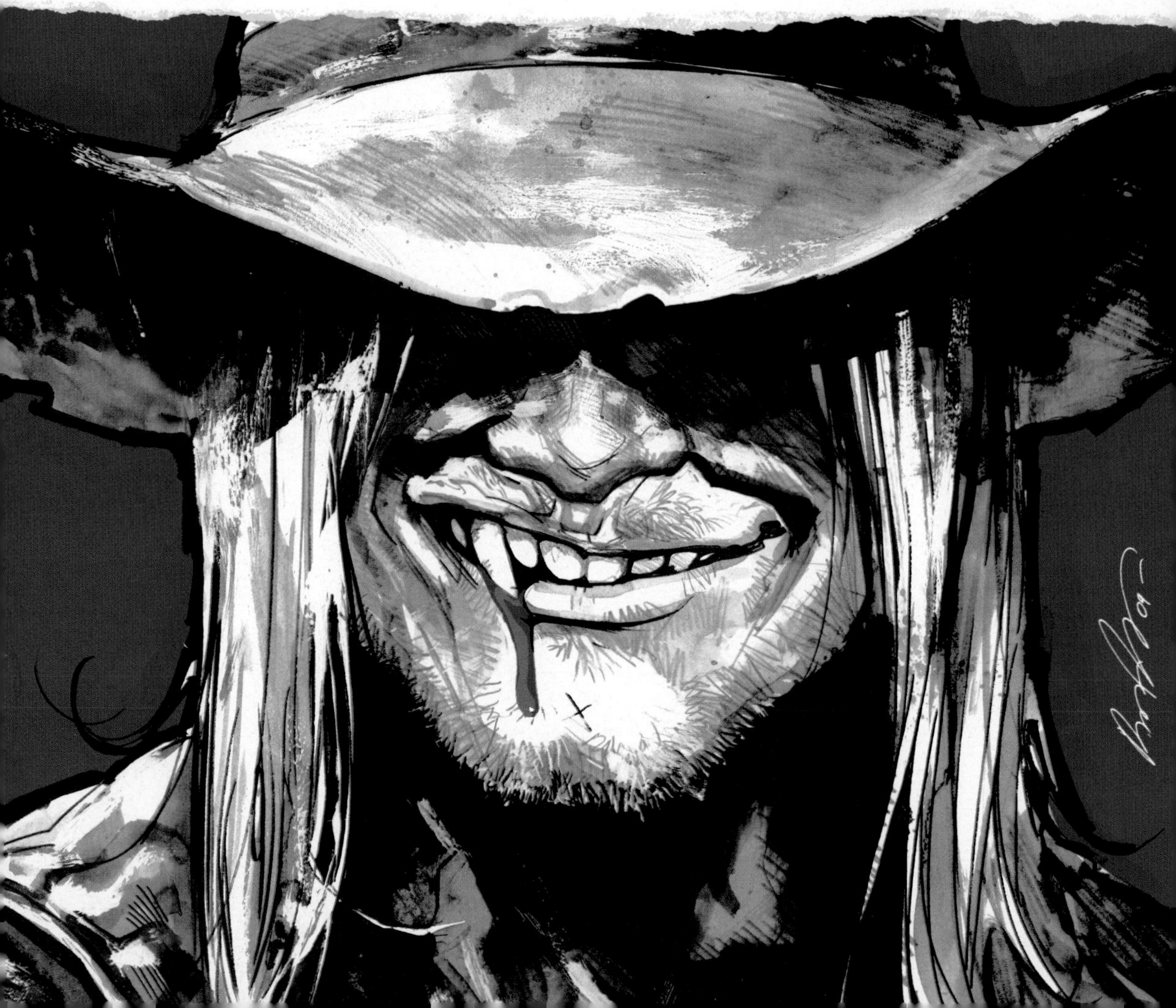

Morning Star
Scott Snyder Writer

❦

Deep Water
Stephen King Writer

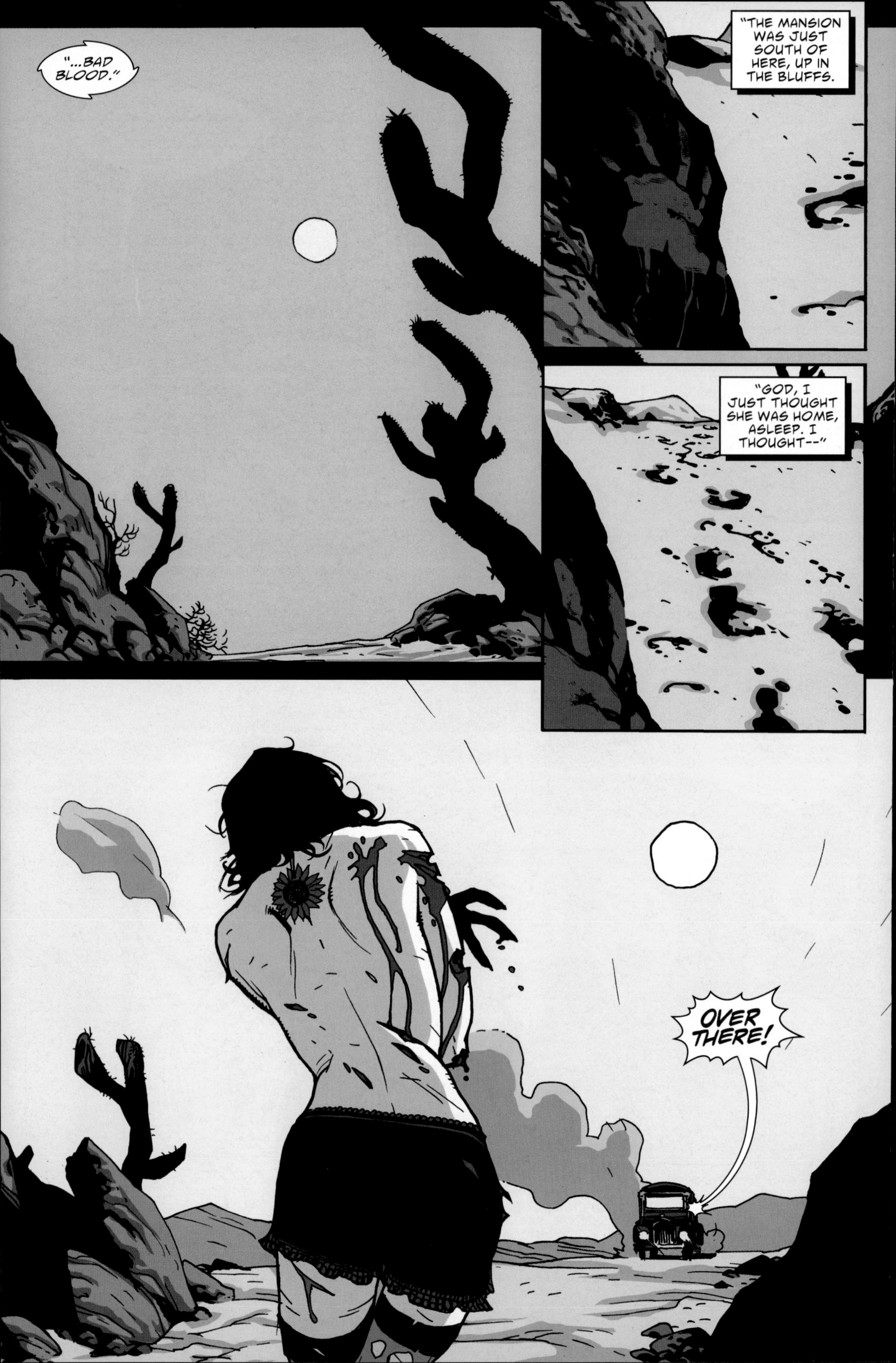
"...BAD BLOOD."
"THE MANSION WAS JUST SOUTH OF HERE, UP IN THE BLUFFS.
"GOD, I JUST THOUGHT SHE WAS HOME, ASLEEP. I THOUGHT--"
OVER THERE!

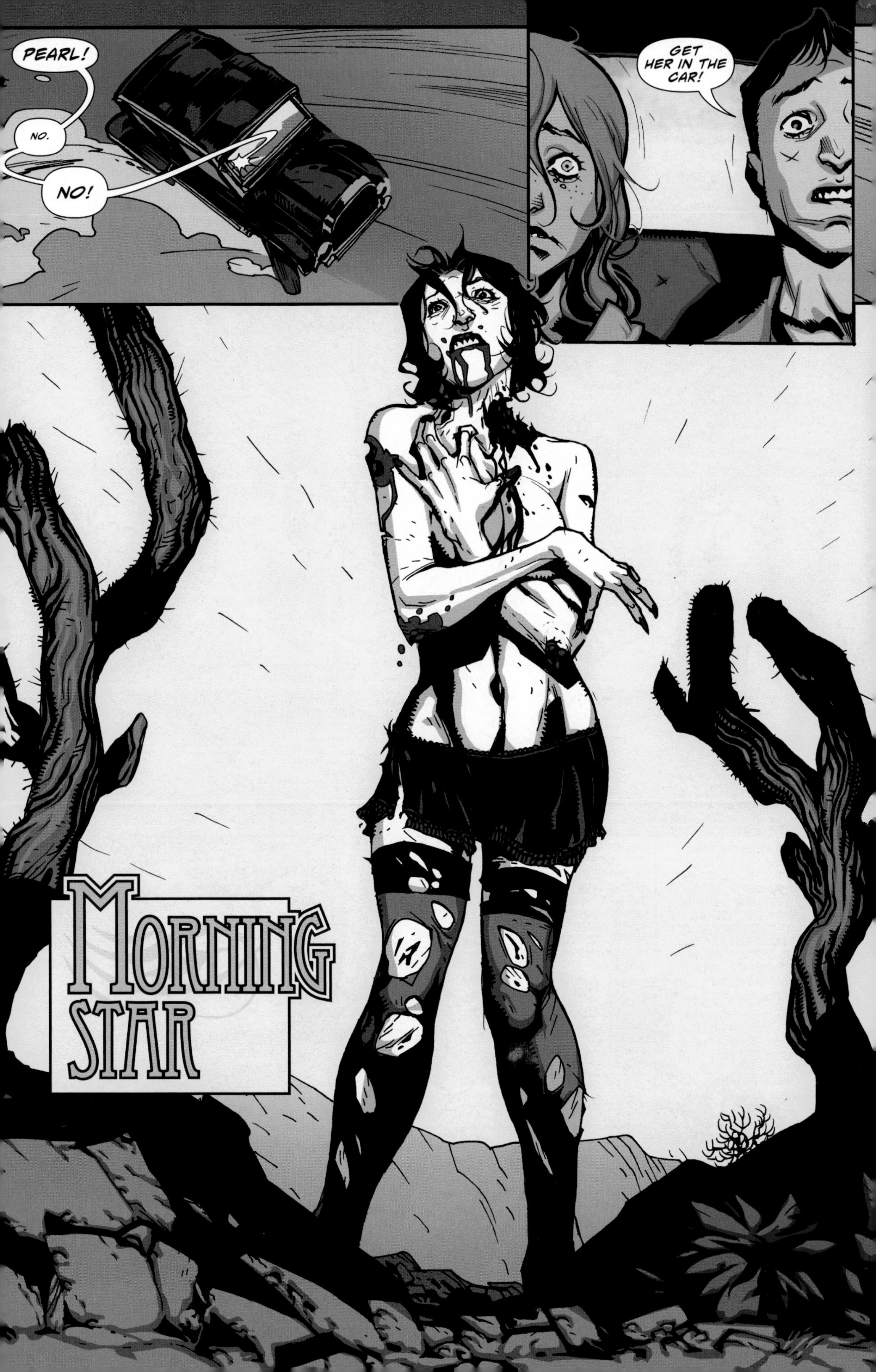
PEARL!
NO.
NO!
GET HER IN THE CAR!
MORNING STAR

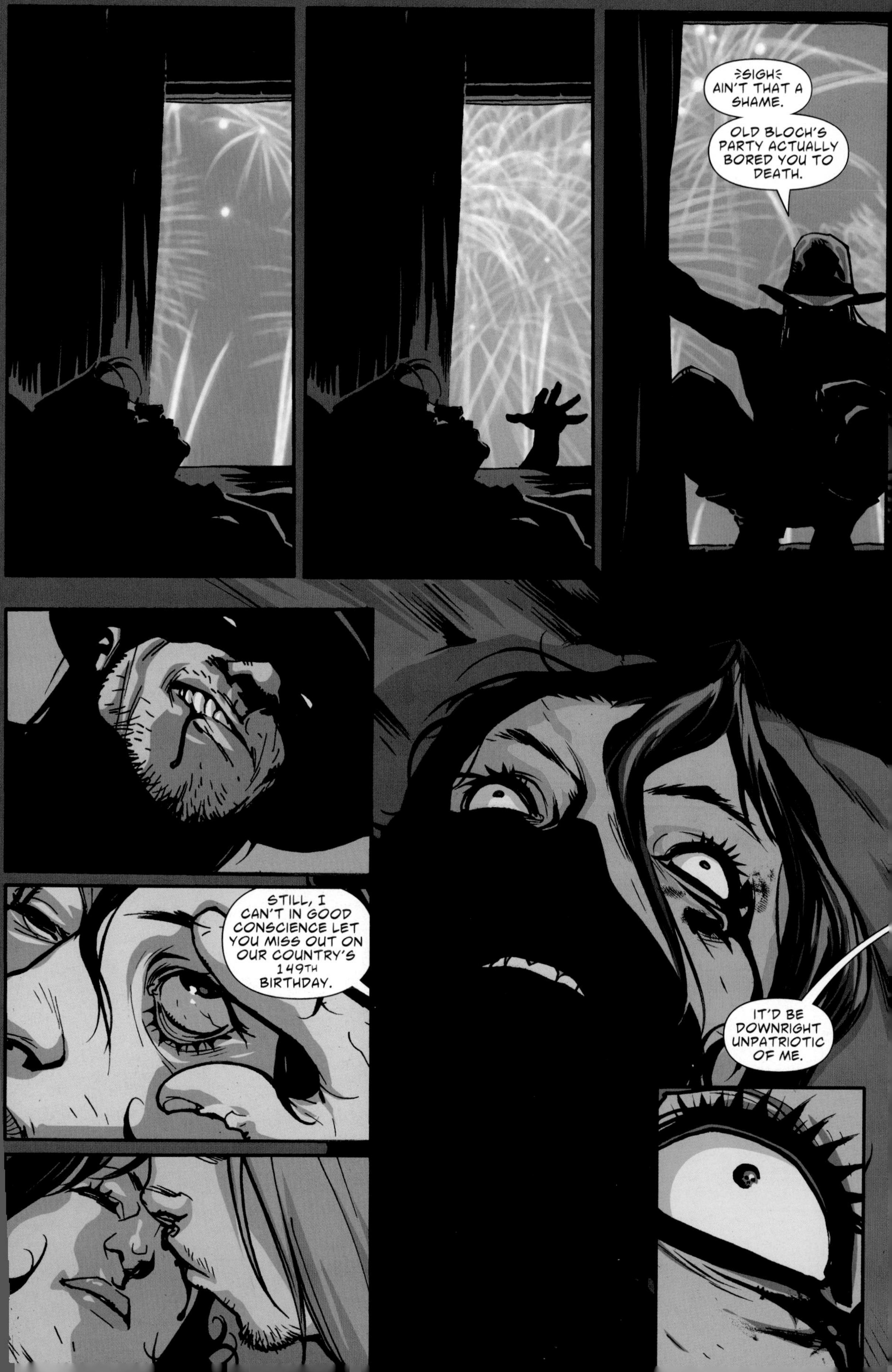

SIGH AIN'T THAT A SHAME.
OLD BLOCH'S PARTY ACTUALLY BORED YOU TO DEATH.
STILL, I CAN'T IN GOOD CONSCIENCE LET YOU MISS OUT ON OUR COUNTRY'S 149TH BIRTHDAY.
IT'D BE DOWNRIGHT UNPATRIOTIC OF ME.

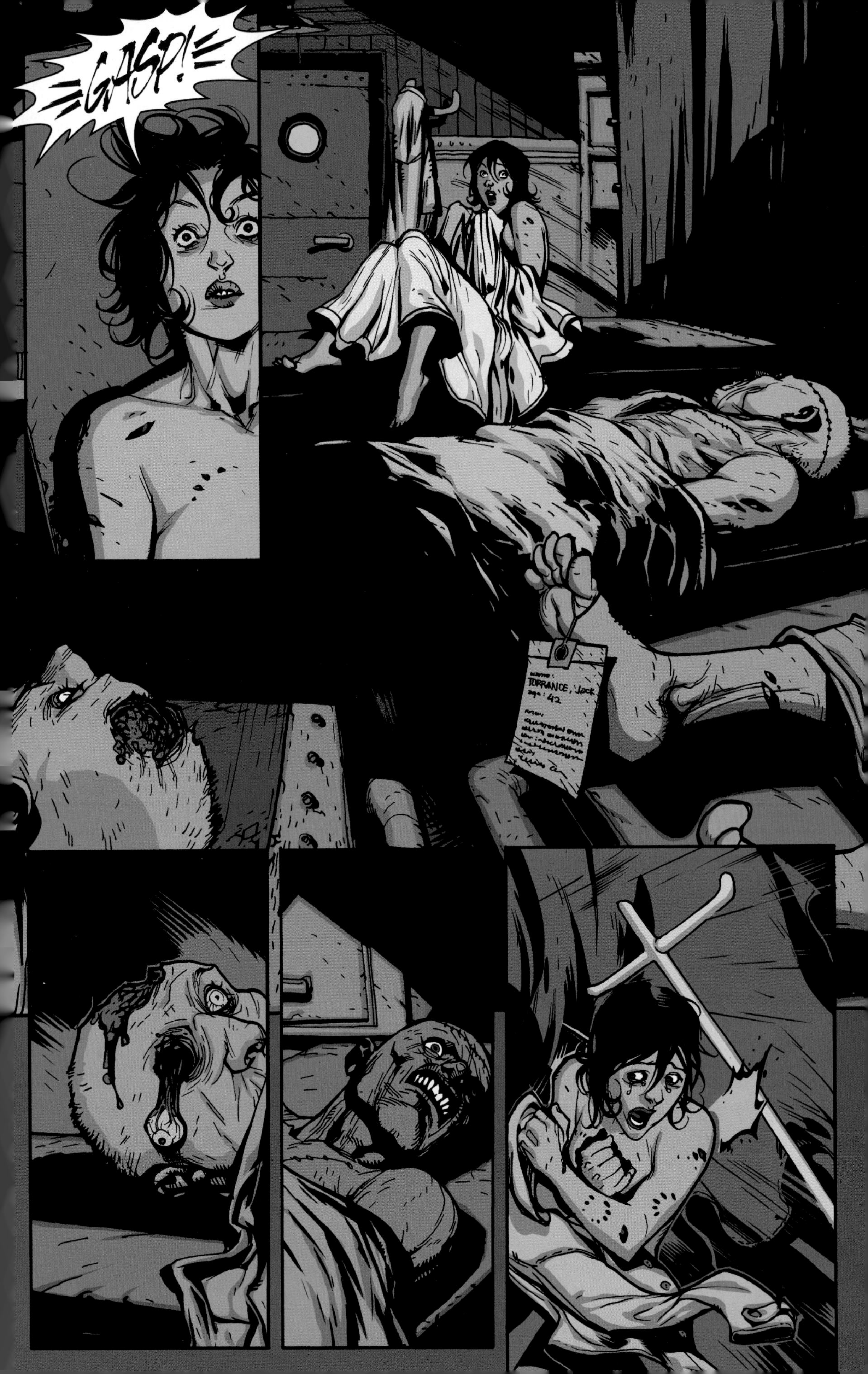
GASP!
TORRANCE, Jack
age: 42

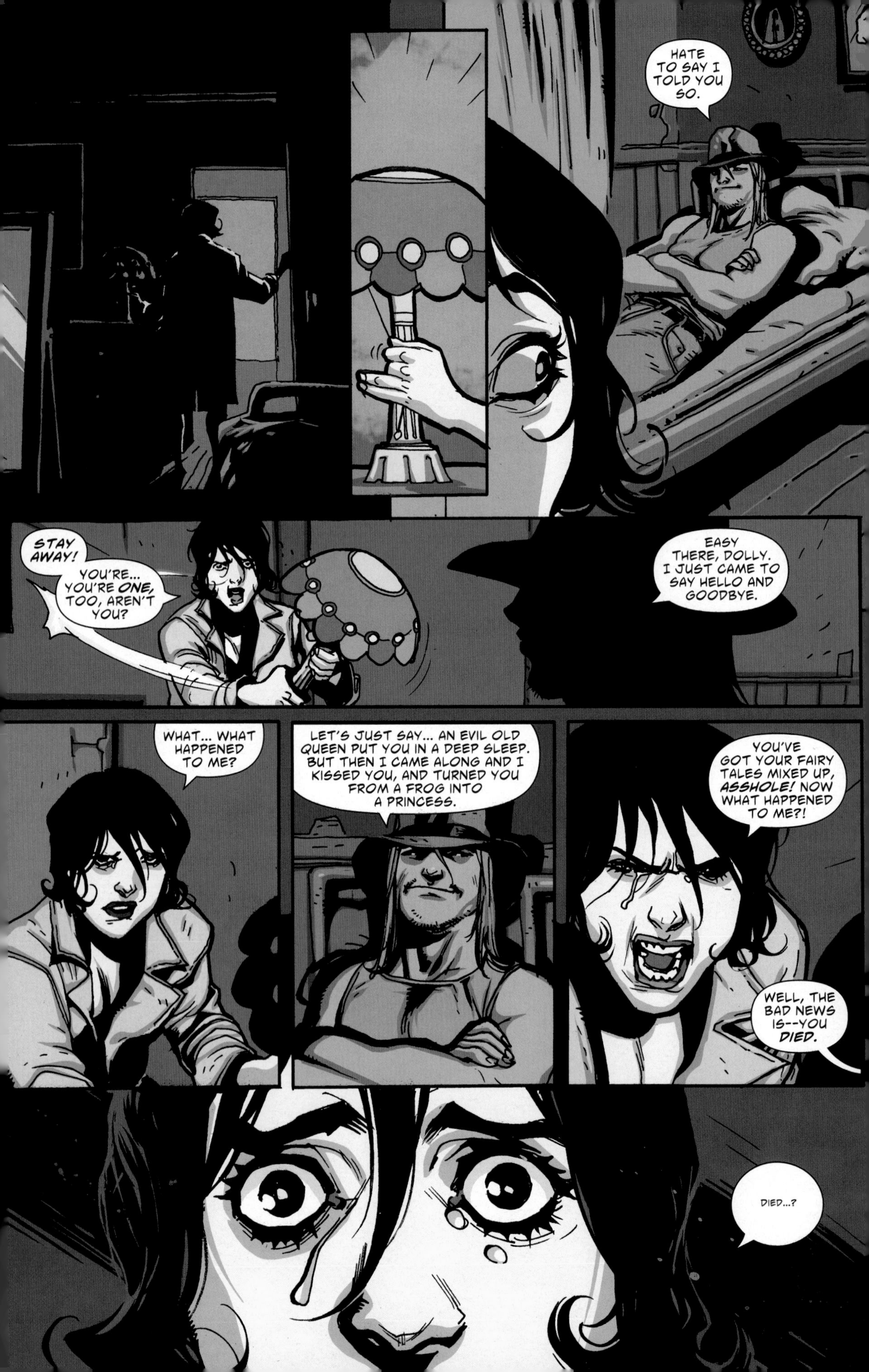
HATE TO SAY I TOLD YOU SO.
STAY AWAY!
YOU'RE... YOU'RE ONE, TOO, AREN'T YOU?
EASY THERE, DOLLY. I JUST CAME TO SAY HELLO AND GOODBYE.
WHAT... WHAT HAPPENED TO ME?
LET'S JUST SAY... AN EVIL OLD QUEEN PUT YOU IN A DEEP SLEEP. BUT THEN I CAME ALONG AND I KISSED YOU, AND TURNED YOU FROM A FROG INTO A PRINCESS.
YOU'VE GOT YOUR FAIRY TALES MIXED UP, ASSHOLE! NOW WHAT HAPPENED TO ME?!
WELL, THE BAD NEWS IS--YOU DIED.
DIED...?

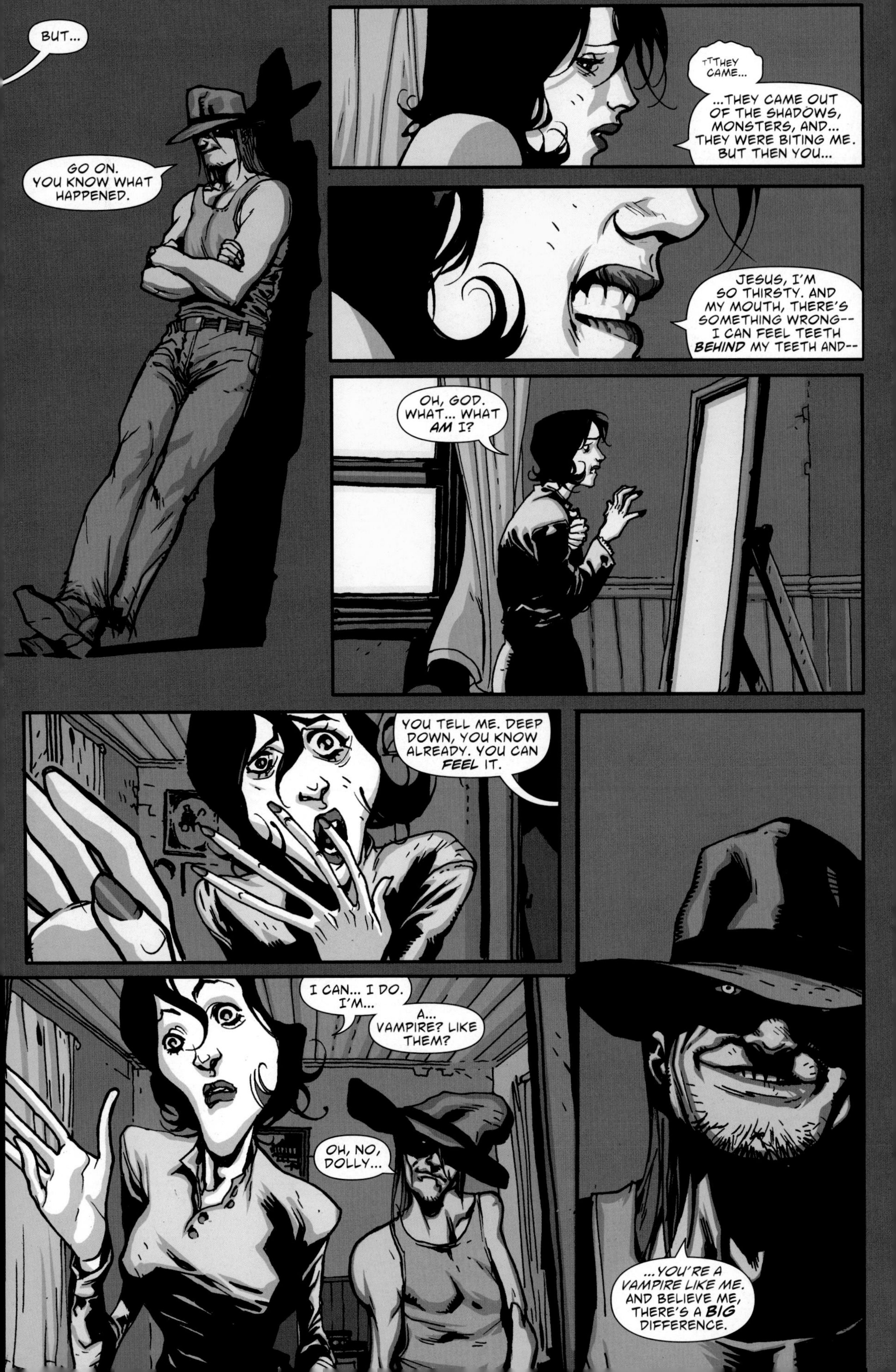
BUT...
GO ON. YOU KNOW WHAT HAPPENED.
T-T-THEY CAME...
...THEY CAME OUT OF THE SHADOWS, MONSTERS, AND... THEY WERE BITING ME. BUT THEN YOU...
JESUS, I'M SO THIRSTY. AND MY MOUTH, THERE'S SOMETHING WRONG-- I CAN FEEL TEETH BEHIND MY TEETH AND--
OH, GOD. WHAT... WHAT AM I?
YOU TELL ME. DEEP DOWN, YOU KNOW ALREADY. YOU CAN FEEL IT.
I CAN... I DO. I'M...
A... VAMPIRE? LIKE THEM?
OH, NO, DOLLY...
...YOU'RE A VAMPIRE LIKE ME. AND BELIEVE ME, THERE'S A BIG DIFFERENCE.

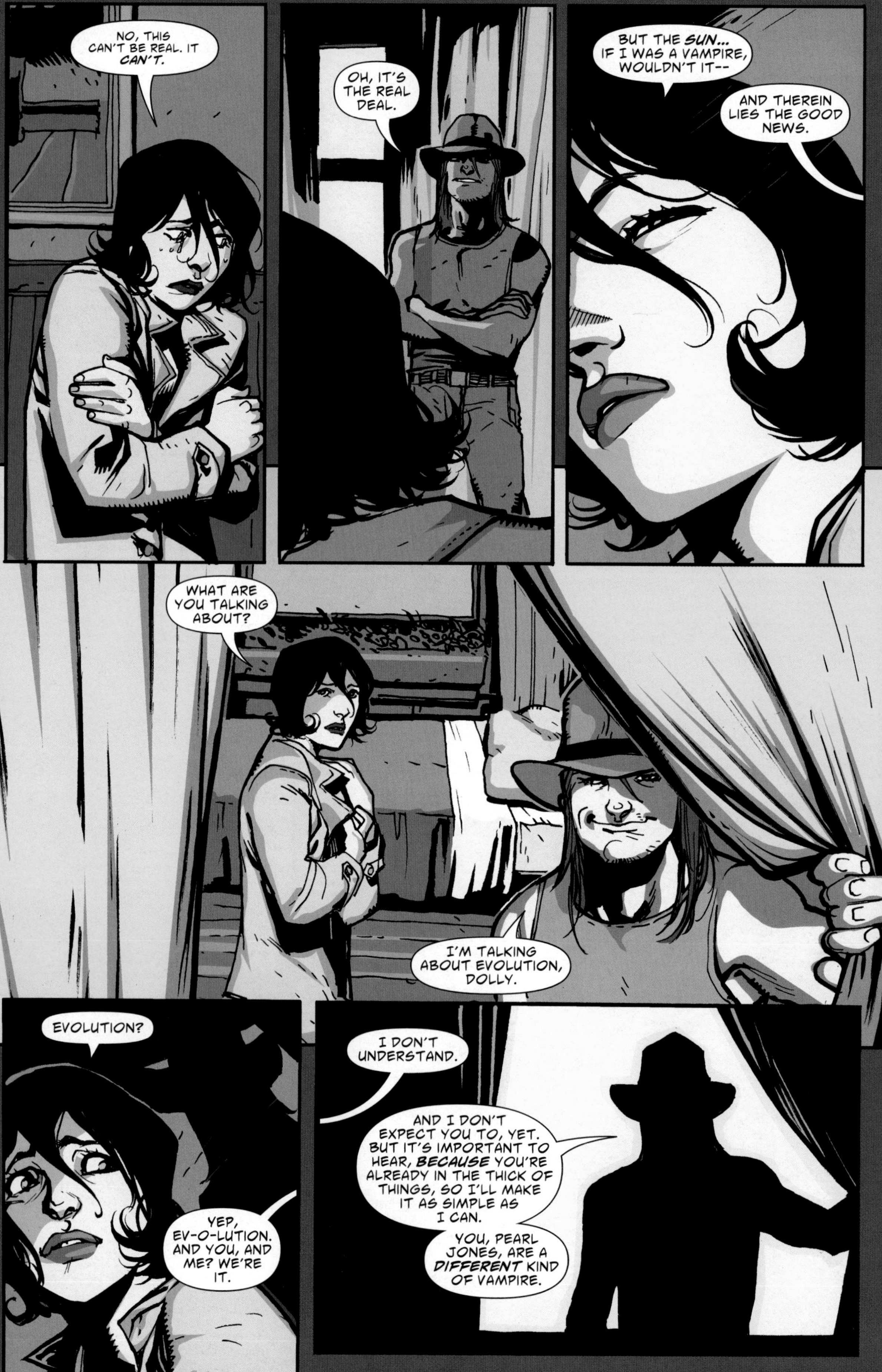
NO, THIS CAN'T BE REAL. IT *CAN'T.*
OH, IT'S THE REAL DEAL.
BUT THE *SUN...* IF I WAS A VAMPIRE, WOULDN'T IT--
AND THEREIN LIES THE GOOD NEWS.
WHAT ARE YOU TALKING ABOUT?
I'M TALKING ABOUT EVOLUTION, DOLLY.
EVOLUTION?
YEP, EV-O-LUTION. AND YOU, AND ME? WE'RE IT.
I DON'T UNDERSTAND.
AND I DON'T EXPECT YOU TO, YET. BUT IT'S IMPORTANT TO HEAR, *BECAUSE* YOU'RE ALREADY IN THE THICK OF THINGS, SO I'LL MAKE IT AS SIMPLE AS I CAN.
YOU, PEARL JONES, ARE A *DIFFERENT* KIND OF VAMPIRE.

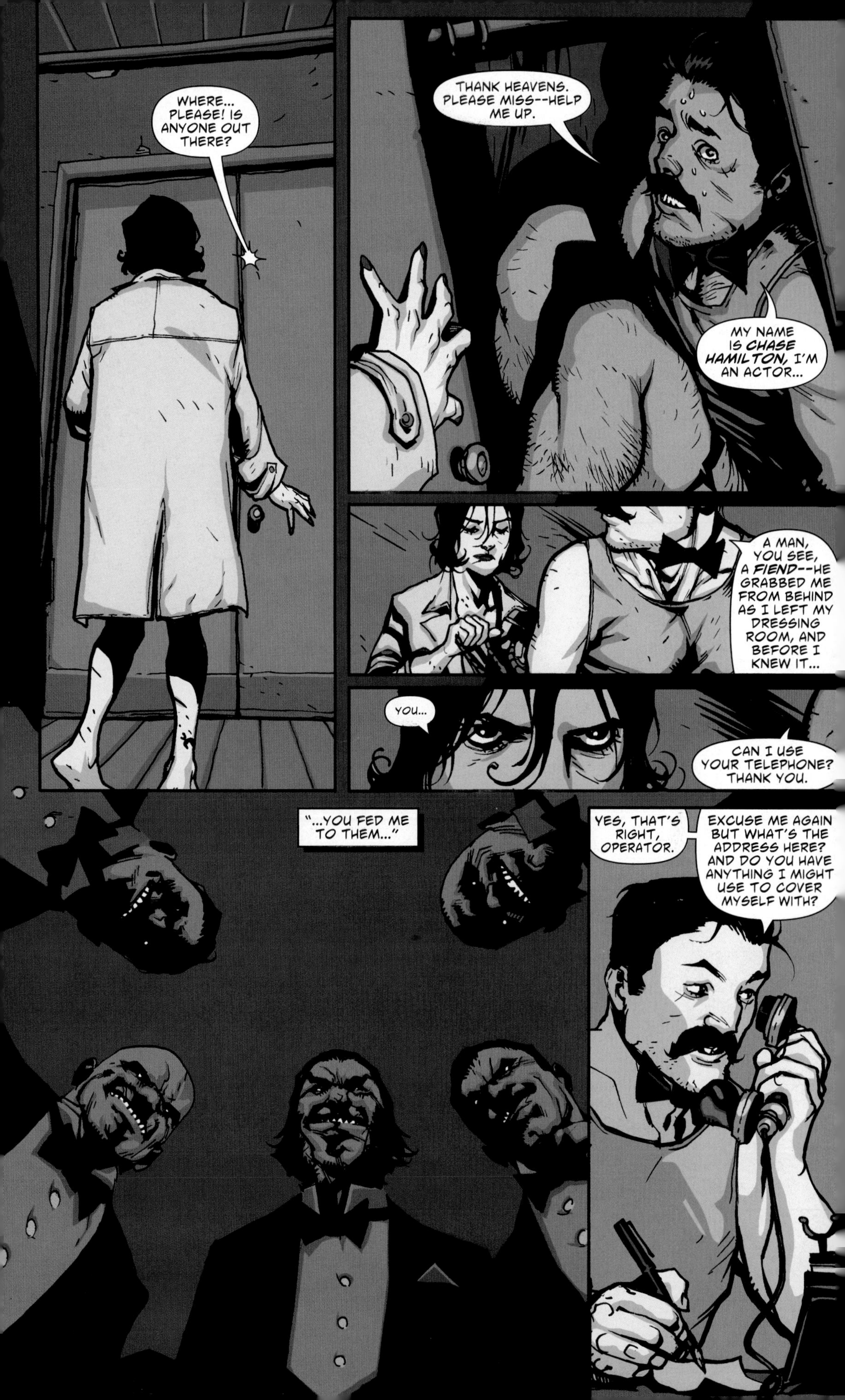

WHERE... PLEASE! IS ANYONE OUT THERE?
THANK HEAVENS. PLEASE MISS--HELP ME UP.
MY NAME IS **CHASE HAMILTON,** I'M AN ACTOR...
A MAN, YOU SEE, A ***FIEND***--HE GRABBED ME FROM BEHIND AS I LEFT MY DRESSING ROOM, AND BEFORE I KNEW IT...
YOU...
CAN I USE YOUR TELEPHONE? THANK YOU.
"...YOU FED ME TO THEM..."
YES, THAT'S RIGHT, OPERATOR.
EXCUSE ME AGAIN BUT WHAT'S THE ADDRESS HERE? AND DO YOU HAVE ANYTHING I MIGHT USE TO COVER MYSELF WITH?

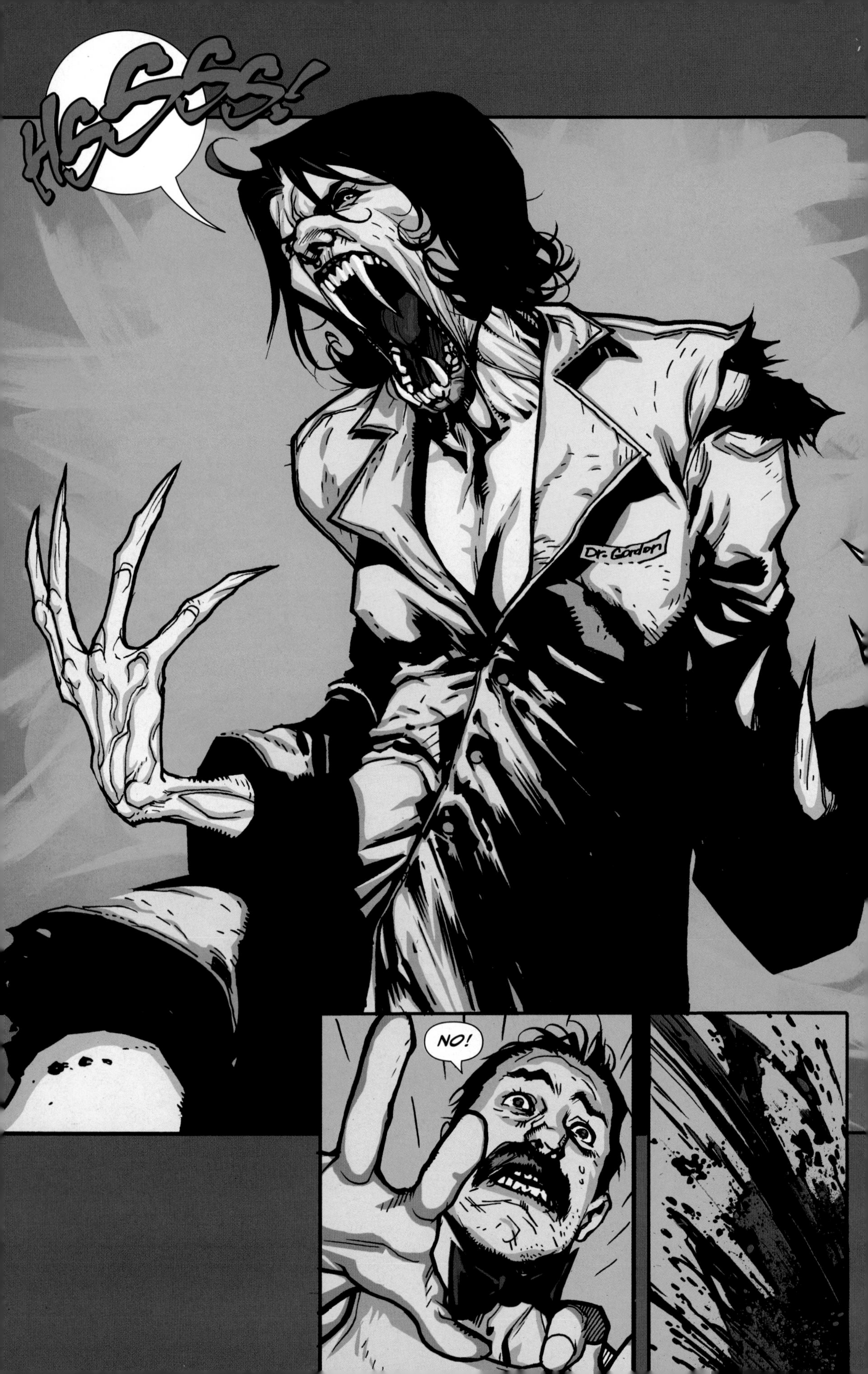
HSSSS!
Dr. Gordon
NO!

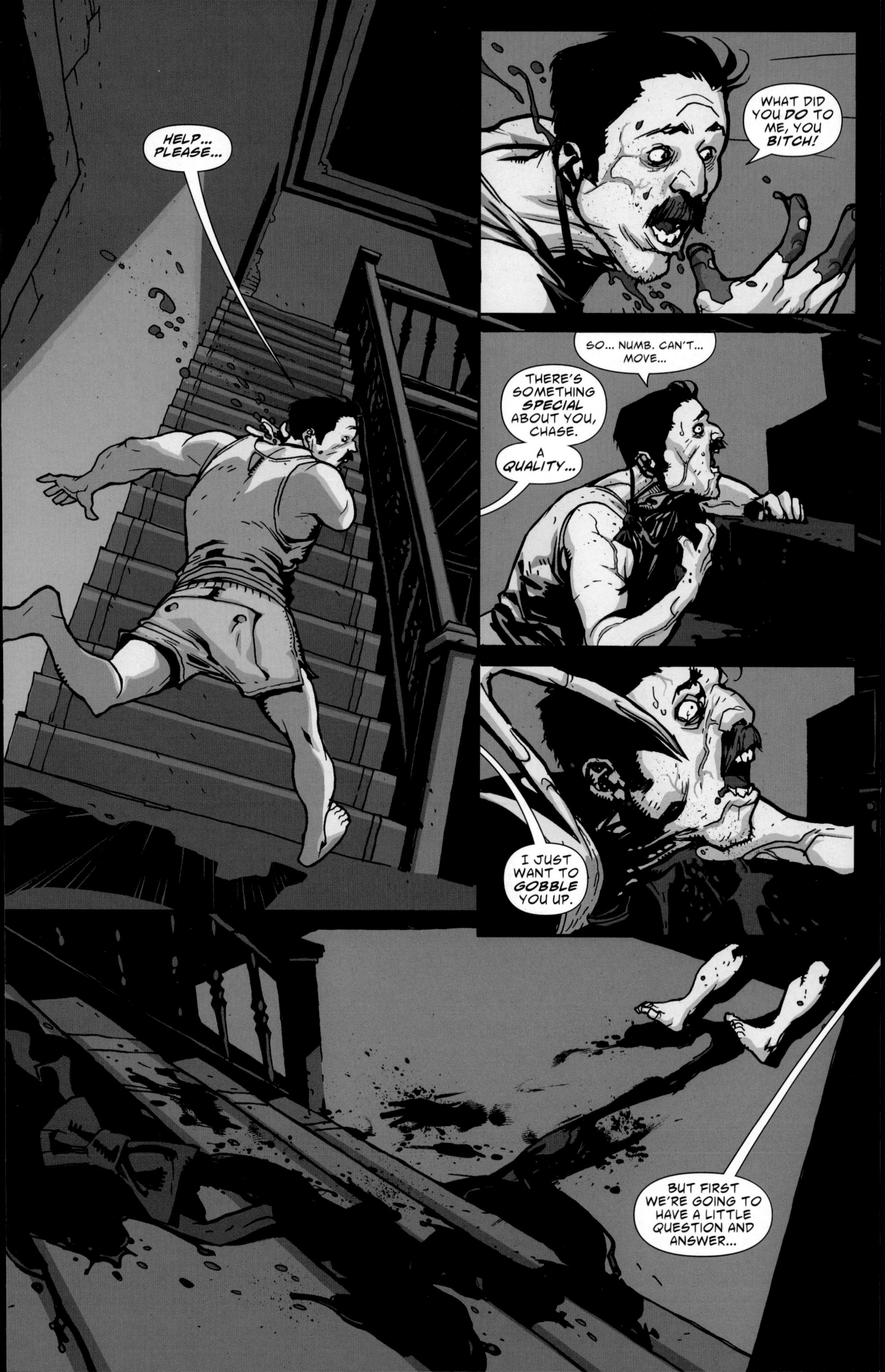
HELP... PLEASE...
WHAT DID YOU DO TO ME, YOU BITCH!
SO... NUMB. CAN'T... MOVE...
THERE'S SOMETHING SPECIAL ABOUT YOU, CHASE.
A QUALITY...
I JUST WANT TO GOBBLE YOU UP.
BUT FIRST WE'RE GOING TO HAVE A LITTLE QUESTION AND ANSWER...

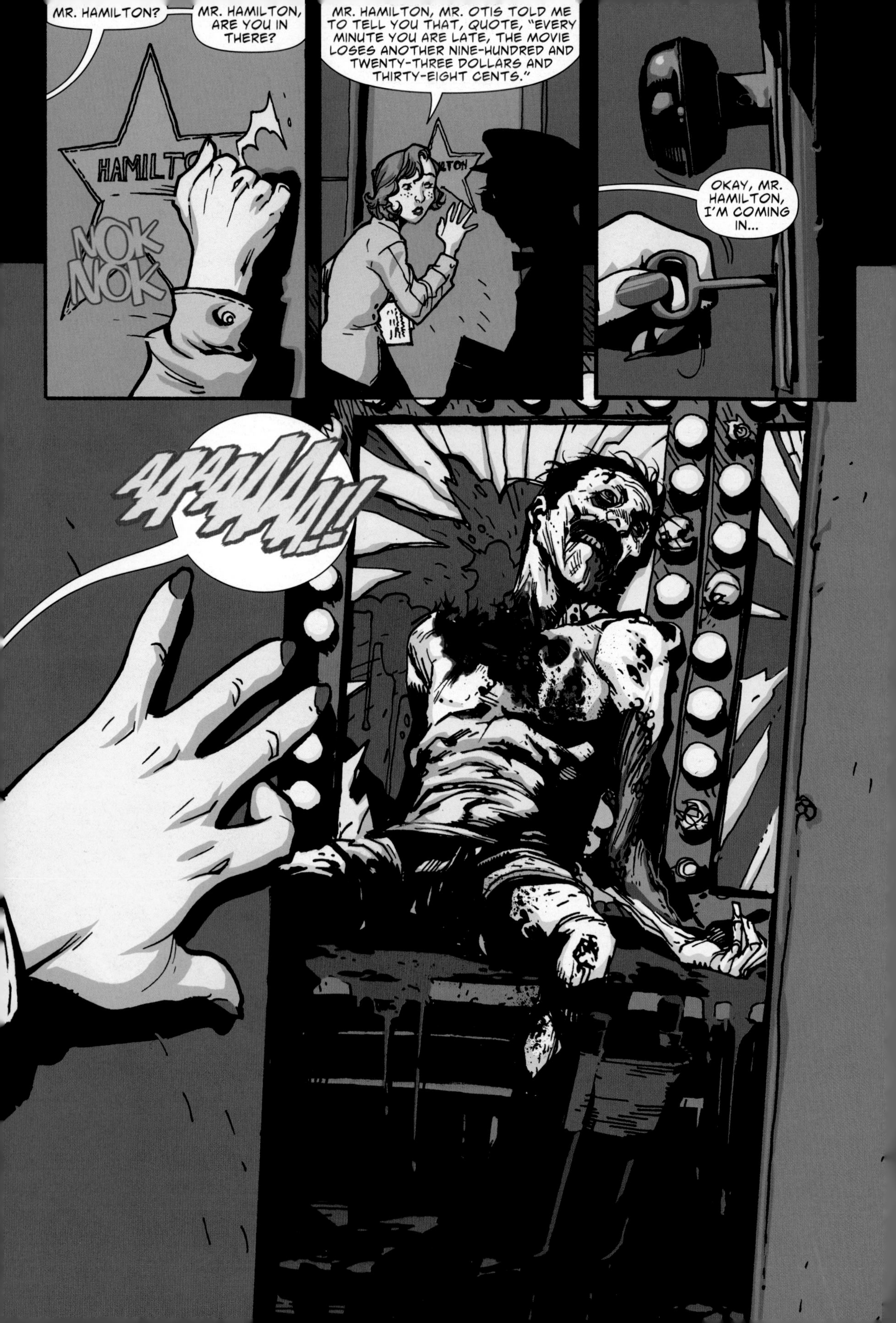
MR. HAMILTON?
MR. HAMILTON, ARE YOU IN THERE?
HAMILTON
NOK NOK
MR. HAMILTON, MR. OTIS TOLD ME TO TELL YOU THAT, QUOTE, "EVERY MINUTE YOU ARE LATE, THE MOVIE LOSES ANOTHER NINE-HUNDRED AND TWENTY-THREE DOLLARS AND THIRTY-EIGHT CENTS."
OKAY, MR. HAMILTON, I'M COMING IN...

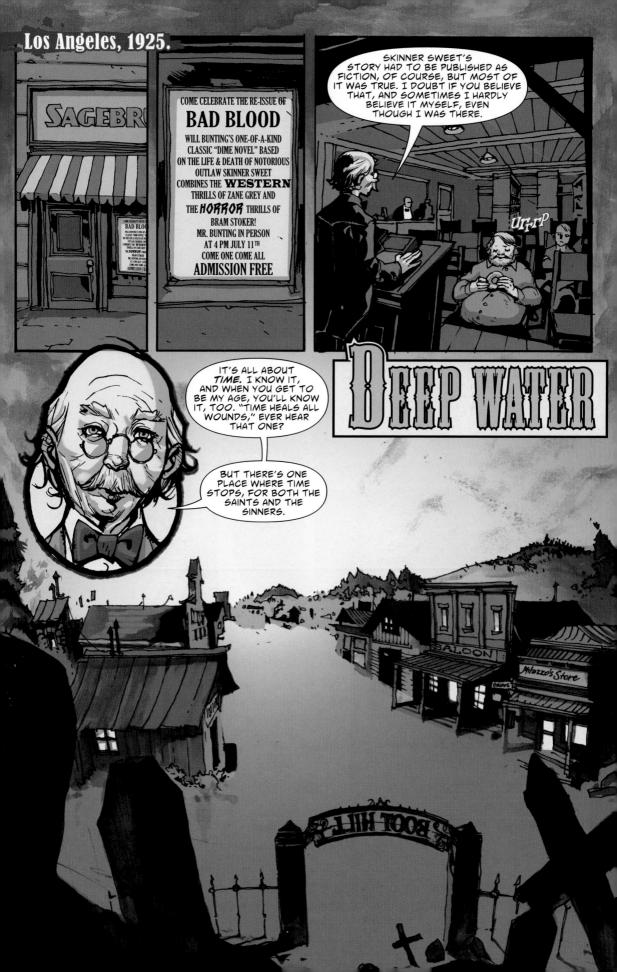

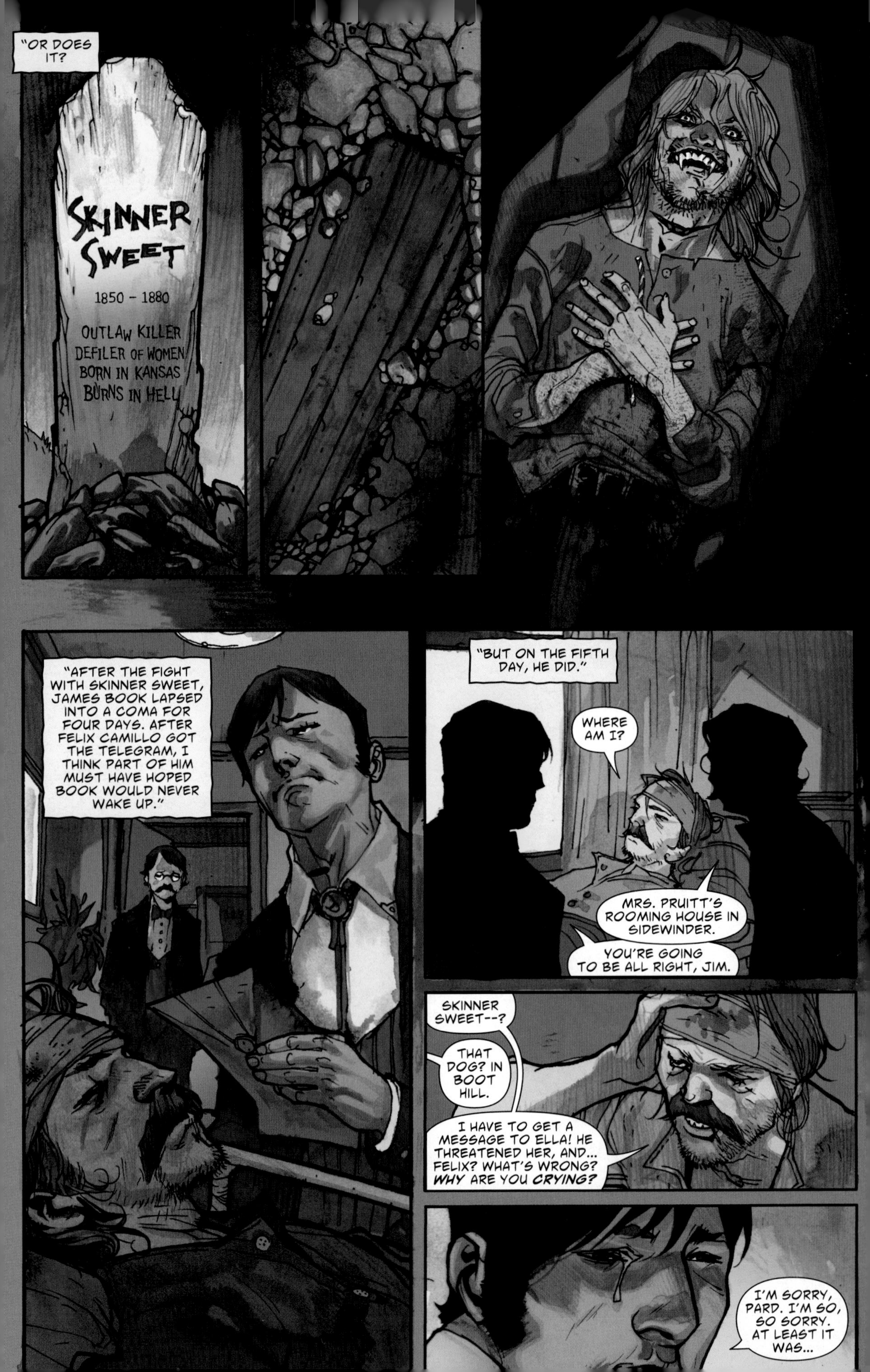
"OR DOES IT?
SKINNER SWEET
1850 – 1880
OUTLAW KILLER
DEFILER OF WOMEN
BORN IN KANSAS
BURNS IN HELL
"AFTER THE FIGHT WITH SKINNER SWEET, JAMES BOOK LAPSED INTO A COMA FOR FOUR DAYS. AFTER FELIX CAMILLO GOT THE TELEGRAM, I THINK PART OF HIM MUST HAVE HOPED BOOK WOULD NEVER WAKE UP."
"BUT ON THE FIFTH DAY, HE DID."
WHERE AM I?
MRS. PRUITT'S ROOMING HOUSE IN SIDEWINDER.
YOU'RE GOING TO BE ALL RIGHT, JIM.
SKINNER SWEET--?
THAT DOG? IN BOOT HILL.
I HAVE TO GET A MESSAGE TO ELLA! HE THREATENED HER, AND... FELIX? WHAT'S WRONG? *WHY* ARE YOU *CRYING*?
I'M SORRY, PARD. I'M SO, SO SORRY. AT LEAST IT WAS...

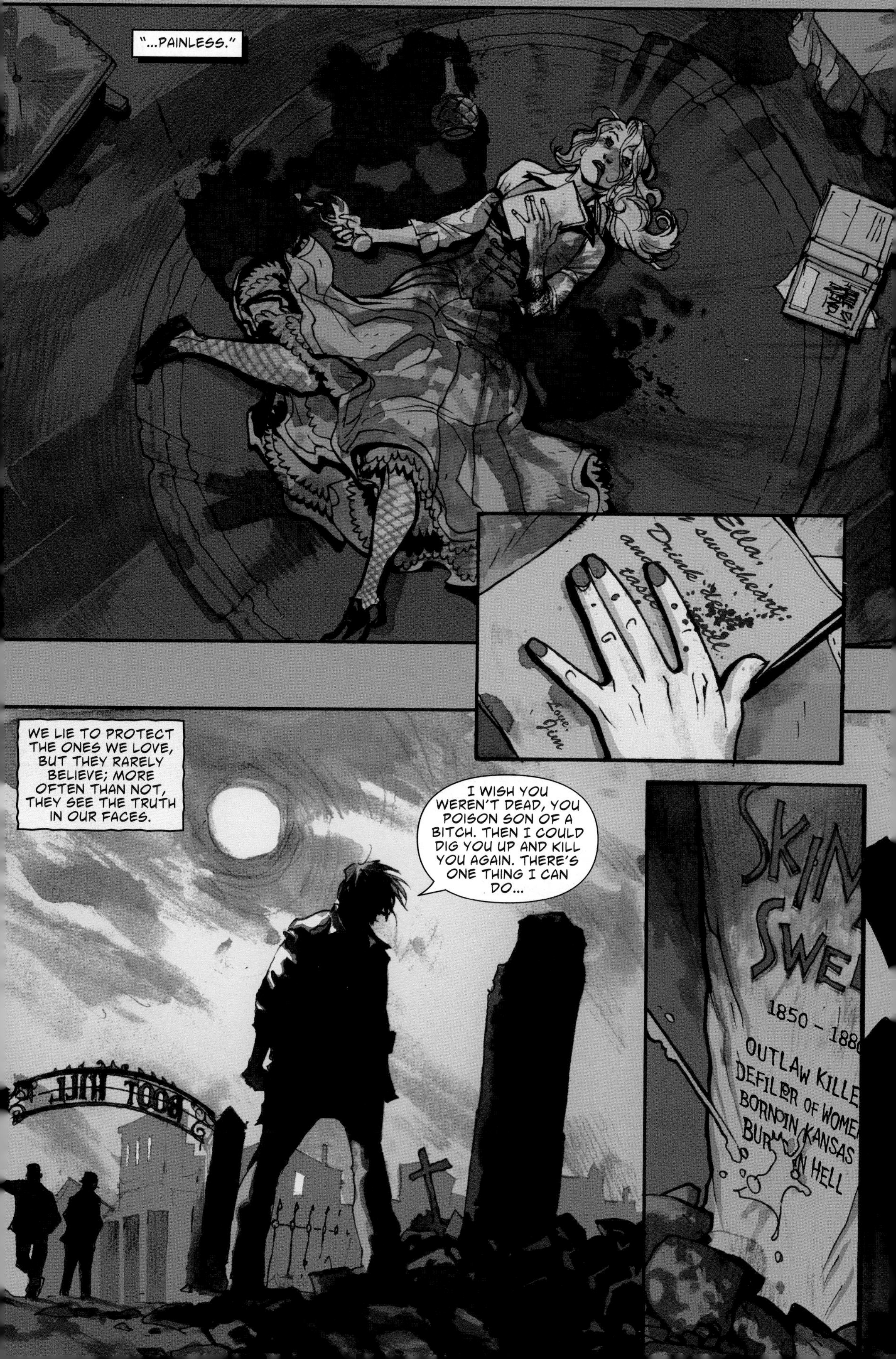
"...PAINLESS."
Ella,
sweetheart,
Love, Jim
WE LIE TO PROTECT THE ONES WE LOVE, BUT THEY RARELY BELIEVE; MORE OFTEN THAN NOT, THEY SEE THE TRUTH IN OUR FACES.
I WISH YOU WEREN'T DEAD, YOU POISON SON OF A BITCH. THEN I COULD DIG YOU UP AND KILL YOU AGAIN. THERE'S ONE THING I CAN DO...
BORN IN KANSAS

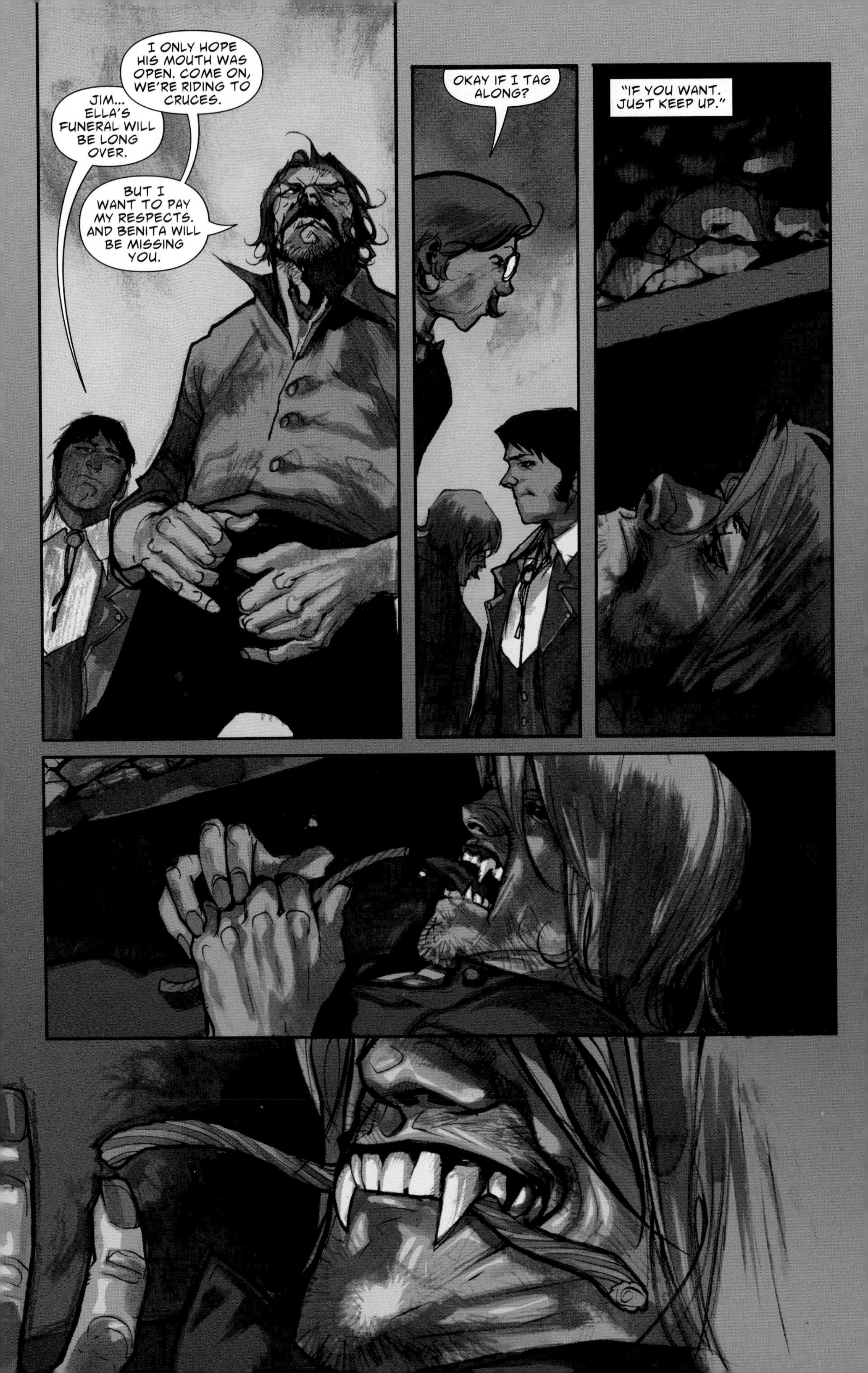
JIM... ELLA'S FUNERAL WILL BE LONG OVER.
I ONLY HOPE HIS MOUTH WAS OPEN. COME ON, WE'RE RIDING TO CRUCES.
BUT I WANT TO PAY MY RESPECTS. AND BENITA WILL BE MISSING YOU.
OKAY IF I TAG ALONG?
"IF YOU WANT. JUST KEEP UP."

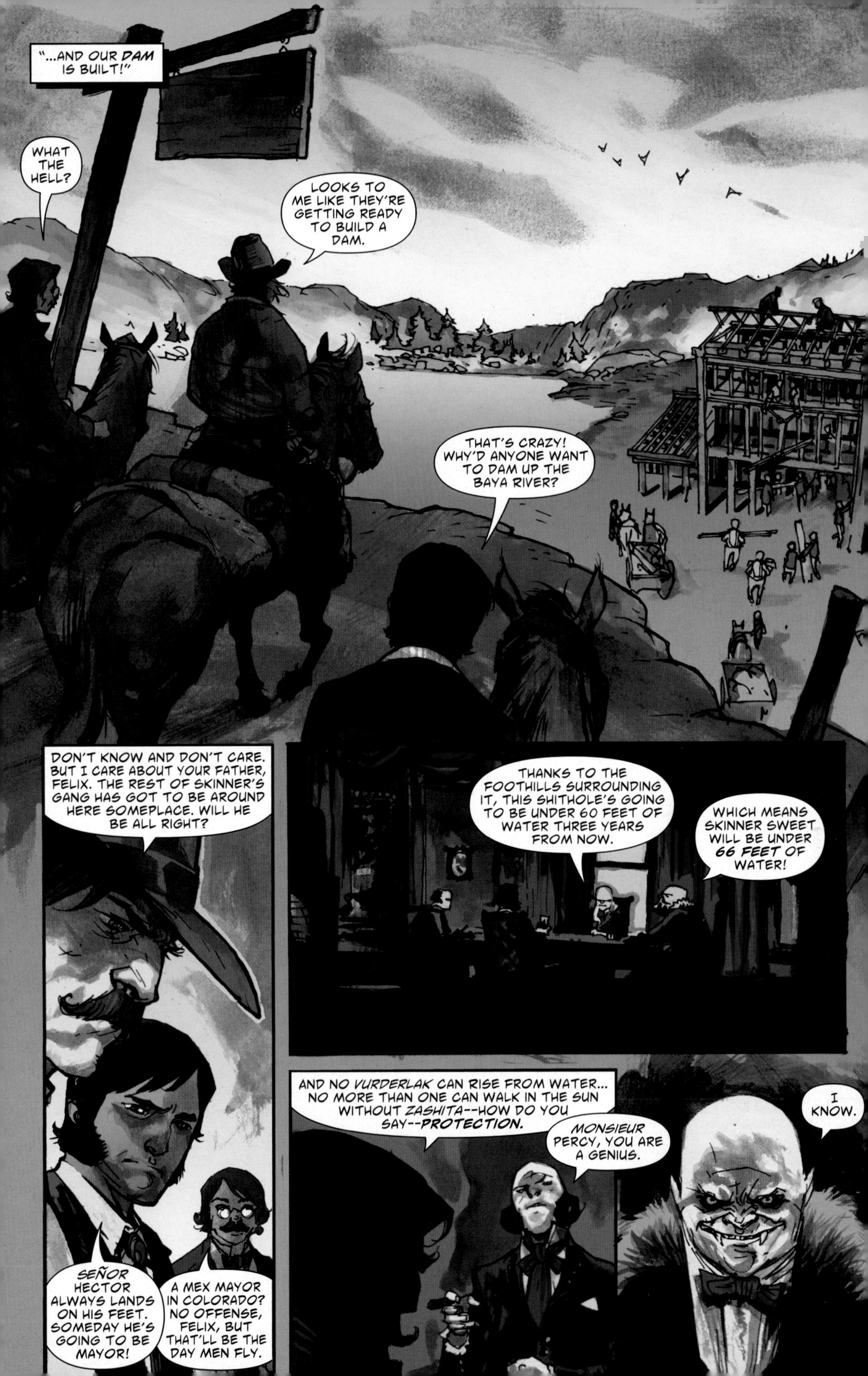
"...AND OUR *DAM* IS BUILT!"
WHAT THE HELL?
LOOKS TO ME LIKE THEY'RE GETTING READY TO BUILD A DAM.
THAT'S CRAZY! WHY'D ANYONE WANT TO DAM UP THE BAYA RIVER?
DON'T KNOW AND DON'T CARE. BUT I CARE ABOUT YOUR FATHER, FELIX. THE REST OF SKINNER'S GANG HAS GOT TO BE AROUND HERE SOMEPLACE. WILL HE BE ALL RIGHT?
SEÑOR HECTOR ALWAYS LANDS ON HIS FEET. SOMEDAY HE'S GOING TO BE MAYOR!
A MEX MAYOR IN COLORADO? NO OFFENSE, FELIX, BUT THAT'LL BE THE DAY MEN FLY.
THANKS TO THE FOOTHILLS SURROUNDING IT, THIS SHITHOLE'S GOING TO BE UNDER 60 FEET OF WATER THREE YEARS FROM NOW.
WHICH MEANS SKINNER SWEET WILL BE UNDER **66 FEET** OF WATER!
AND NO *VURDERLAK* CAN RISE FROM WATER... NO MORE THAN ONE CAN WALK IN THE SUN WITHOUT *ZASHITA*--HOW DO YOU SAY--***PROTECTION.***
MONSIEUR PERCY, YOU ARE A GENIUS.
I KNOW.

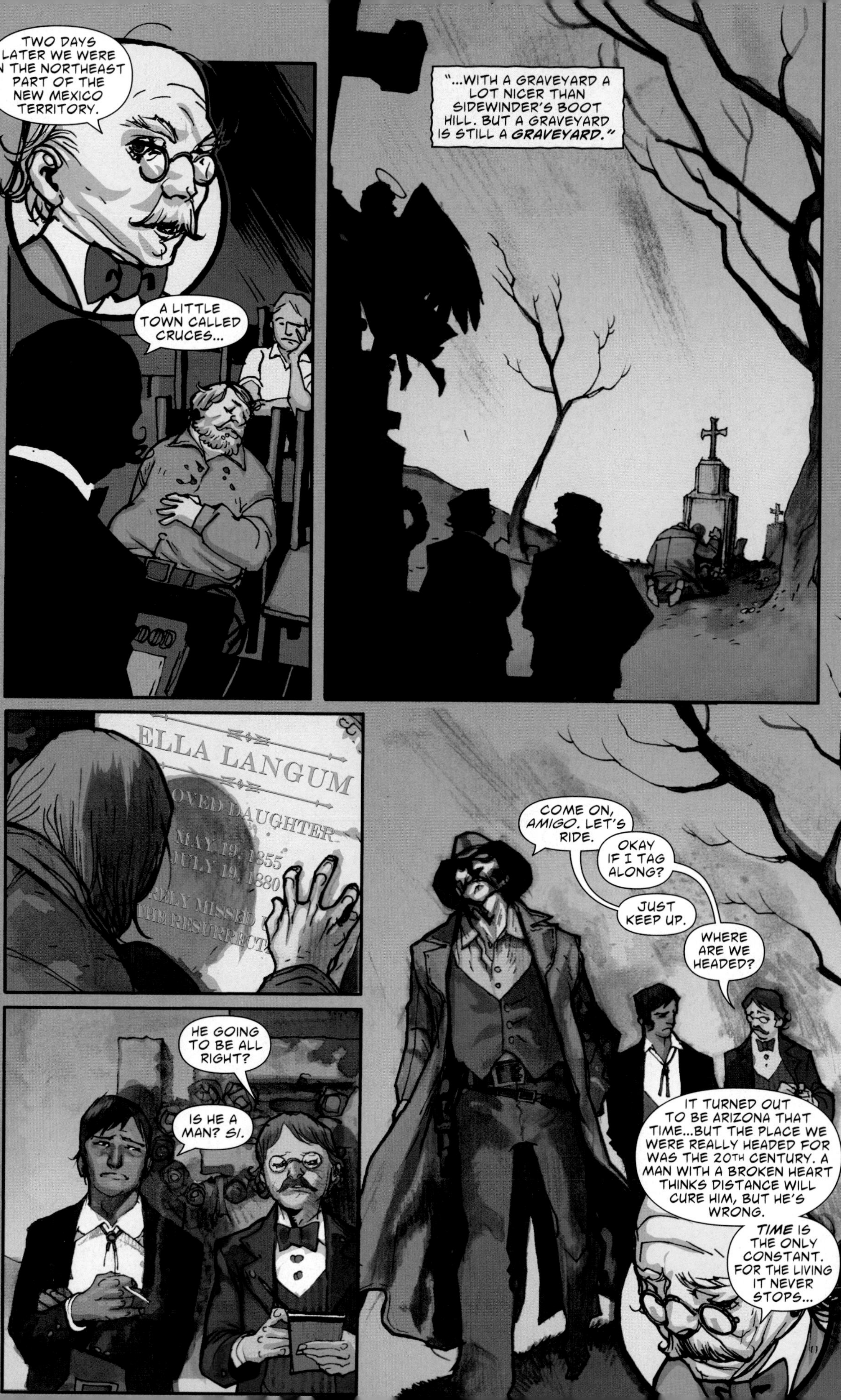
TWO DAYS LATER WE WERE IN THE NORTHEAST PART OF THE NEW MEXICO TERRITORY.
A LITTLE TOWN CALLED CRUCES...
"...WITH A GRAVEYARD A LOT NICER THAN SIDEWINDER'S BOOT HILL. BUT A GRAVEYARD IS STILL A *GRAVEYARD*."
ELLA LANGUM
HE GOING TO BE ALL RIGHT?
IS HE A MAN? *SI*.
COME ON, *AMIGO*. LET'S RIDE.
OKAY IF I TAG ALONG?
JUST KEEP UP.
WHERE ARE WE HEADED?
IT TURNED OUT TO BE ARIZONA THAT TIME...BUT THE PLACE WE WERE REALLY HEADED FOR WAS THE 20TH CENTURY. A MAN WITH A BROKEN HEART THINKS DISTANCE WILL CURE HIM, BUT HE'S WRONG.
TIME IS THE ONLY CONSTANT. FOR THE LIVING IT NEVER STOPS...

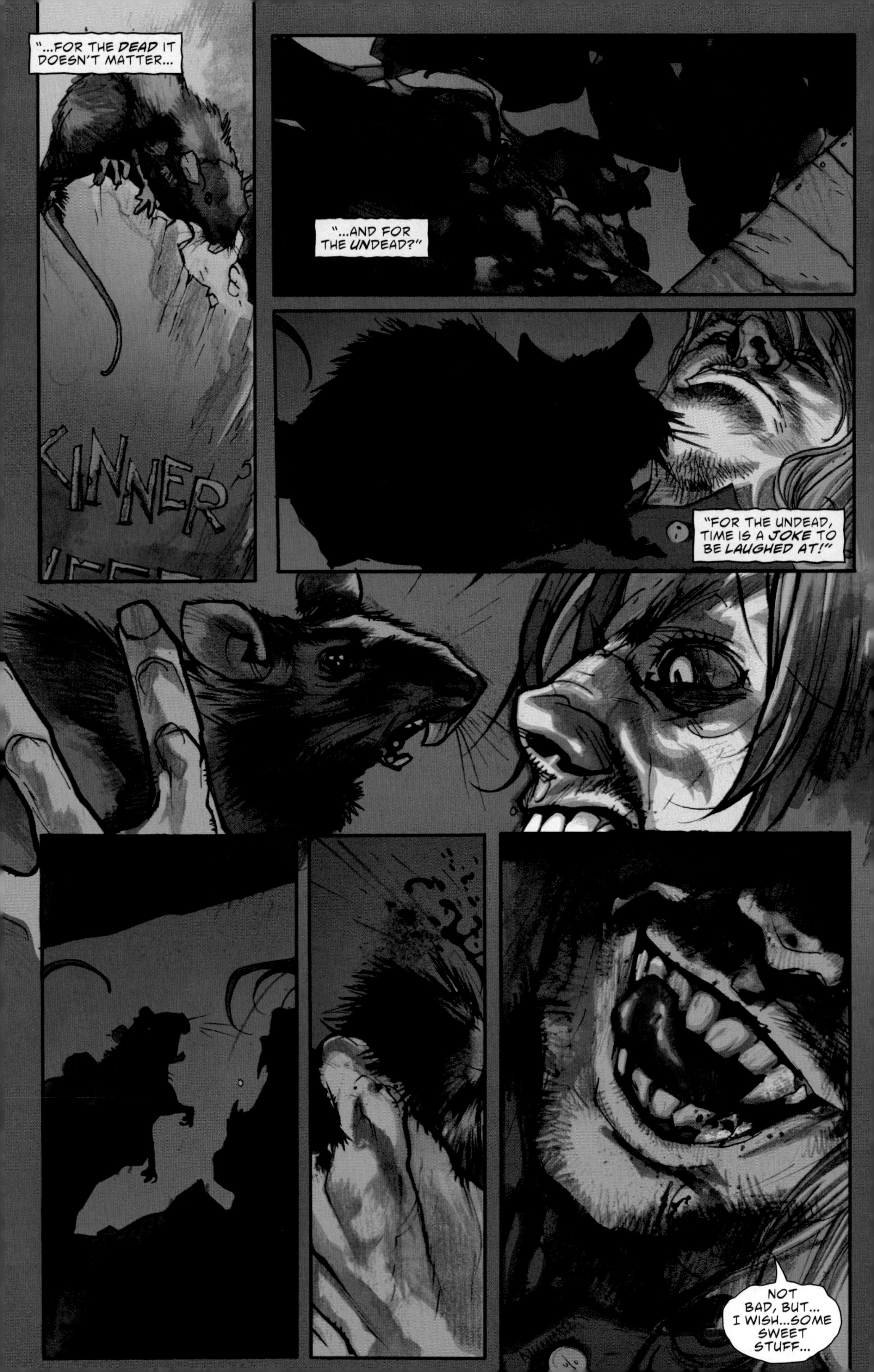
"...FOR THE DEAD IT DOESN'T MATTER...
"...AND FOR THE UNDEAD?"
"FOR THE UNDEAD, TIME IS A JOKE TO BE LAUGHED AT!"
NOT BAD, BUT... I WISH...SOME SWEET STUFF...

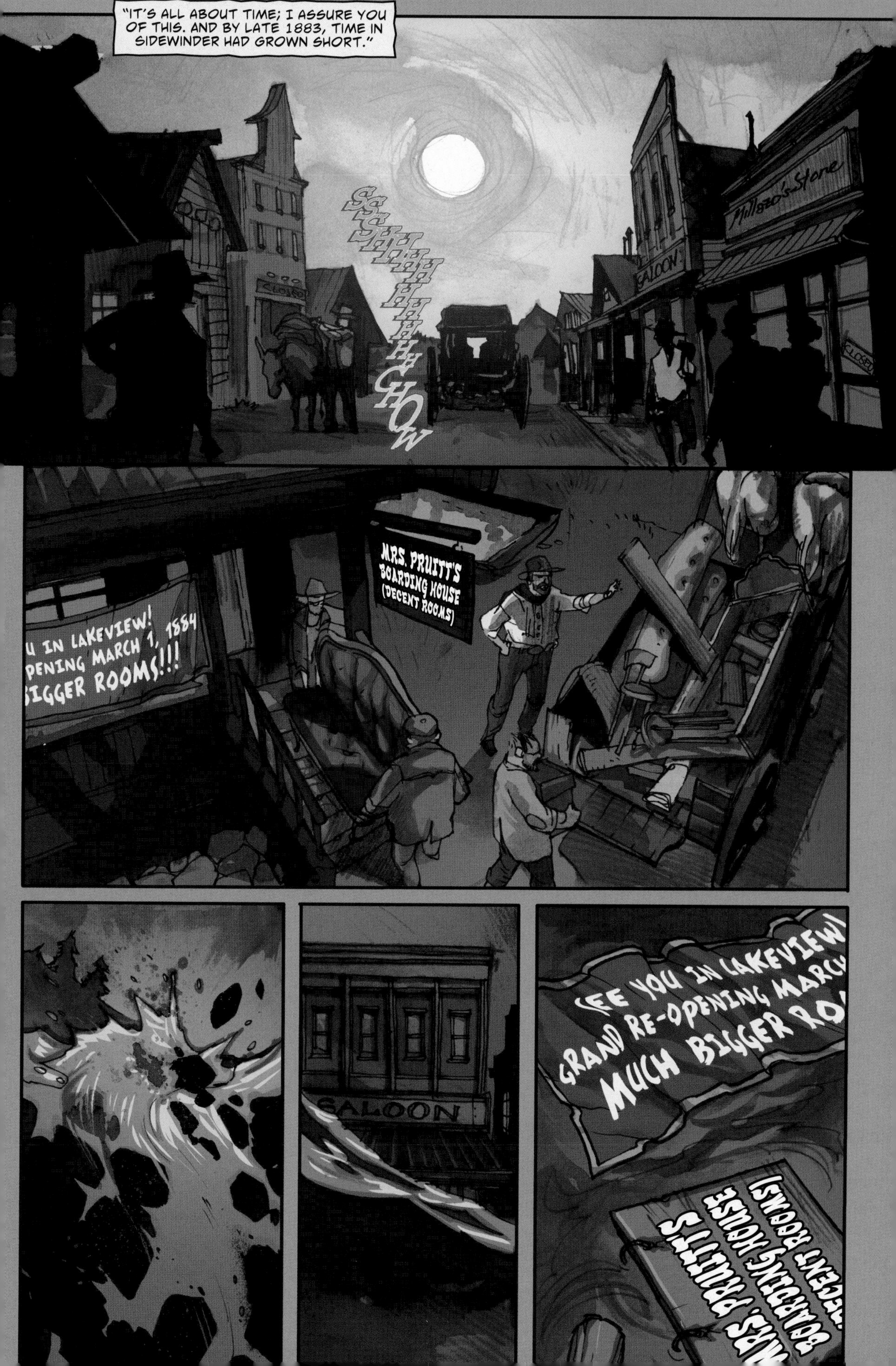
"IT'S ALL ABOUT TIME; I ASSURE YOU OF THIS. AND BY LATE 1883, TIME IN SIDEWINDER HAD GROWN SHORT."
CLOSED
SALOON
CLOSED
SSSHHHHHHHHCHOW
MRS. PRUITT'S BOARDING HOUSE (DECENT ROOMS)
U IN LAKEVIEW!
PENING MARCH 1, 1884
BIGGER ROOMS!!!
SALOON
SEE YOU IN LAKEVIEW!
GRAND RE-OPENING MARC
MUCH BIGGER RO
MRS. PRUITT'S BOARDING HOUSE (DECENT ROOMS)

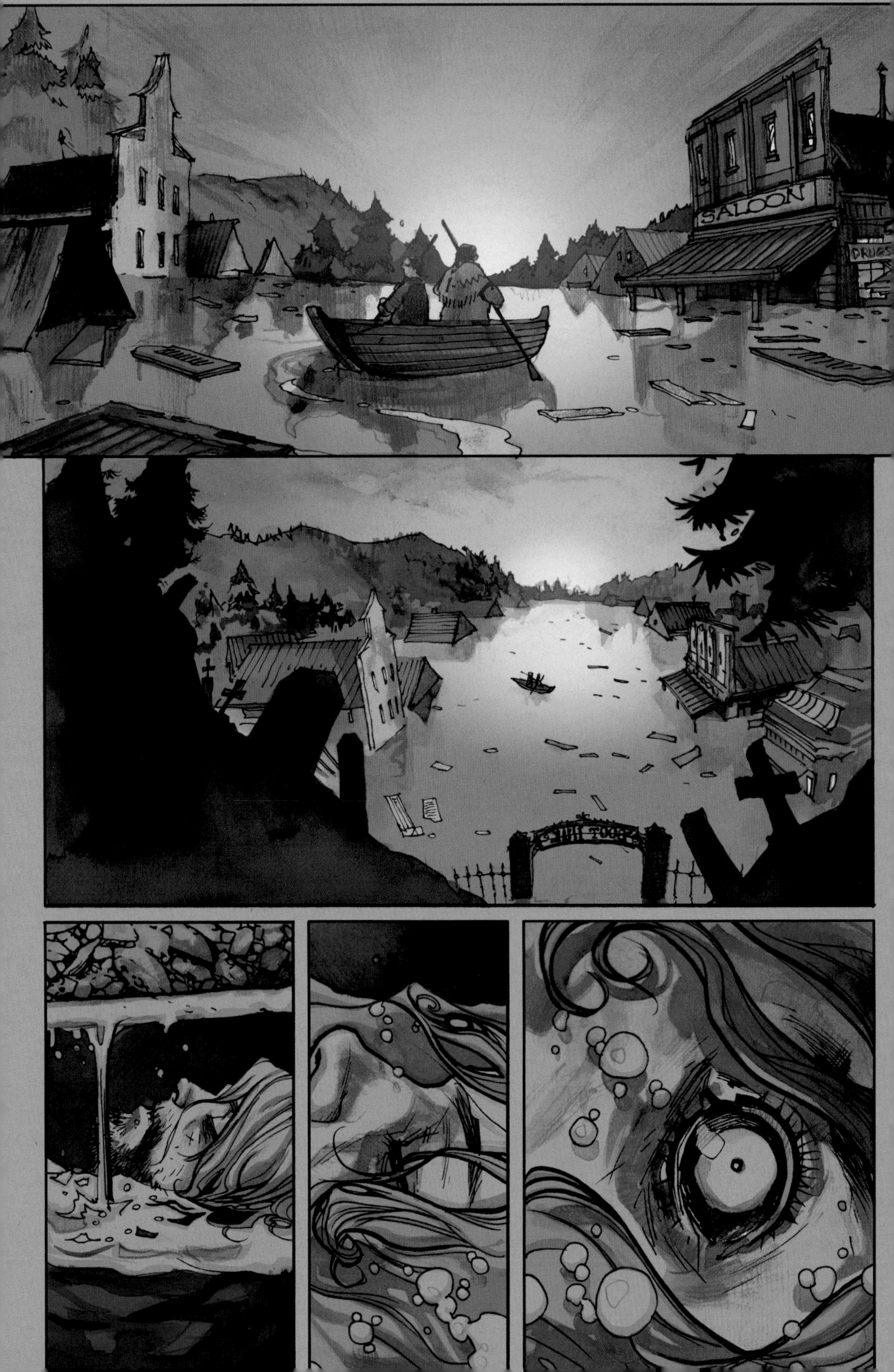
SALOON
DRUGS

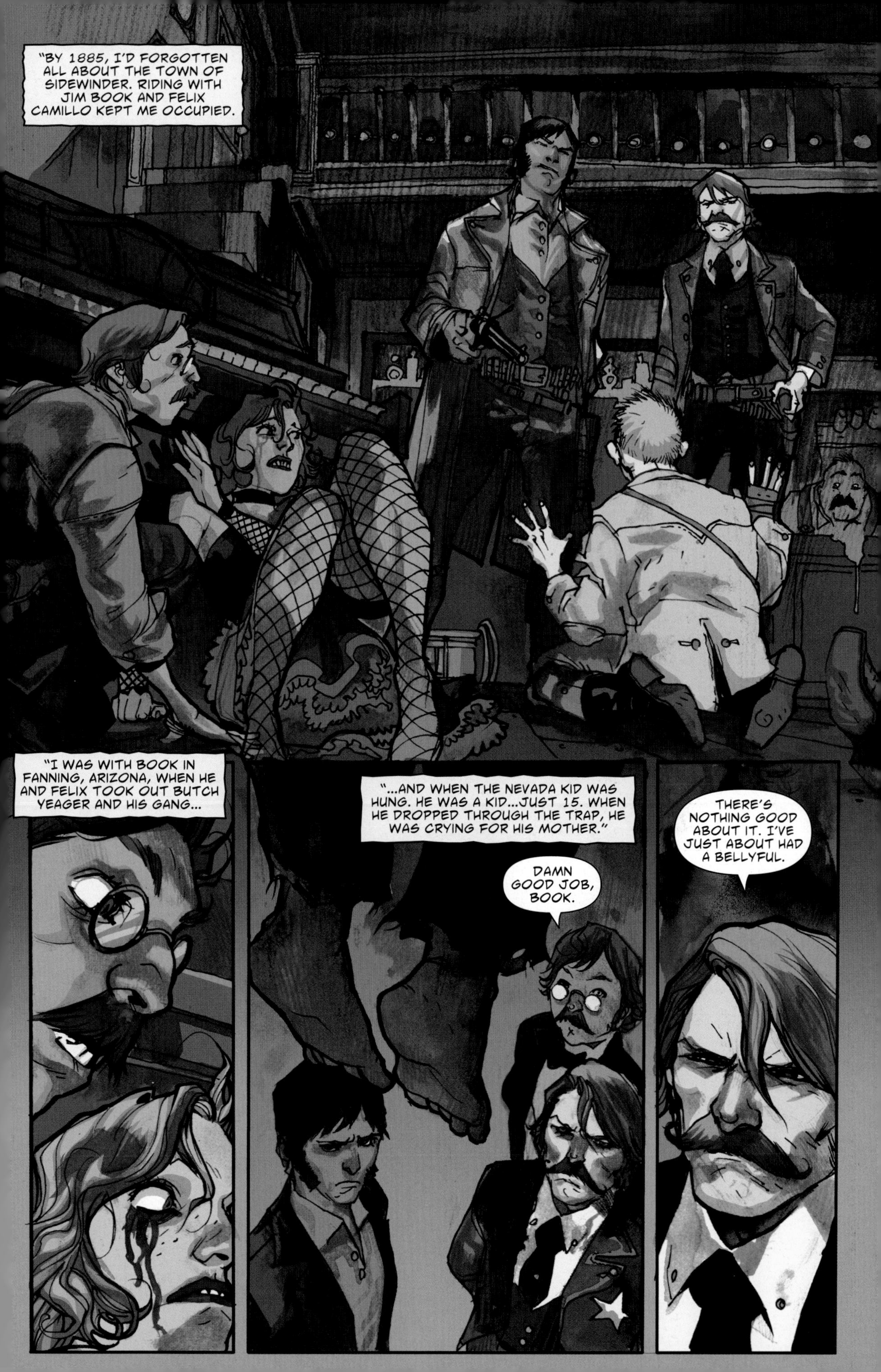
"BY 1885, I'D FORGOTTEN ALL ABOUT THE TOWN OF SIDEWINDER. RIDING WITH JIM BOOK AND FELIX CAMILLO KEPT ME OCCUPIED.
"I WAS WITH BOOK IN FANNING, ARIZONA, WHEN HE AND FELIX TOOK OUT BUTCH YEAGER AND HIS GANG...
"...AND WHEN THE NEVADA KID WAS HUNG. HE WAS A KID...JUST 15. WHEN HE DROPPED THROUGH THE TRAP, HE WAS CRYING FOR HIS MOTHER."
DAMN GOOD JOB, BOOK.
THERE'S NOTHING GOOD ABOUT IT. I'VE JUST ABOUT HAD A BELLYFUL.

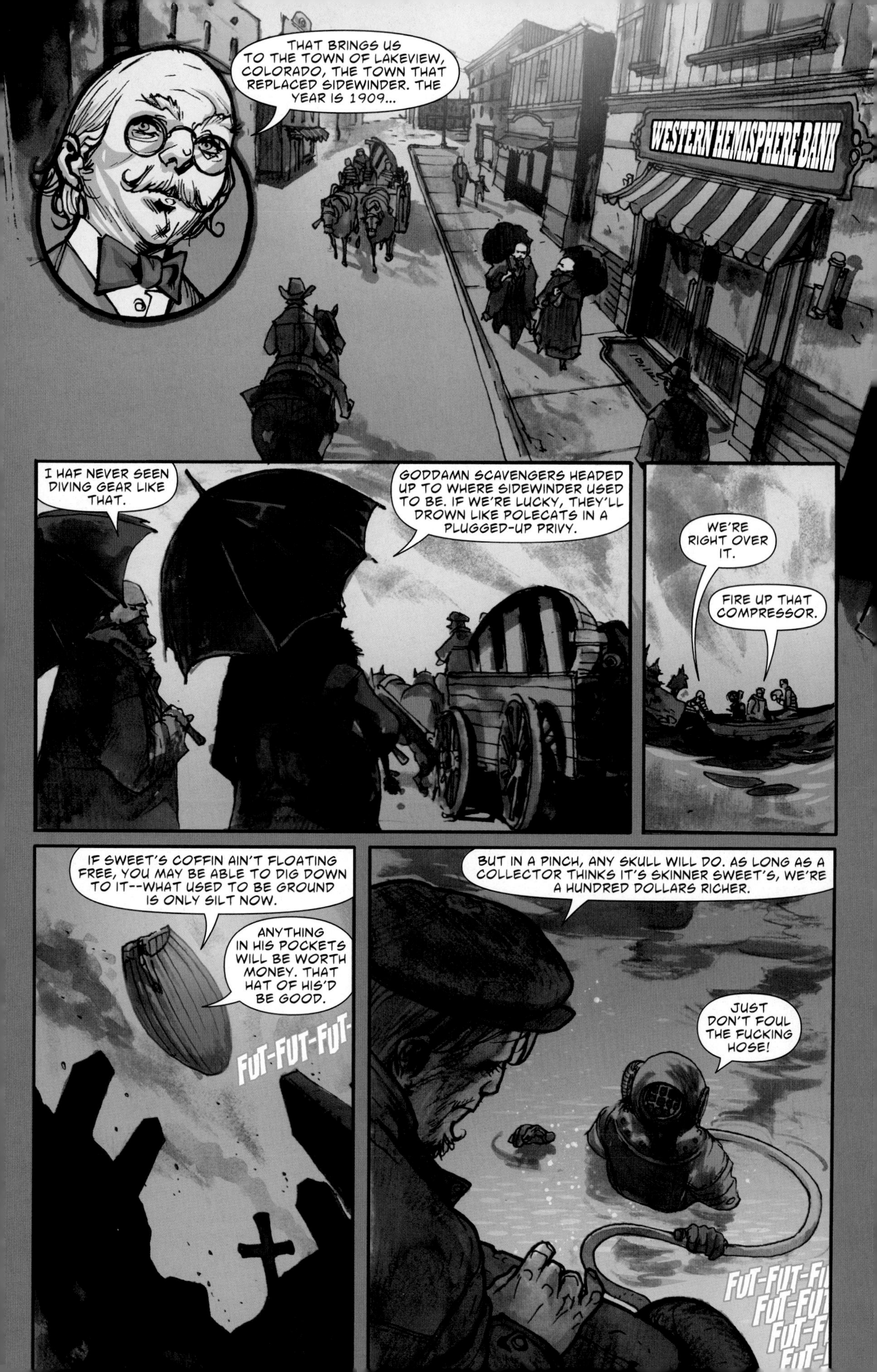
THAT BRINGS US TO THE TOWN OF LAKEVIEW, COLORADO, THE TOWN THAT REPLACED SIDEWINDER. THE YEAR IS 1909...
WESTERN HEMISPHERE BANK
I HAF NEVER SEEN DIVING GEAR LIKE THAT.
GODDAMN SCAVENGERS HEADED UP TO WHERE SIDEWINDER USED TO BE. IF WE'RE LUCKY, THEY'LL DROWN LIKE POLECATS IN A PLUGGED-UP PRIVY.
WE'RE RIGHT OVER IT.
FIRE UP THAT COMPRESSOR.
IF SWEET'S COFFIN AIN'T FLOATING FREE, YOU MAY BE ABLE TO DIG DOWN TO IT--WHAT USED TO BE GROUND IS ONLY SILT NOW.
ANYTHING IN HIS POCKETS WILL BE WORTH MONEY. THAT HAT OF HIS'D BE GOOD.
FUT-FUT-FUT-
BUT IN A PINCH, ANY SKULL WILL DO. AS LONG AS A COLLECTOR THINKS IT'S SKINNER SWEET'S, WE'RE A HUNDRED DOLLARS RICHER.
JUST DON'T FOUL THE FUCKING HOSE!

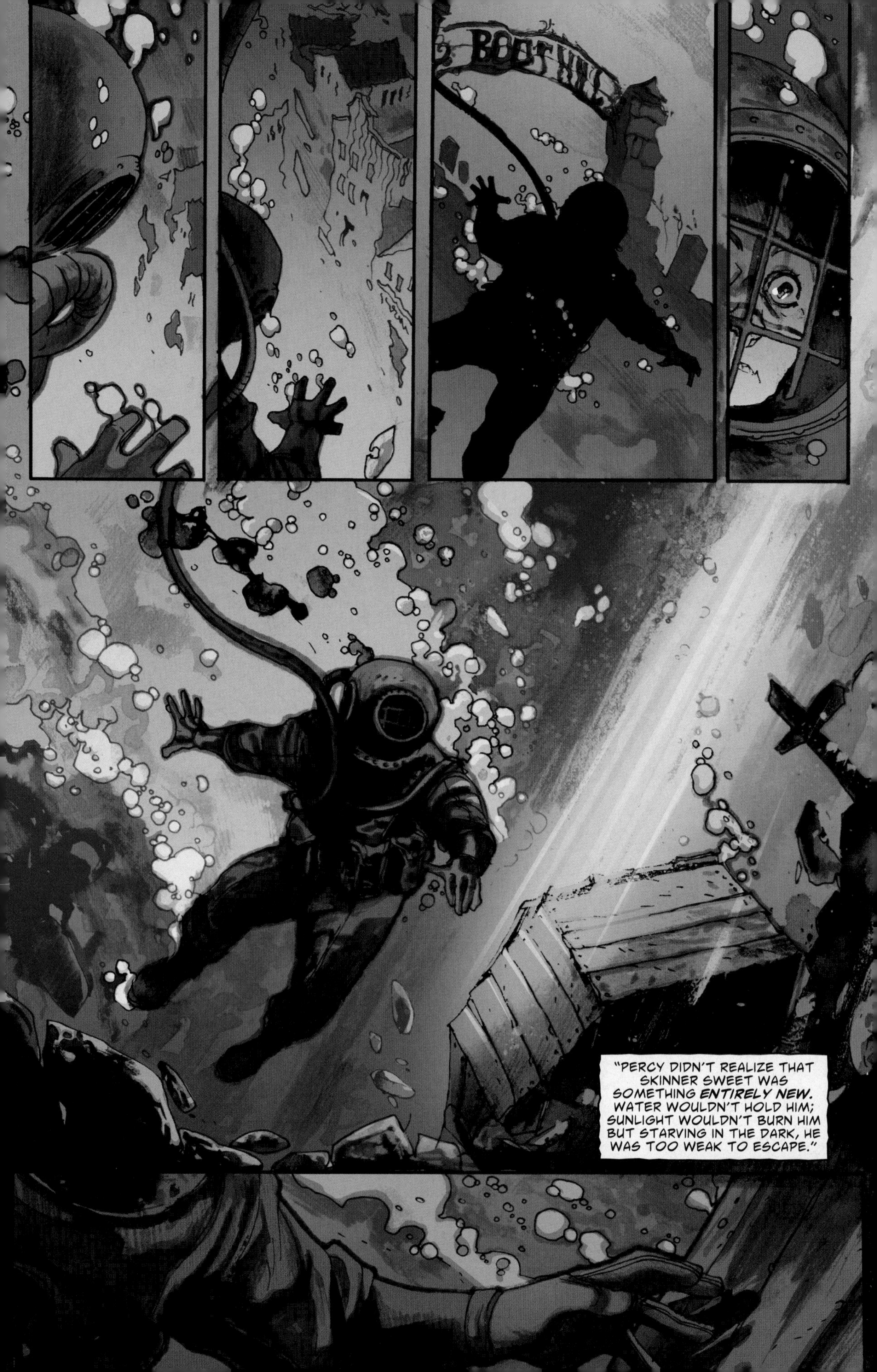
BOOT HILL
"PERCY DIDN'T REALIZE THAT SKINNER SWEET WAS SOMETHING *ENTIRELY NEW.* WATER WOULDN'T HOLD HIM; SUNLIGHT WOULDN'T BURN HIM BUT STARVING IN THE DARK, HE WAS TOO WEAK TO ESCAPE."

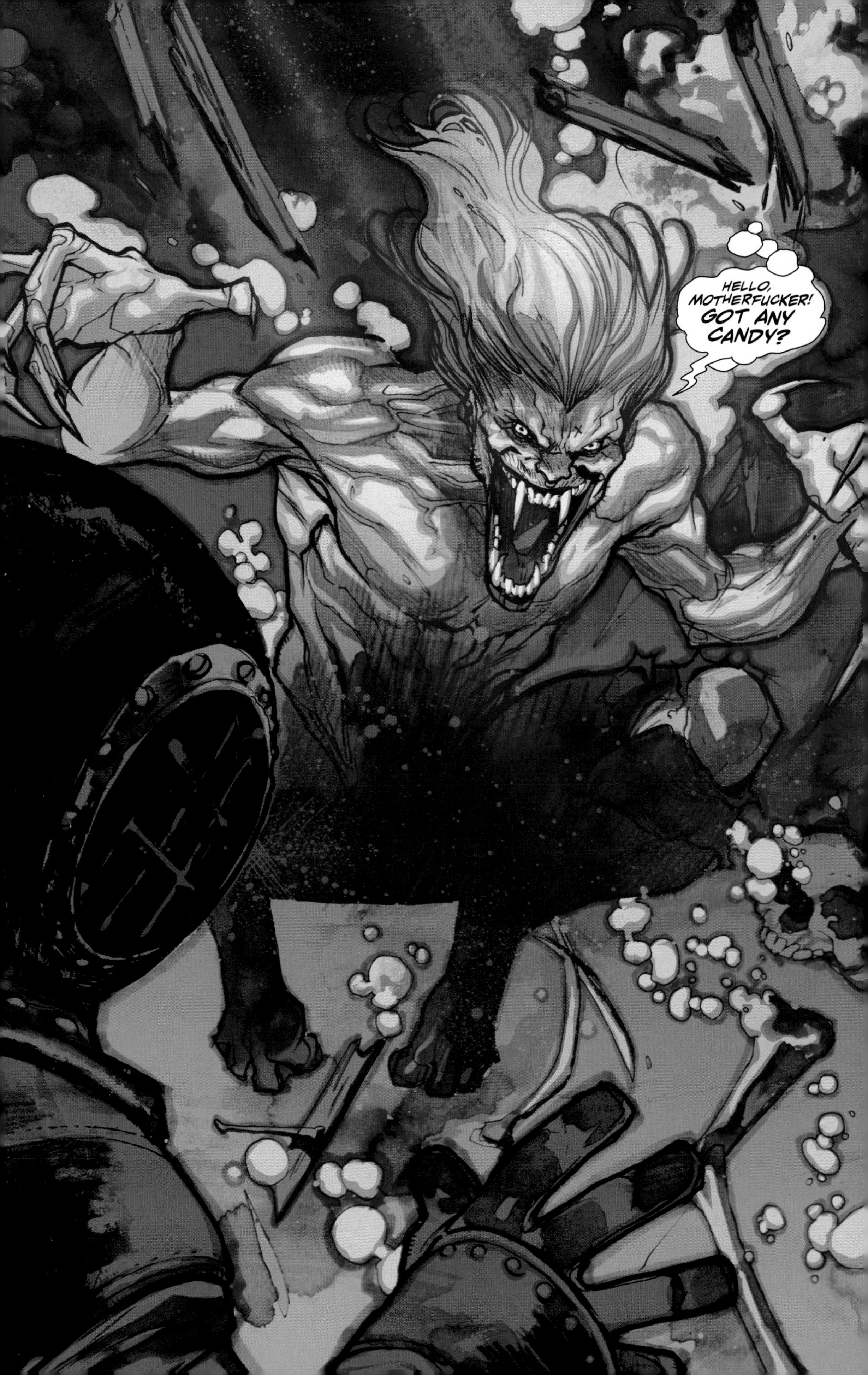
HELLO, MOTHERFUCKER! GOT ANY CANDY?

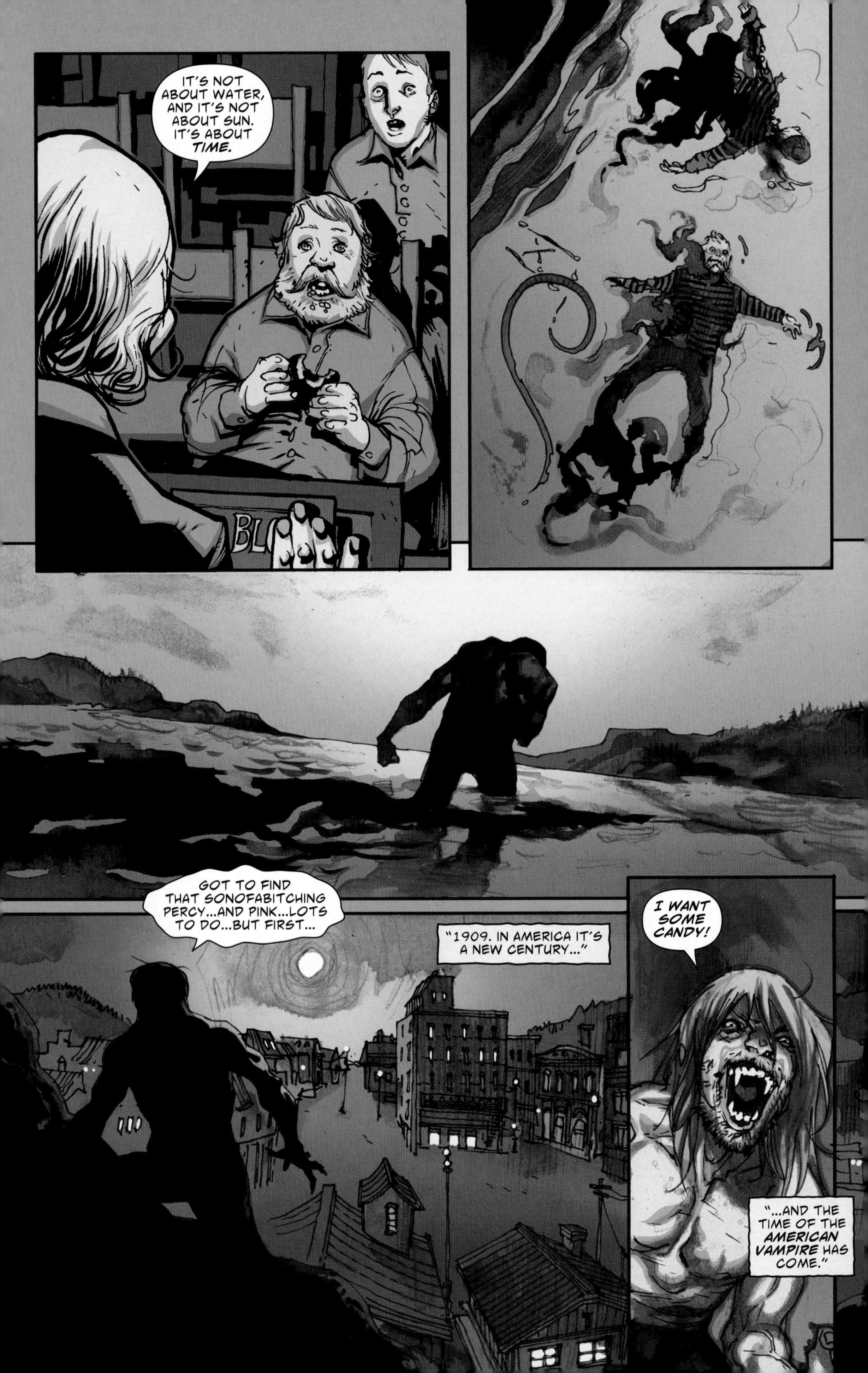
IT'S NOT ABOUT WATER, AND IT'S NOT ABOUT SUN. IT'S ABOUT *TIME.*
GOT TO FIND THAT SONOFABITCHING PERCY...AND PINK...LOTS TO DO...BUT FIRST...
"1909. IN AMERICA IT'S A NEW CENTURY..."
I WANT SOME CANDY!
"...AND THE TIME OF THE *AMERICAN VAMPIRE* HAS COME."

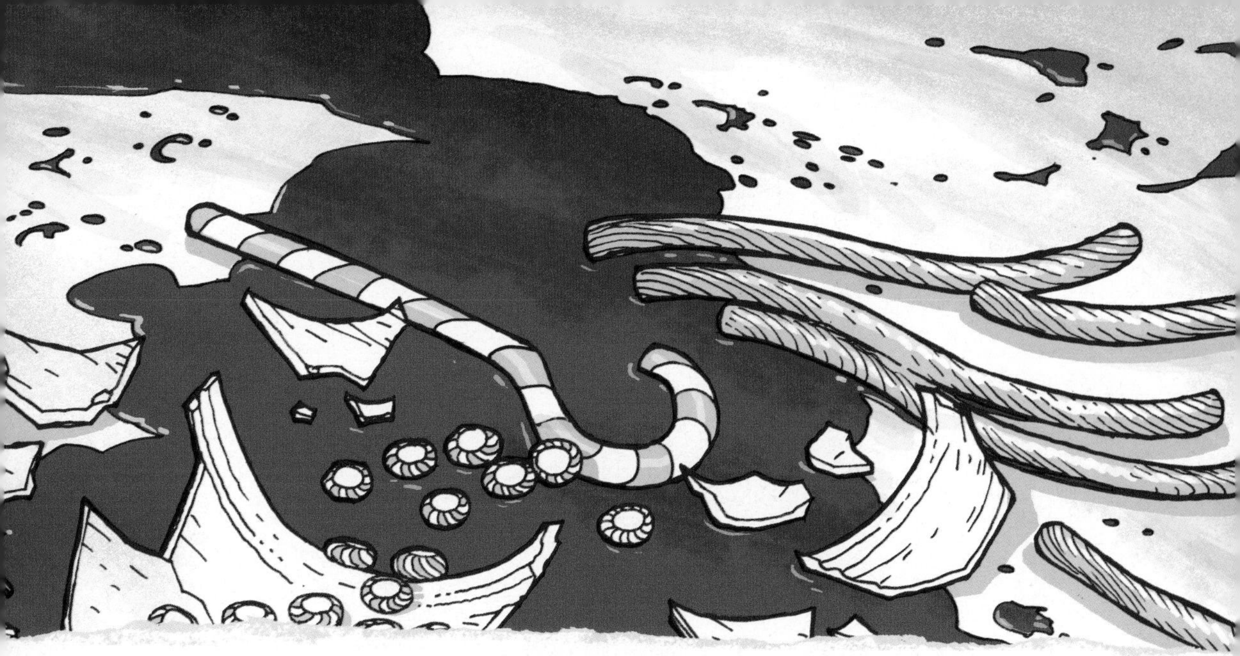

Chapter Three

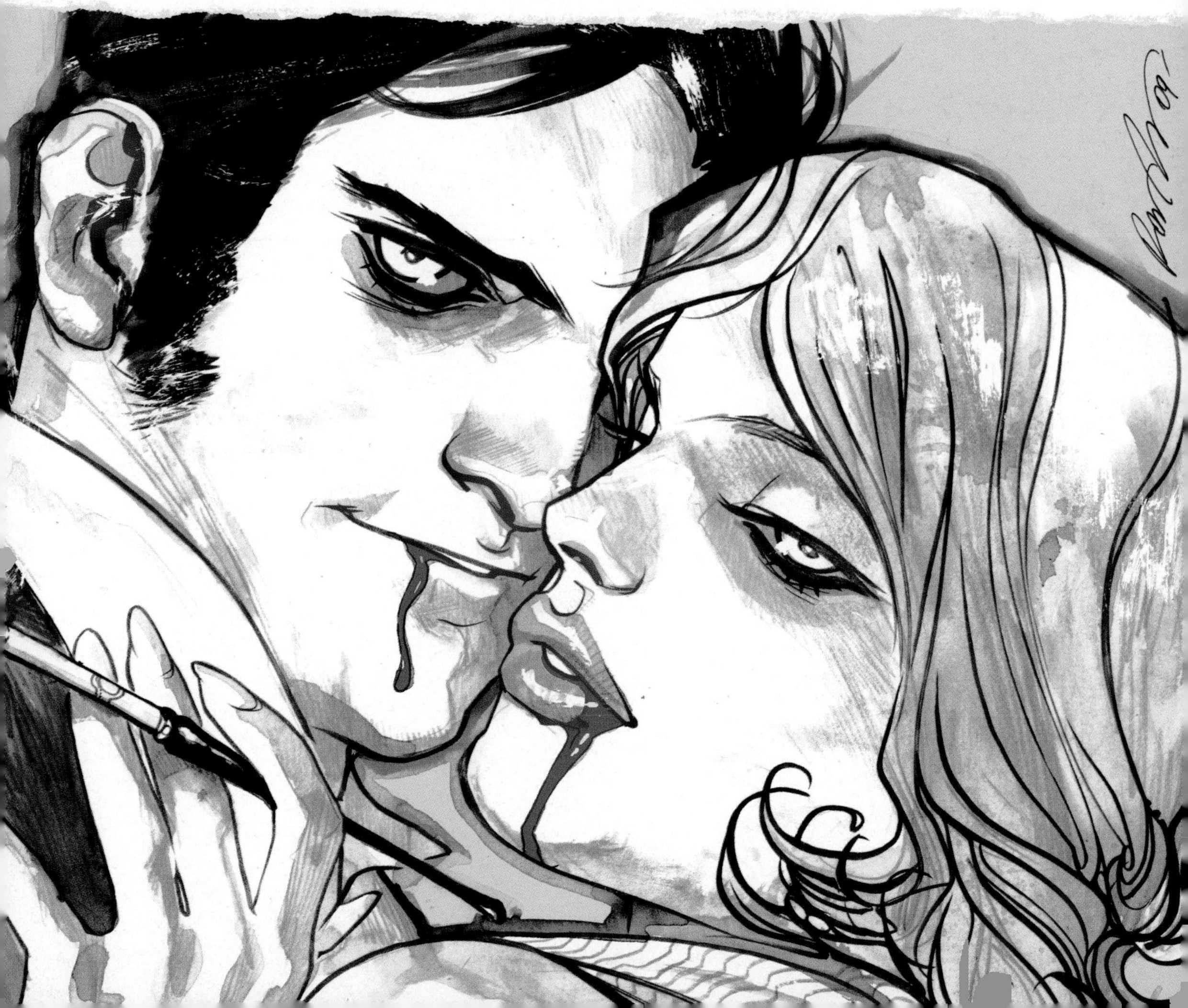

Rough Cut
Scott Snyder Writer

Blood Vengeance
Stephen King Writer

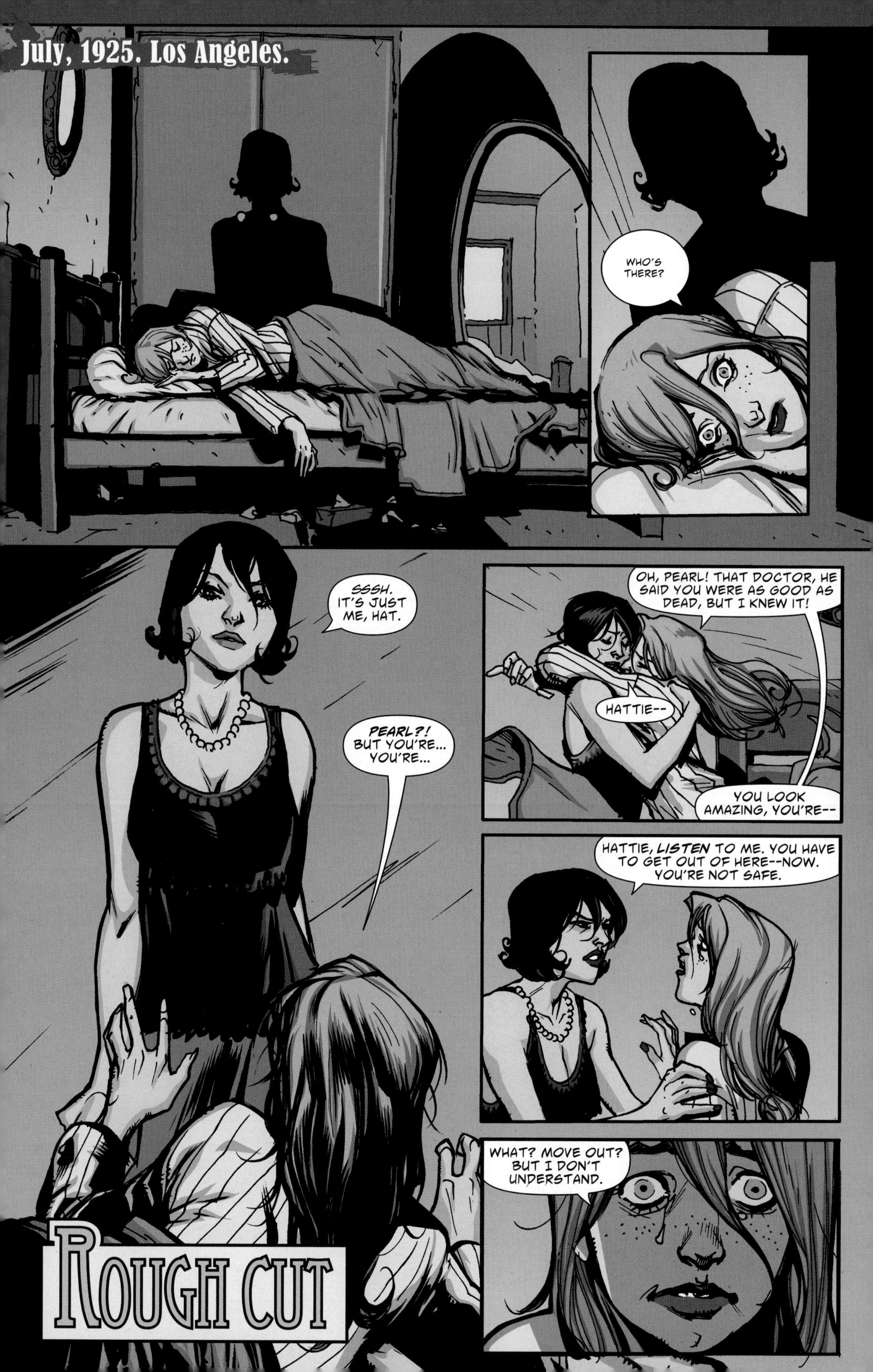
July, 1925. Los Angeles.
WHO'S THERE?
SSSH. IT'S JUST ME, HAT.
PEARL?! BUT YOU'RE... YOU'RE...
OH, PEARL! THAT DOCTOR, HE SAID YOU WERE AS GOOD AS DEAD, BUT I KNEW IT!
HATTIE--
YOU LOOK AMAZING, YOU'RE--
HATTIE, LISTEN TO ME. YOU HAVE TO GET OUT OF HERE--NOW. YOU'RE NOT SAFE.
WHAT? MOVE OUT? BUT I DON'T UNDERSTAND.
ROUGH CUT

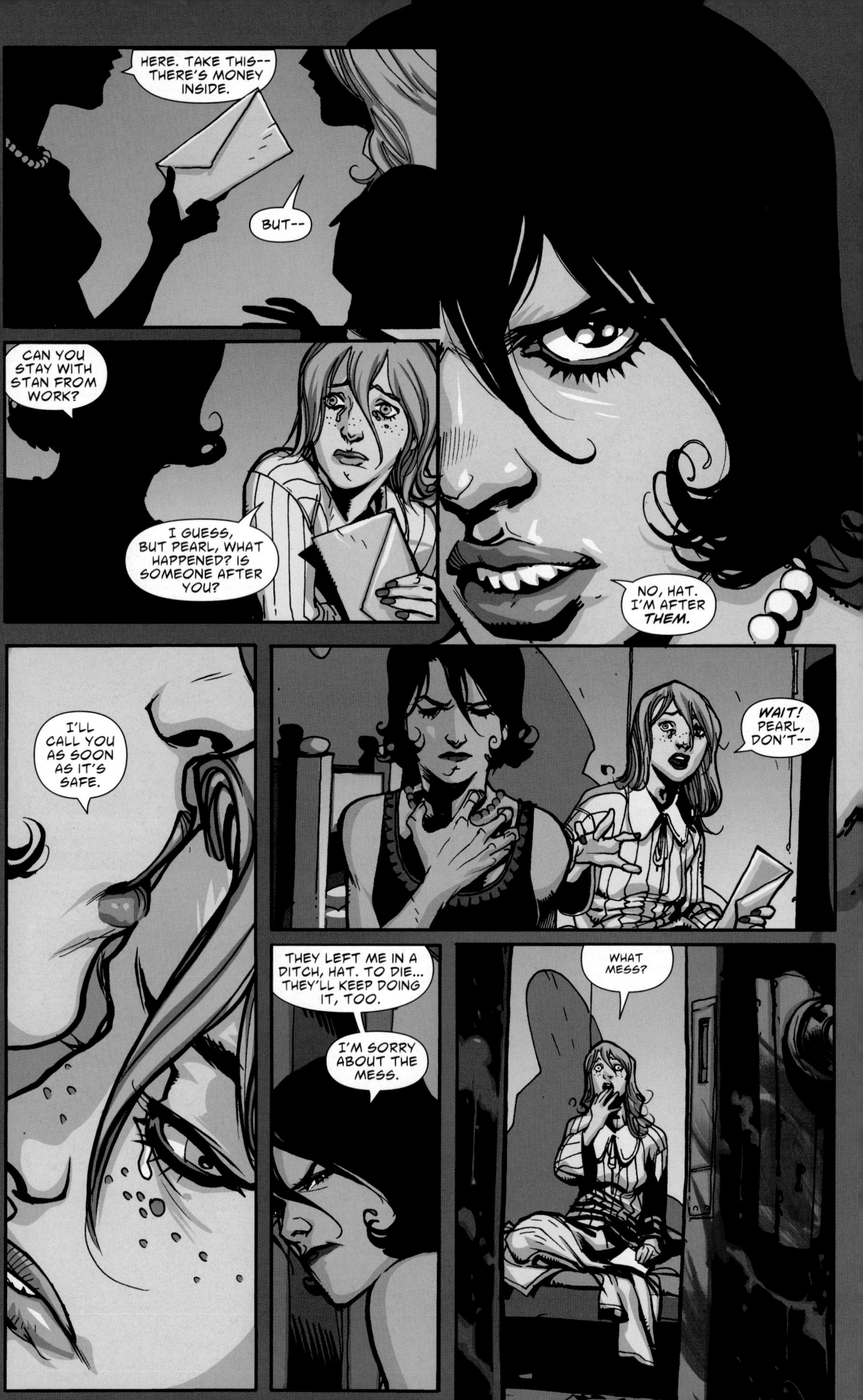
HERE. TAKE THIS-- THERE'S MONEY INSIDE.
BUT--
CAN YOU STAY WITH STAN FROM WORK?
I GUESS, BUT PEARL, WHAT HAPPENED? IS SOMEONE AFTER YOU?
NO, HAT. I'M AFTER *THEM.*
I'LL CALL YOU AS SOON AS IT'S SAFE.
WAIT! PEARL, DON'T--
THEY LEFT ME IN A DITCH, HAT. TO DIE... THEY'LL KEEP DOING IT, TOO.
I'M SORRY ABOUT THE MESS.
WHAT MESS?

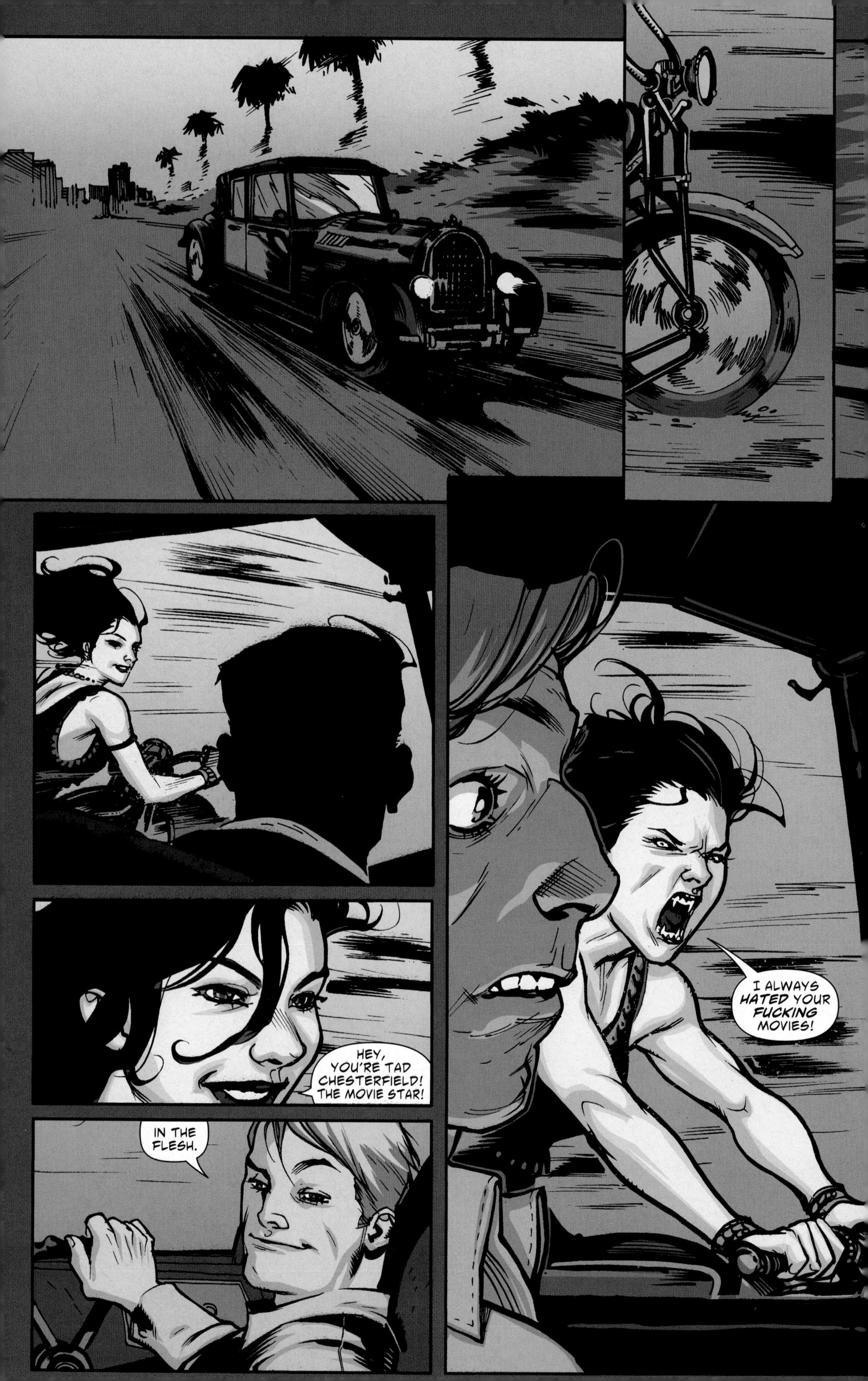
HEY, YOU'RE TAD CHESTERFIELD! THE MOVIE STAR!
IN THE FLESH.
I ALWAYS HATED YOUR FUCKING MOVIES!

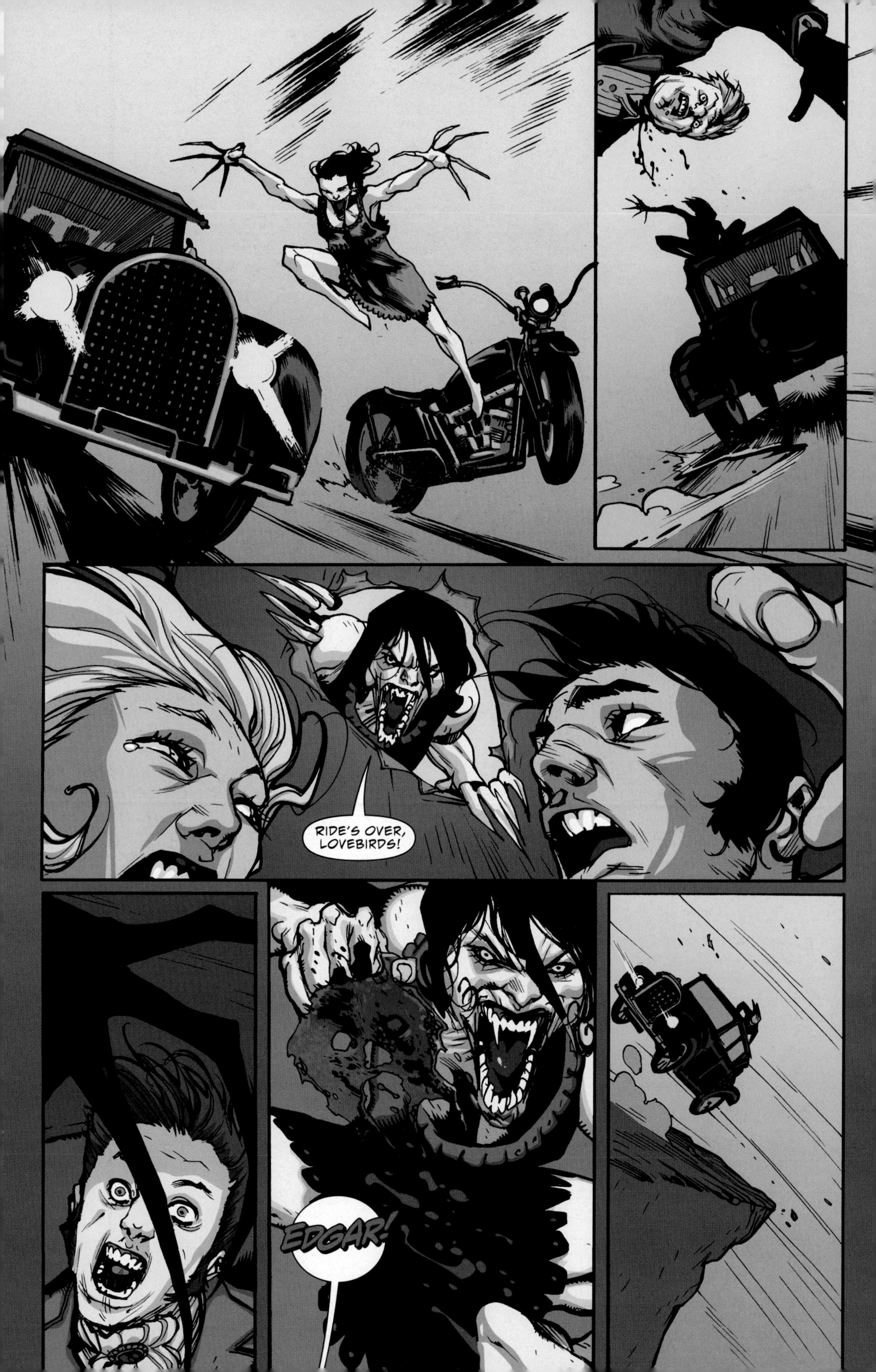

RIDE'S OVER, LOVEBIRDS!
EDGAR!

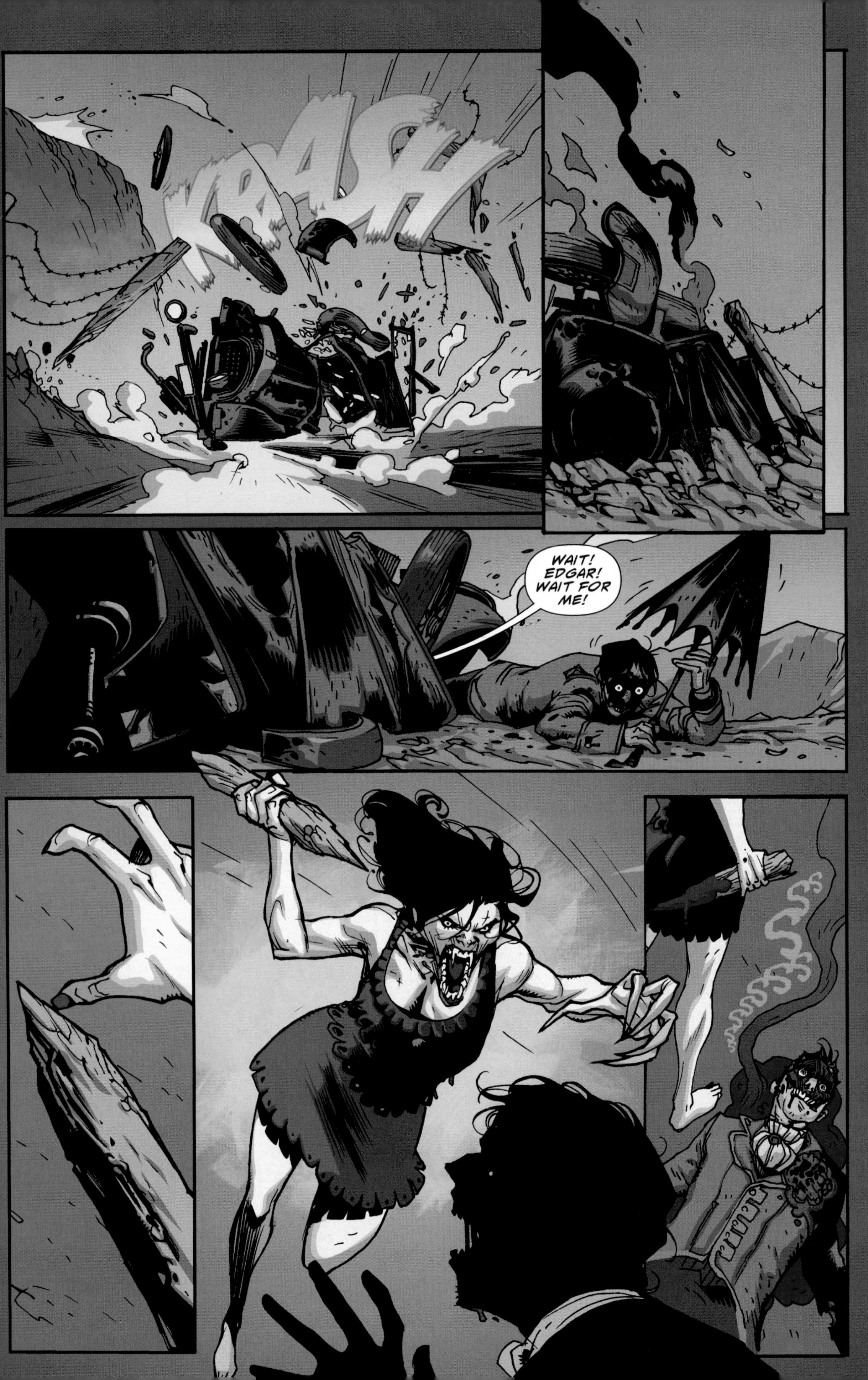
KRASH
WAIT! EDGAR! WAIT FOR ME!

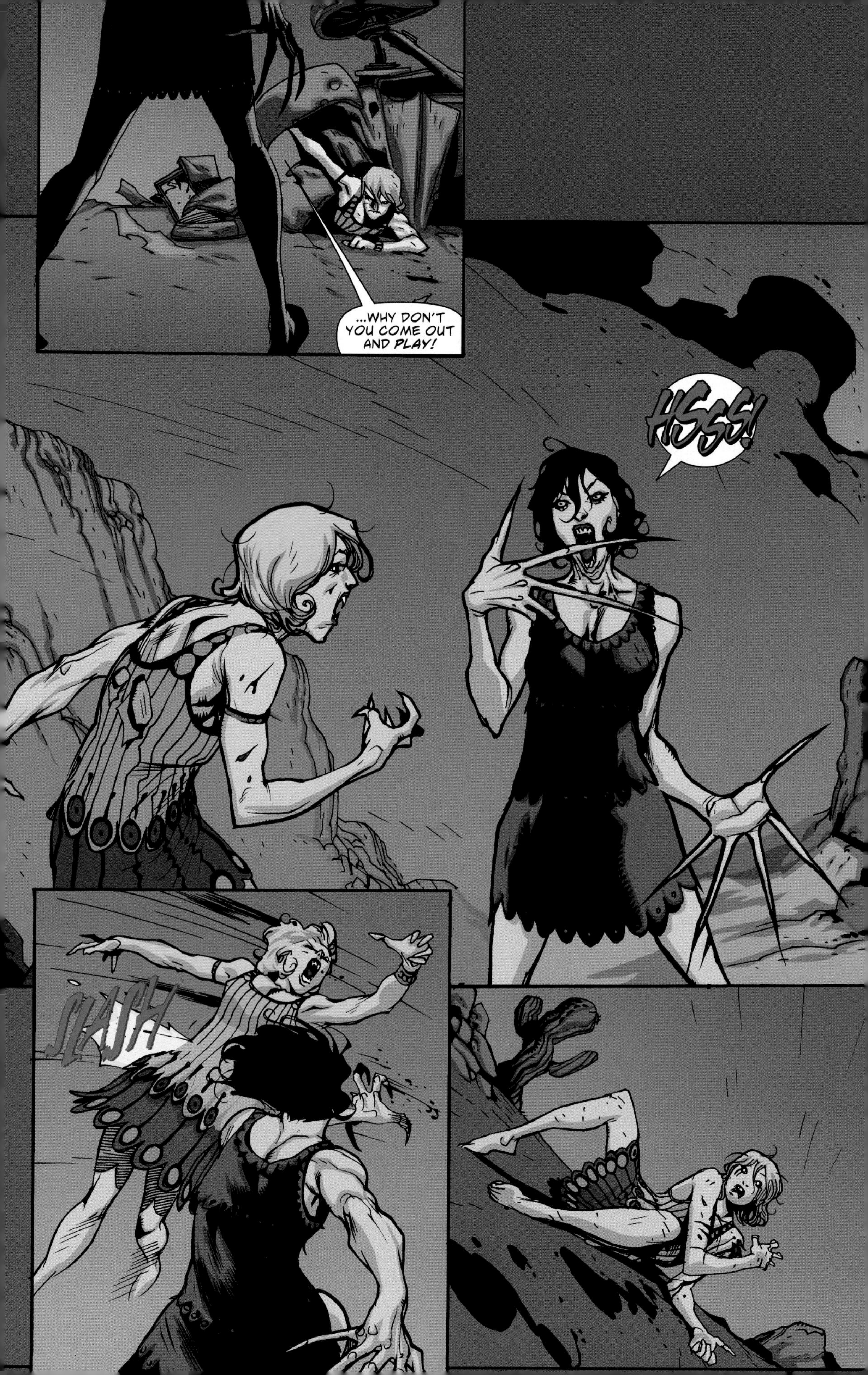
...WHY DON'T YOU COME OUT AND PLAY!
HSSS!
SLASH

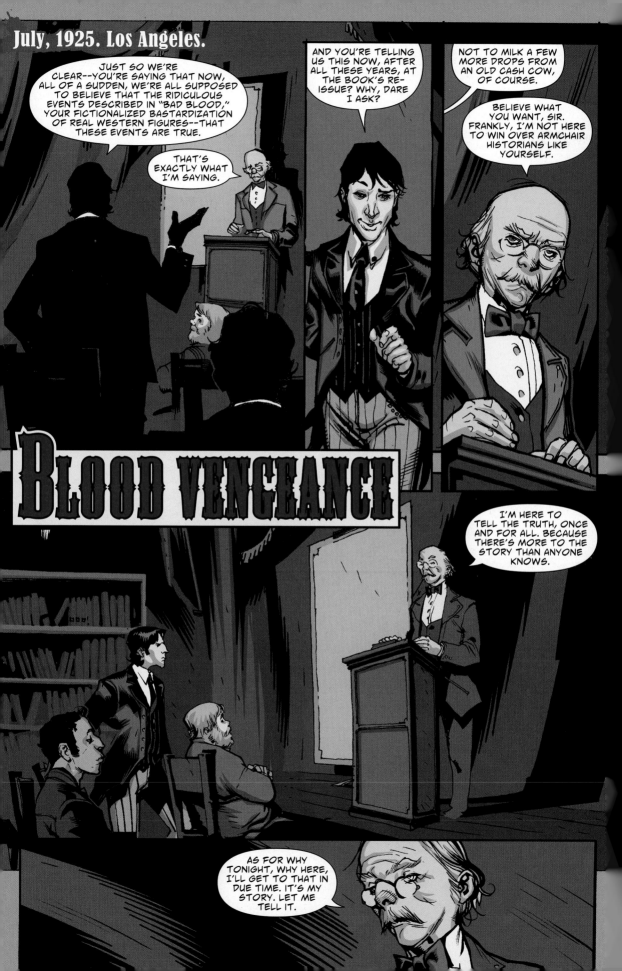

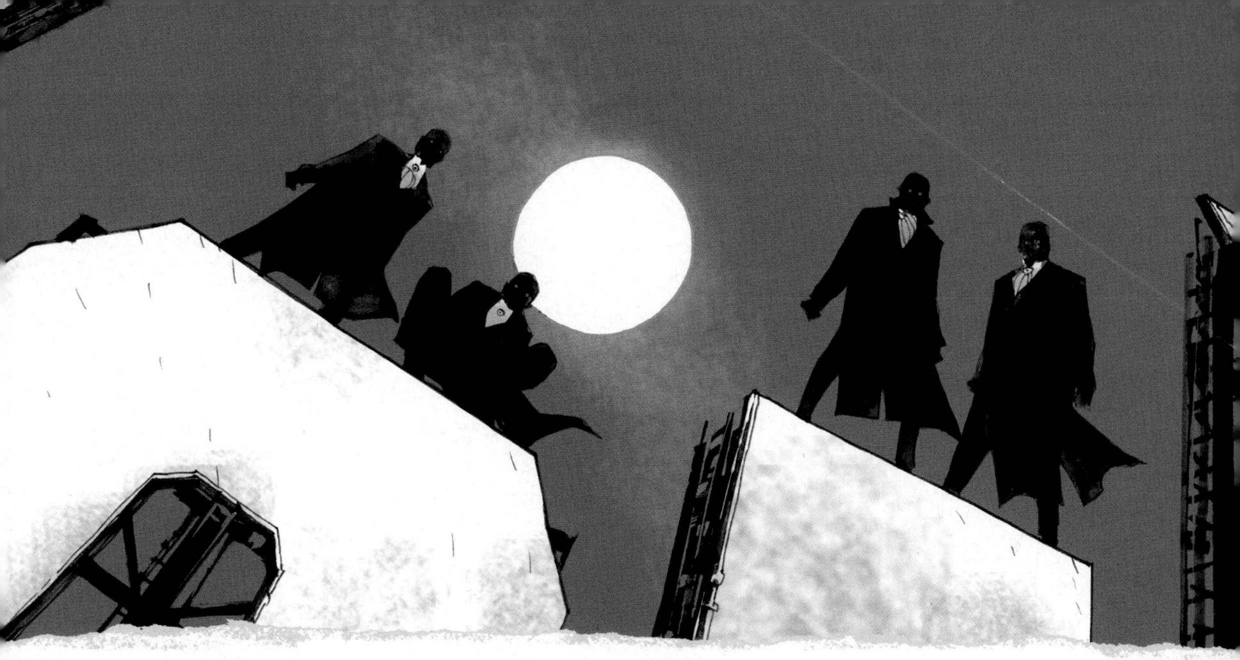

Chapter Four

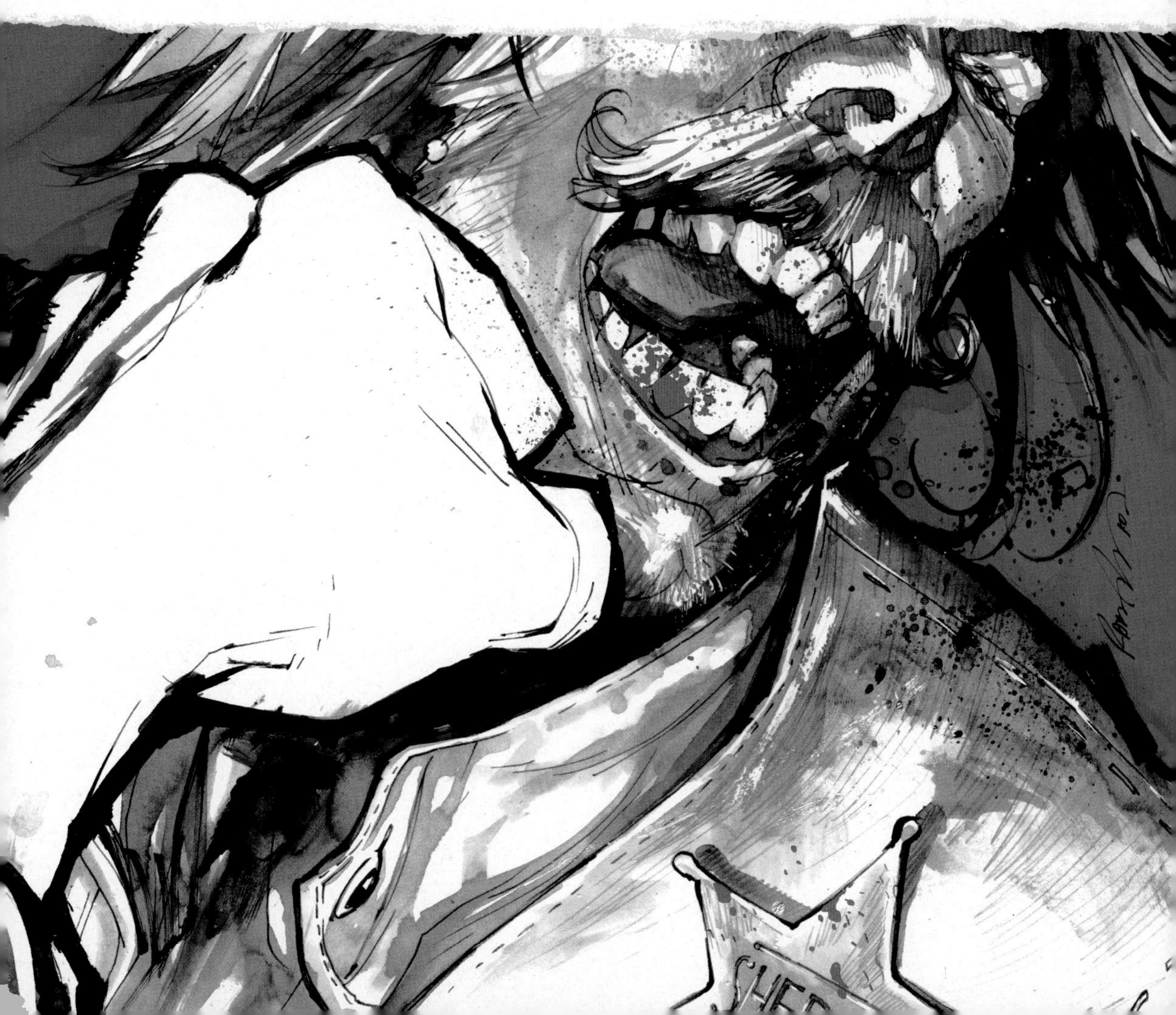

Double Exposure
Scott Snyder Writer

One Drop of Blood
Stephen King Writer

DOUBLE EXPOSURE

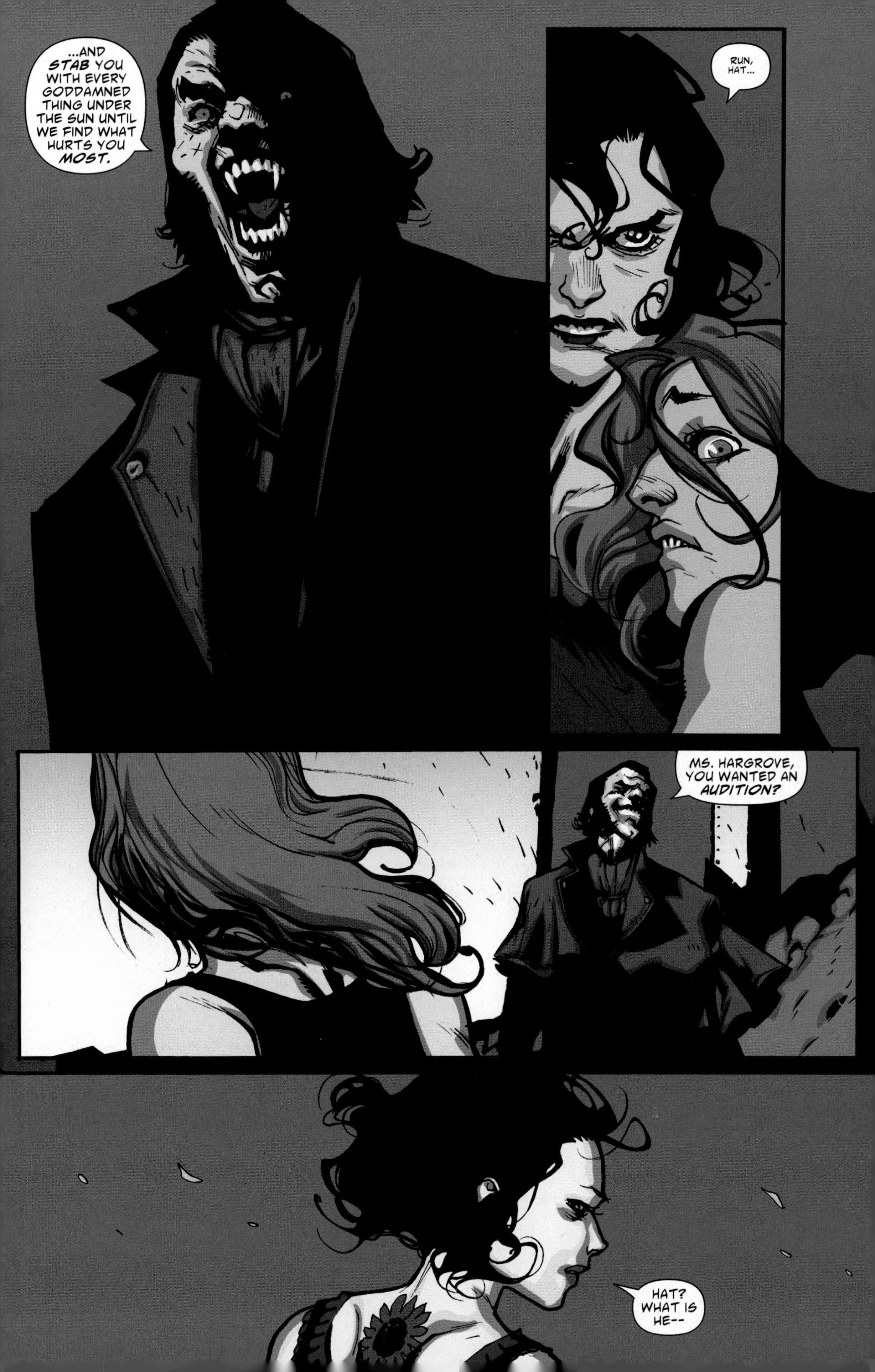
...AND STAB YOU WITH EVERY GODDAMNED THING UNDER THE SUN UNTIL WE FIND WHAT HURTS YOU MOST.
RUN, HAT...
MS. HARGROVE, YOU WANTED AN AUDITION?
HAT? WHAT IS HE--

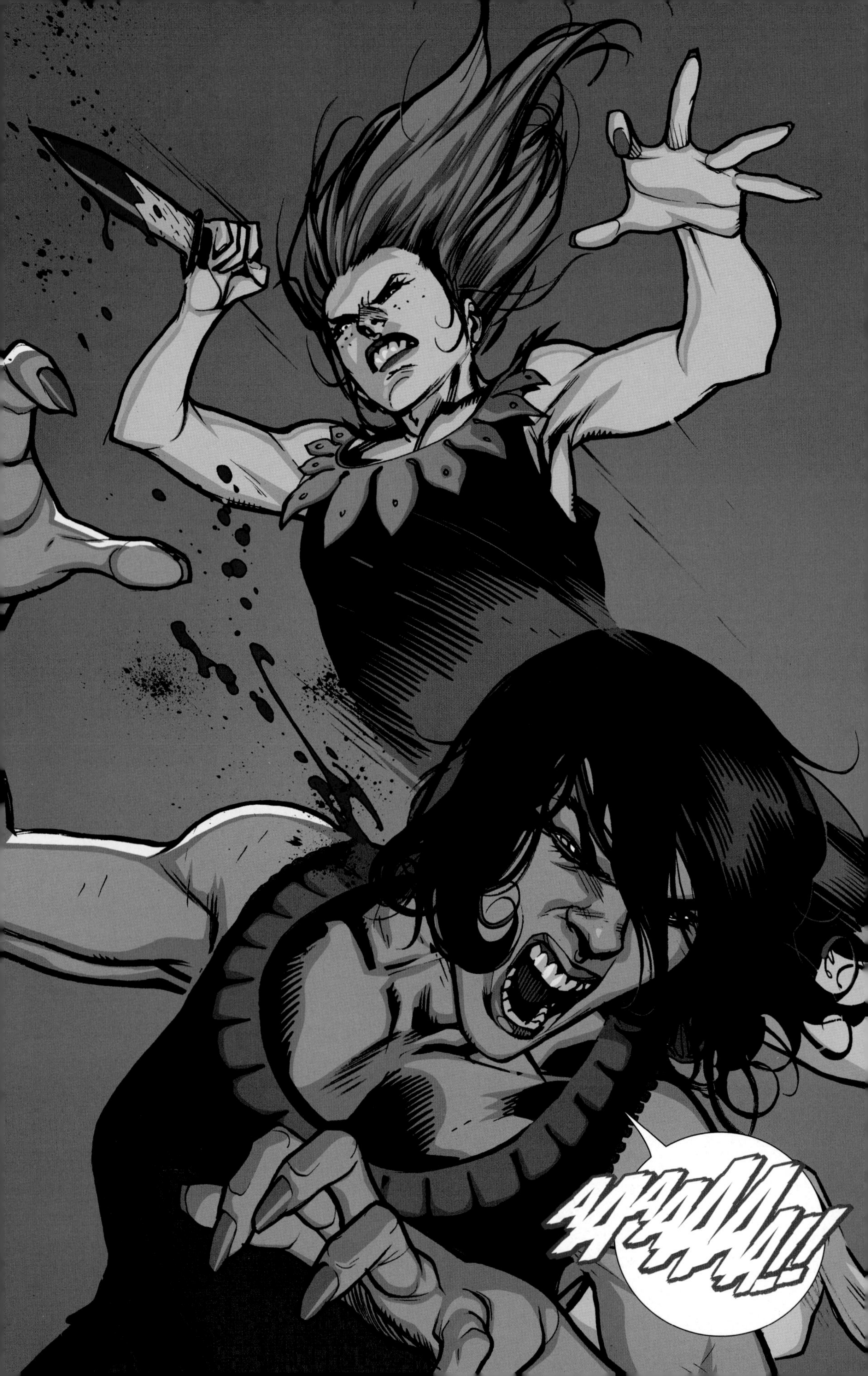
AAAAAAH!!

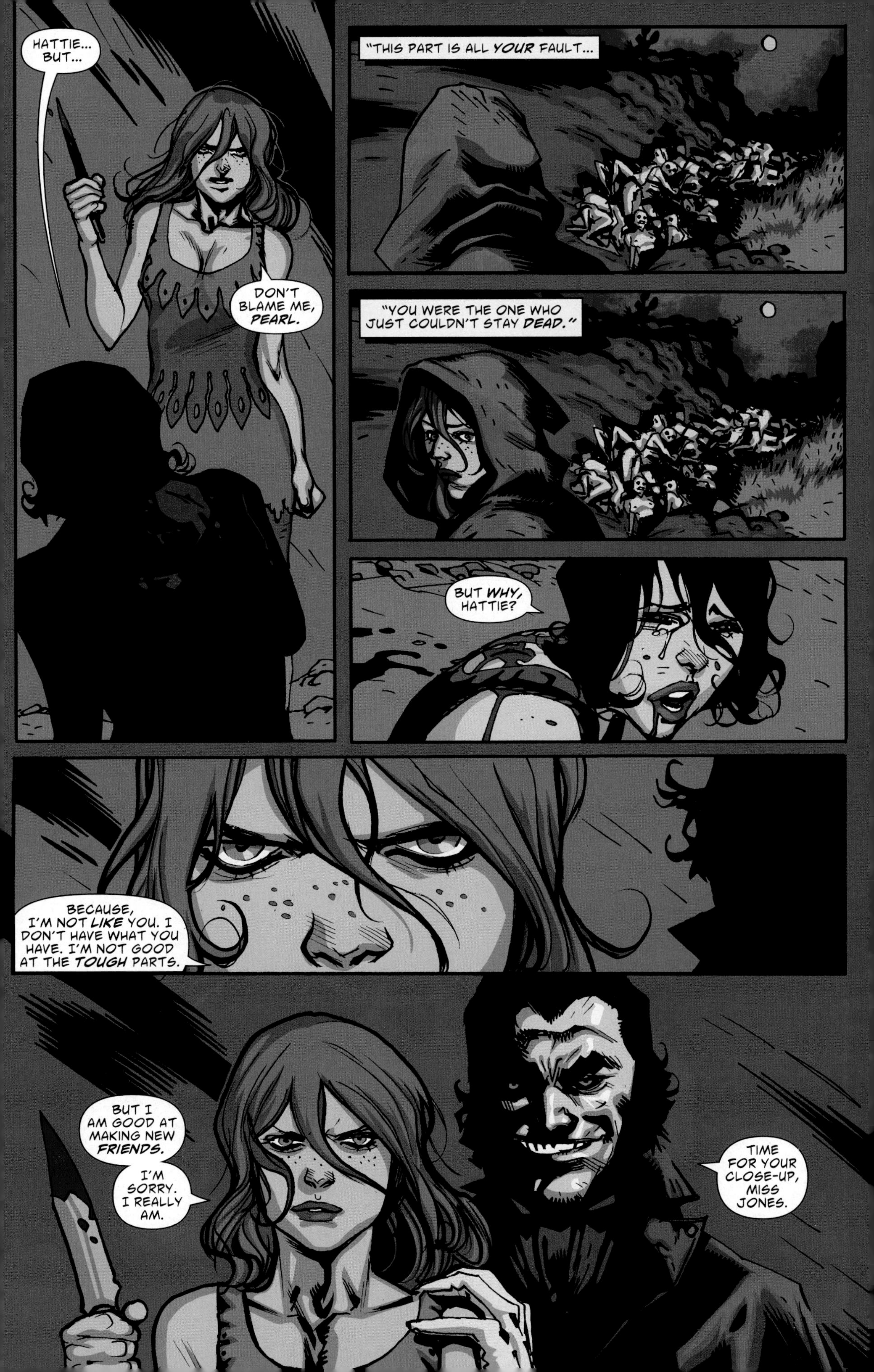
HATTIE... BUT...
DON'T BLAME ME, PEARL.
"THIS PART IS ALL YOUR FAULT...
"YOU WERE THE ONE WHO JUST COULDN'T STAY DEAD."
BUT WHY, HATTIE?
BECAUSE, I'M NOT LIKE YOU. I DON'T HAVE WHAT YOU HAVE. I'M NOT GOOD AT THE TOUGH PARTS.
BUT I AM GOOD AT MAKING NEW FRIENDS.
I'M SORRY. I REALLY AM.
TIME FOR YOUR CLOSE-UP, MISS JONES.

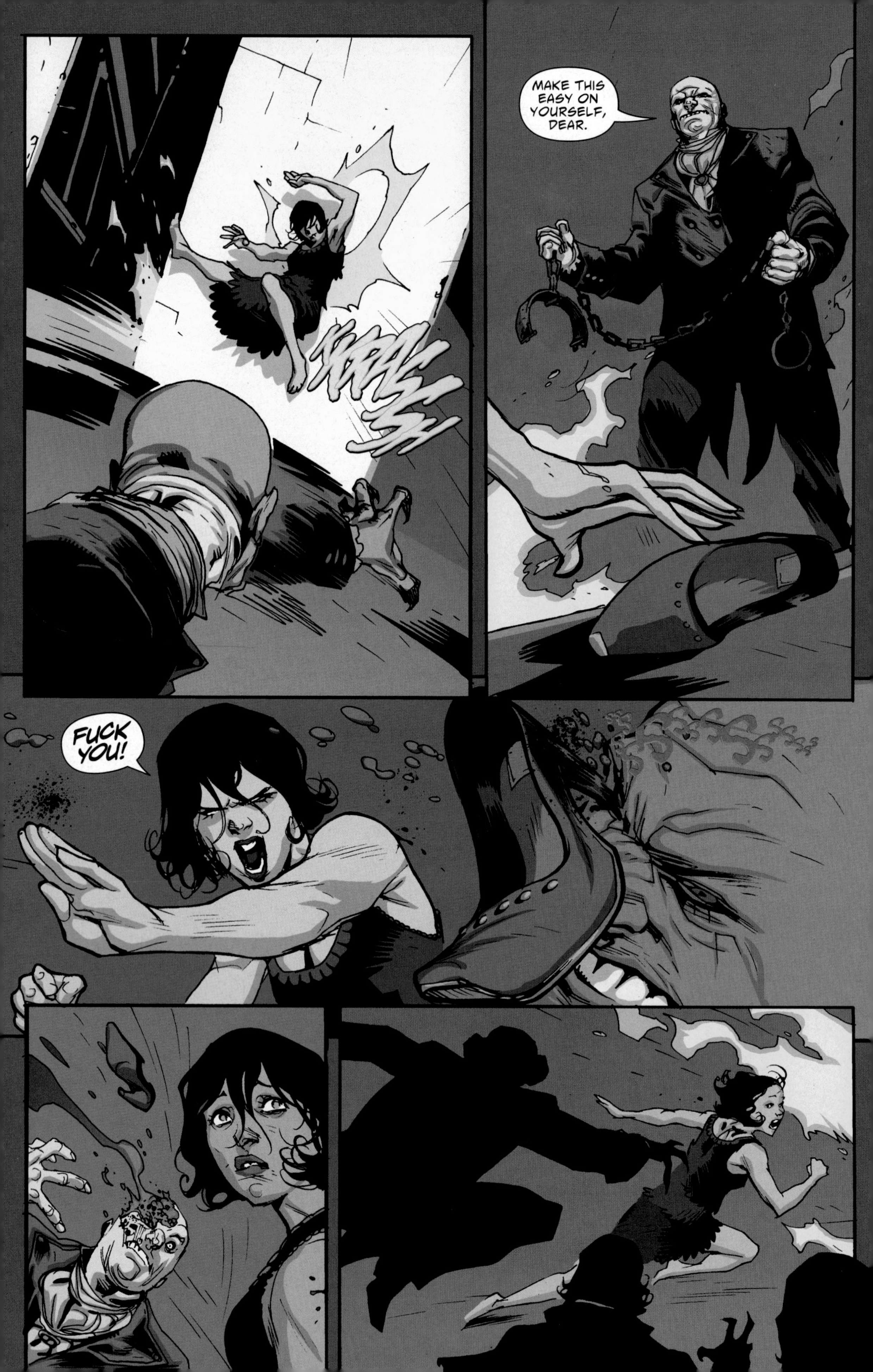
KRAAAASH
MAKE THIS EASY ON YOURSELF, DEAR.
FUCK YOU!

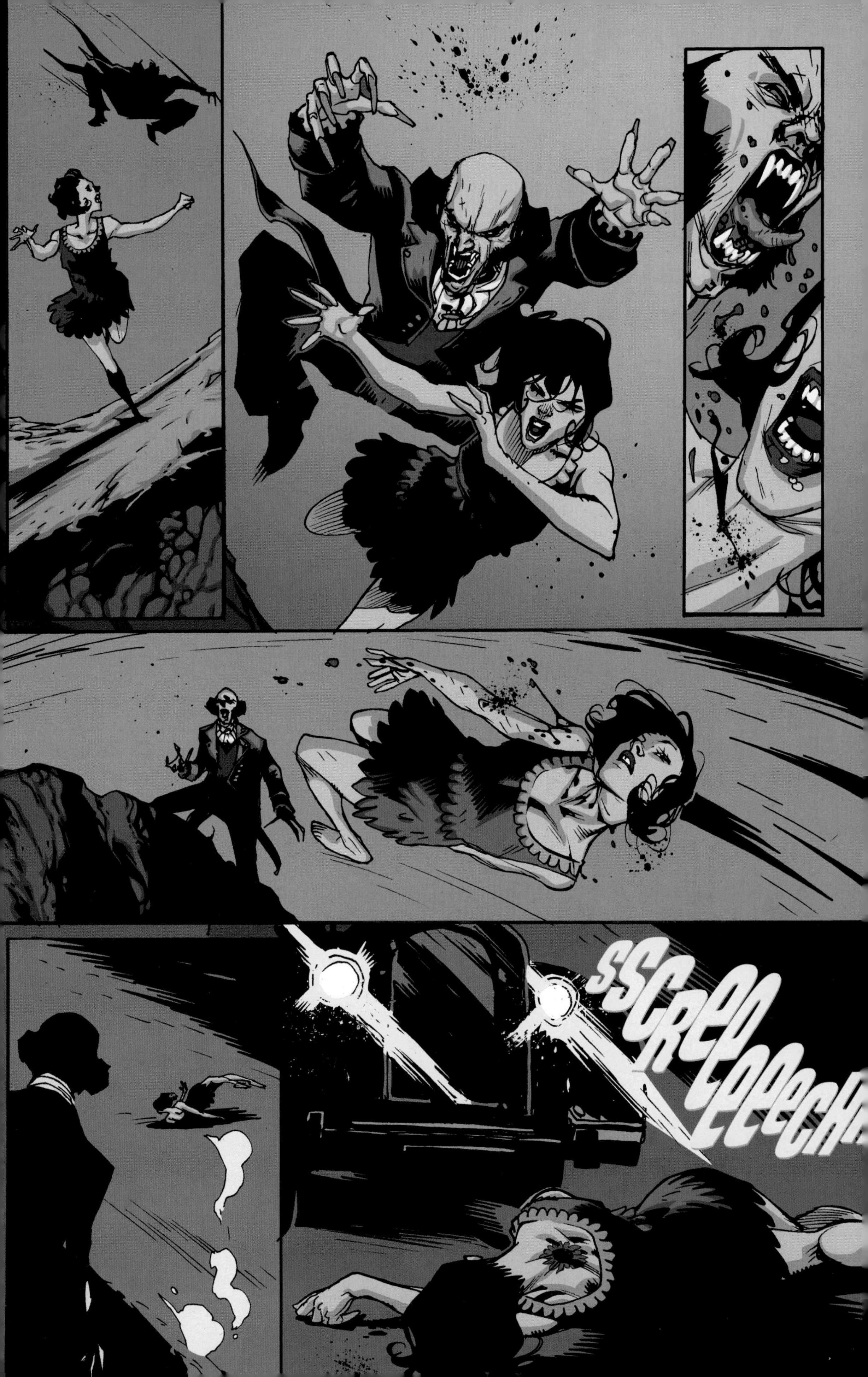
SSCREEEEEECH

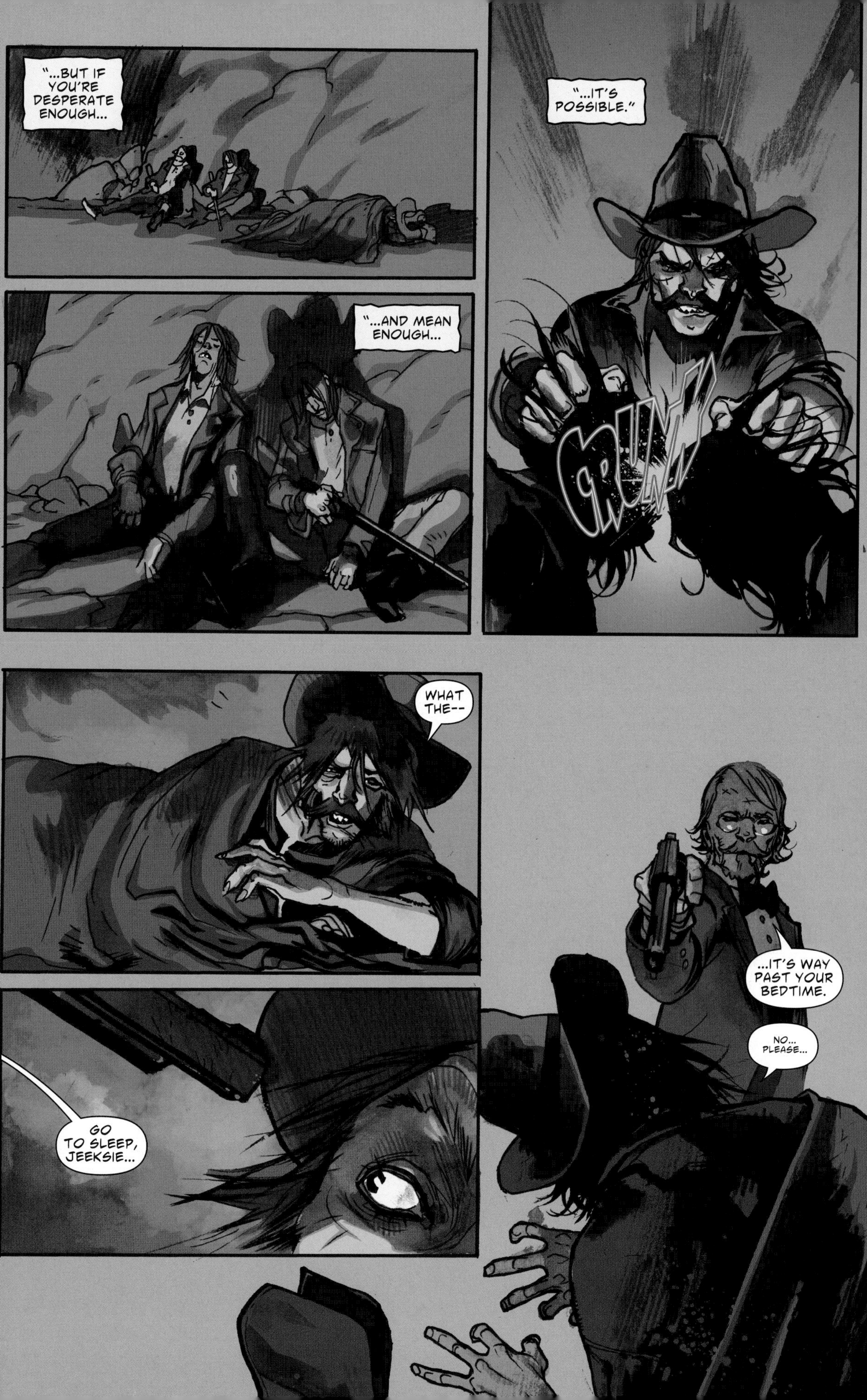
"...BUT IF YOU'RE DESPERATE ENOUGH...
"...AND MEAN ENOUGH...
"...IT'S POSSIBLE."
CRUNCH
WHAT THE--
...IT'S WAY PAST YOUR BEDTIME.
NO... PLEASE...
GO TO SLEEP, JEEKSIE...

LIFE IS VARIOUS AND NEW, GENTLEMEN. MY HOPES PLUMMETED WHEN THEY AMBUSHED JEEKS, BUT NOW THEY BEGIN TO RISE AGAIN.

THE GIRL AND THE WRITER ARE STAYING PUT. SO IT'S JUST BOOK AND CAMILLO.

I FEEL A BIT SORRY FOR MONSIEUR SWEET...*DOULEUR*... HE IS, AFTER ALL, ONE OF US...

HE IS *NOT* LIKE US! IF YOU MAKE THE MISTAKE OF THINKING HE IS, IT'S APT TO BE YOUR *LAST* MISTAKE!

MEIN GOTT, I'M SO *HUNGRY*...

...LET'S GET SOMEONE TO EAT!

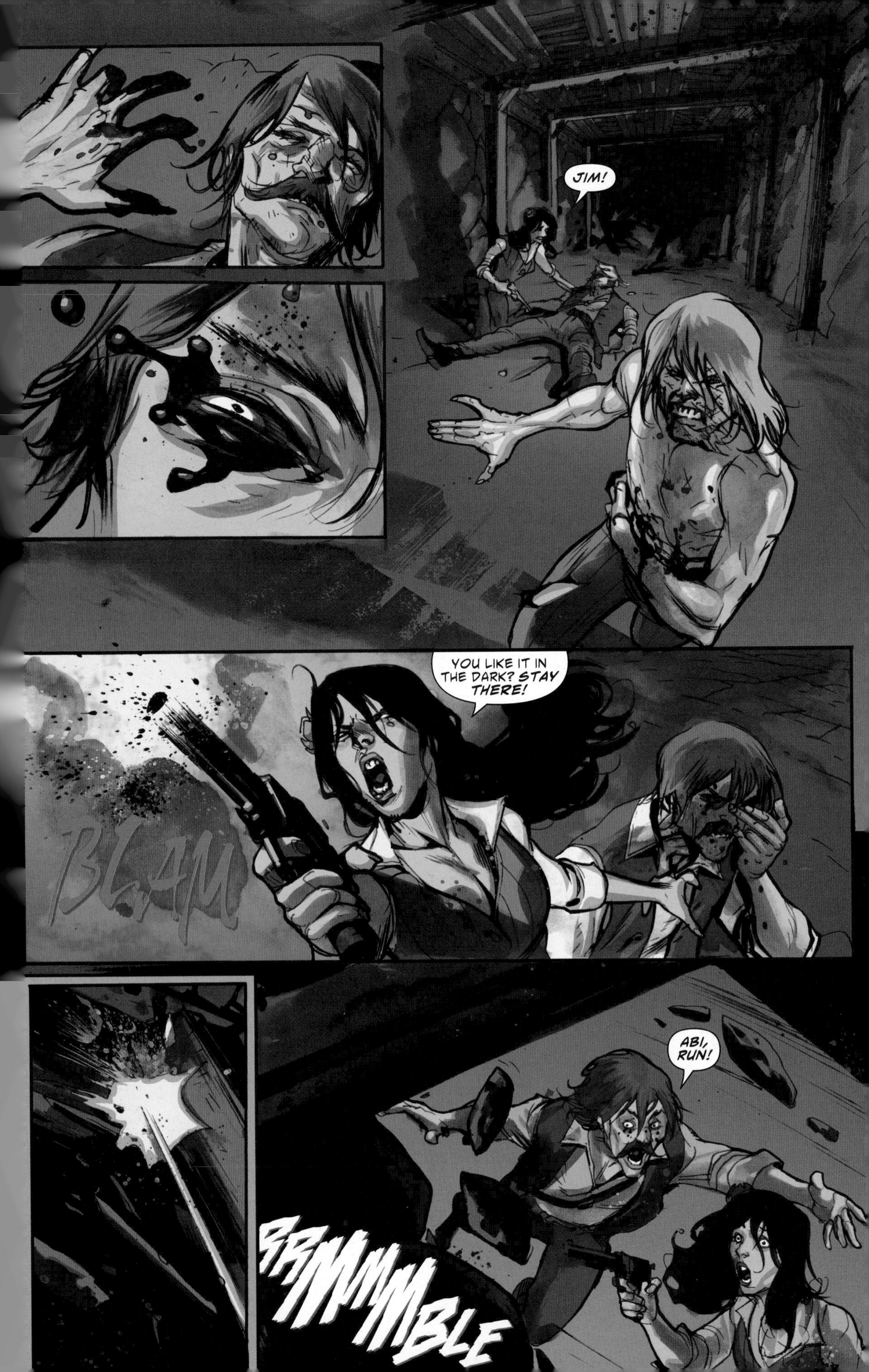
JIM!
YOU LIKE IT IN THE DARK? STAY THERE!
BLAM
ABI, RUN!
RRMMMBLE

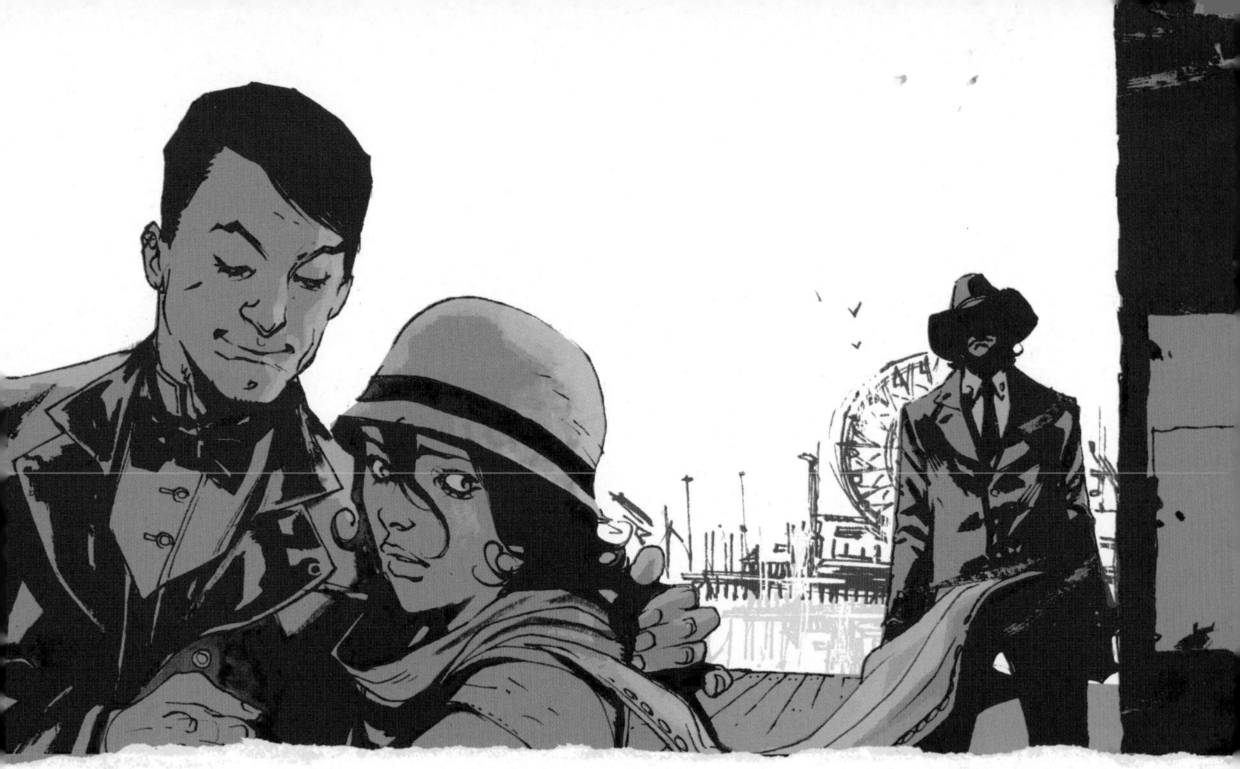

Chapter Five

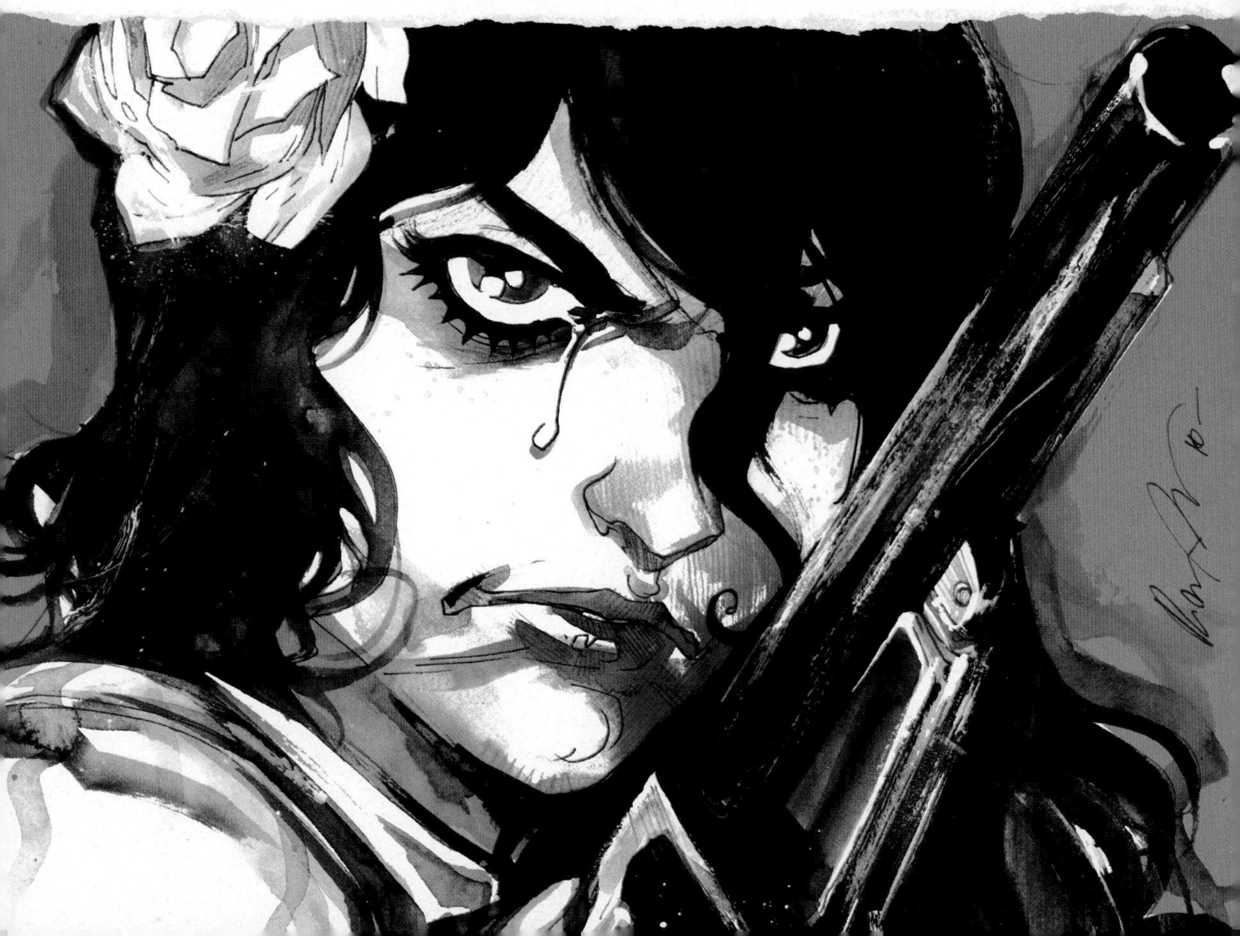

Curtain Call
Scott Snyder Writer

If Thy Right Hand
Offend Thee...
Stephen King Writer

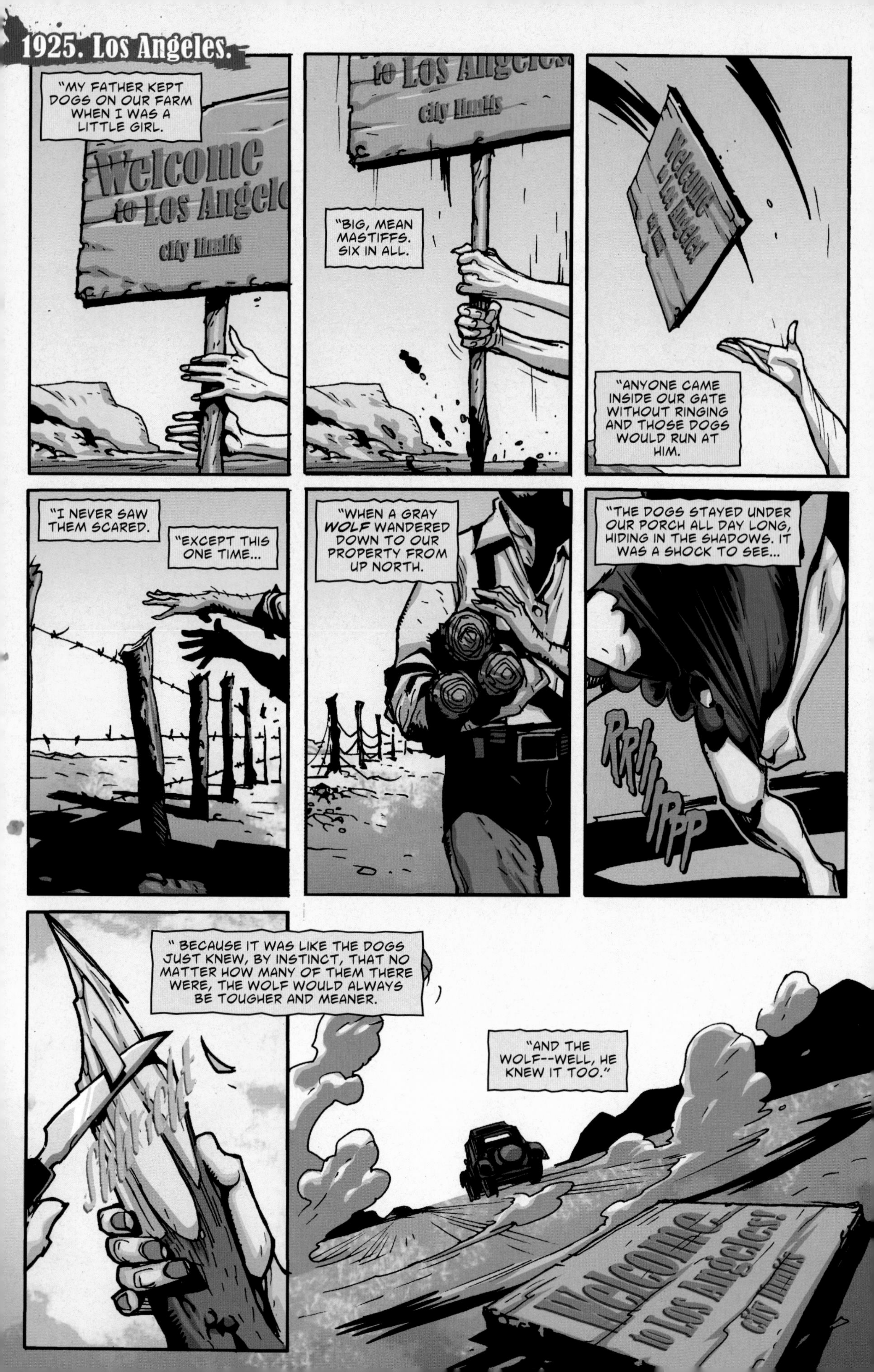
1925. Los Angeles.
"MY FATHER KEPT DOGS ON OUR FARM WHEN I WAS A LITTLE GIRL.
Welcome to Los Angeles city limits
"BIG, MEAN MASTIFFS. SIX IN ALL.
"ANYONE CAME INSIDE OUR GATE WITHOUT RINGING AND THOSE DOGS WOULD RUN AT HIM.
"I NEVER SAW THEM SCARED.
"EXCEPT THIS ONE TIME...
"WHEN A GRAY WOLF WANDERED DOWN TO OUR PROPERTY FROM UP NORTH.
"THE DOGS STAYED UNDER OUR PORCH ALL DAY LONG, HIDING IN THE SHADOWS. IT WAS A SHOCK TO SEE...
RRIIIIRPP
" BECAUSE IT WAS LIKE THE DOGS JUST KNEW, BY INSTINCT, THAT NO MATTER HOW MANY OF THEM THERE WERE, THE WOLF WOULD ALWAYS BE TOUGHER AND MEANER.
"AND THE WOLF--WELL, HE KNEW IT TOO."
Welcome to Los Angeles! city limits

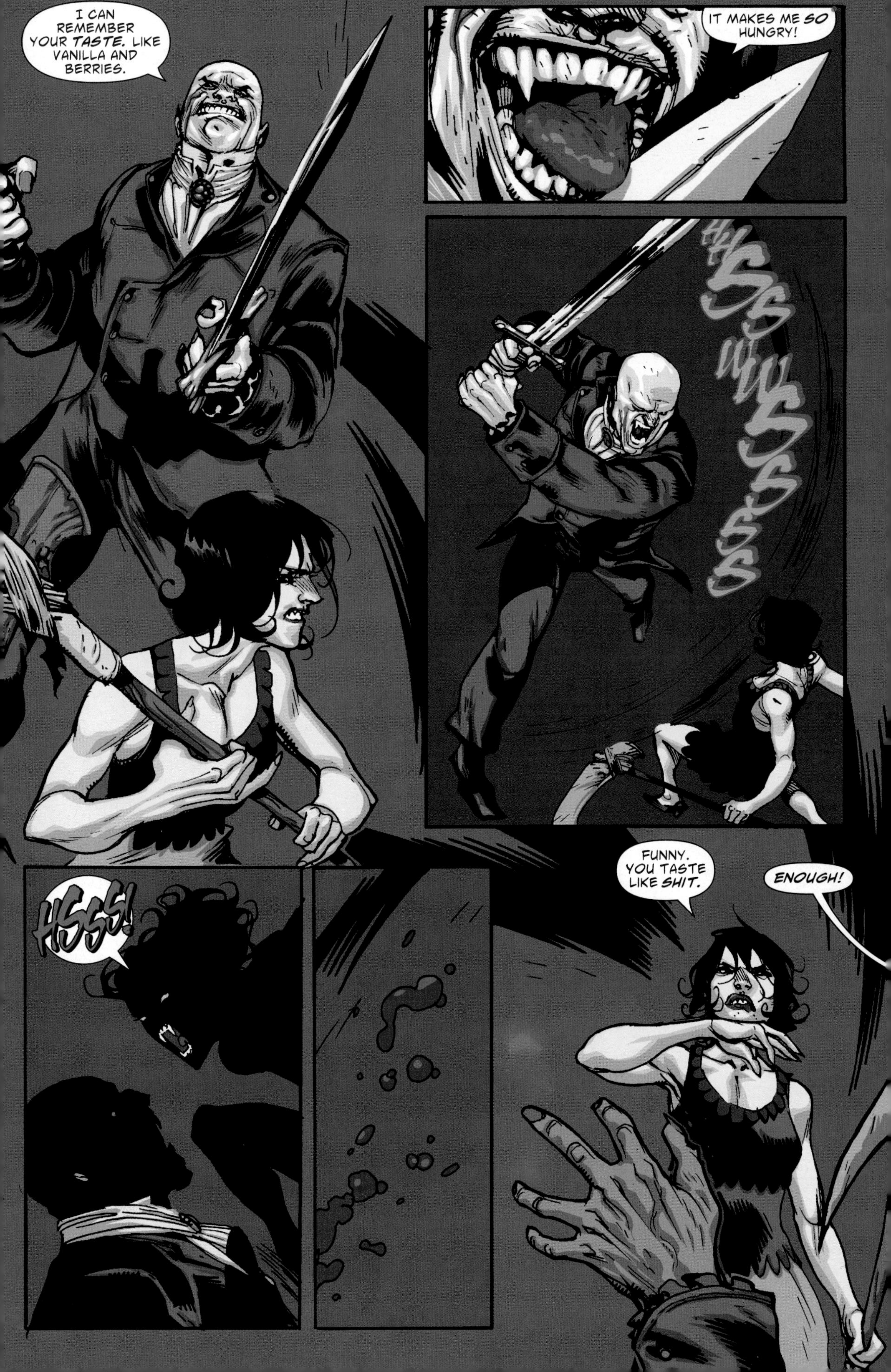
I CAN REMEMBER YOUR TASTE. LIKE VANILLA AND BERRIES.
IT MAKES ME SO HUNGRY!
HHSSWWSSSSS
HSSS!
FUNNY. YOU TASTE LIKE SHIT.
ENOUGH!

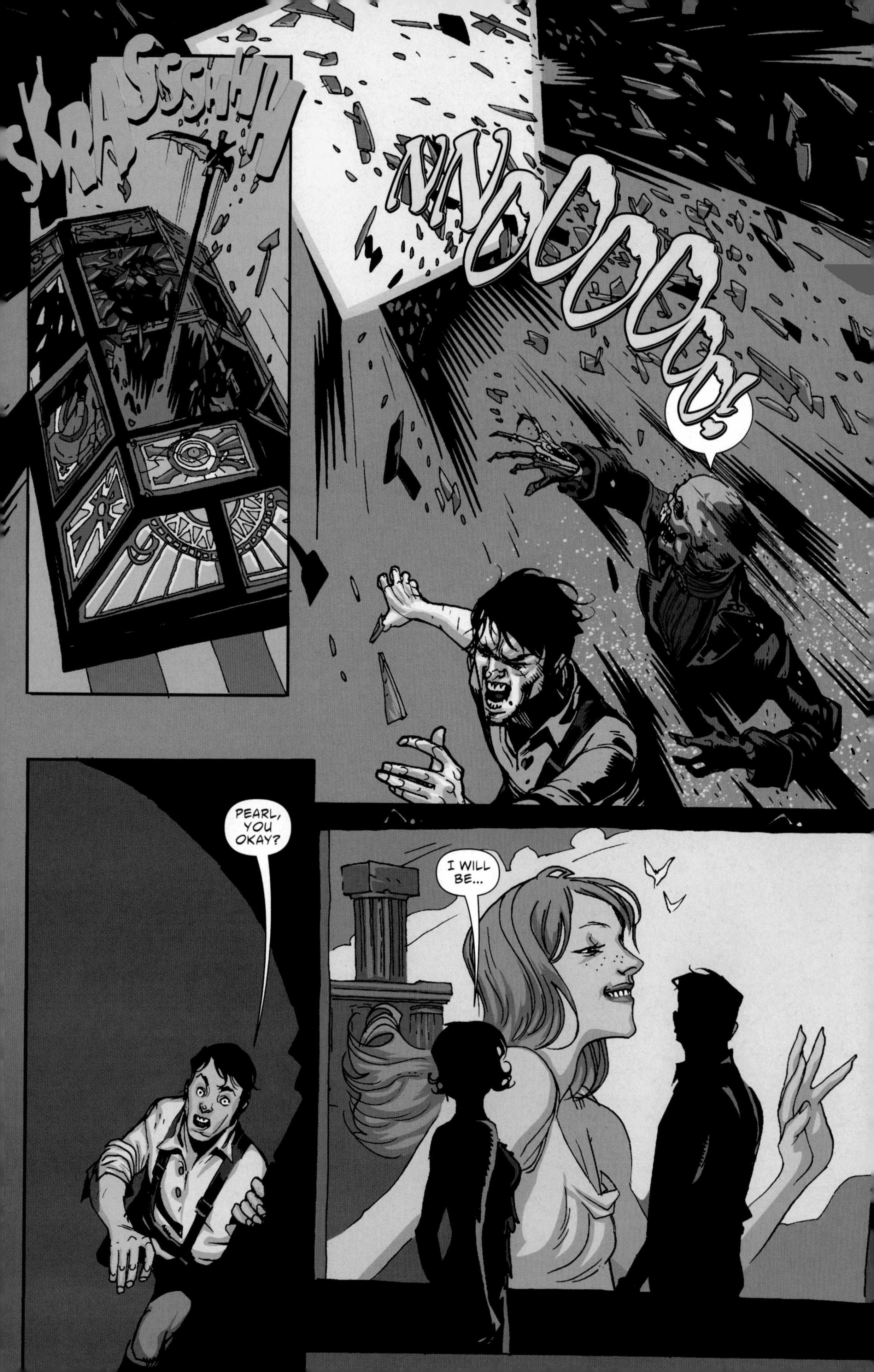
SKRASSSSHHH
NNOOOOOO!
PEARL, YOU OKAY?
I WILL BE...

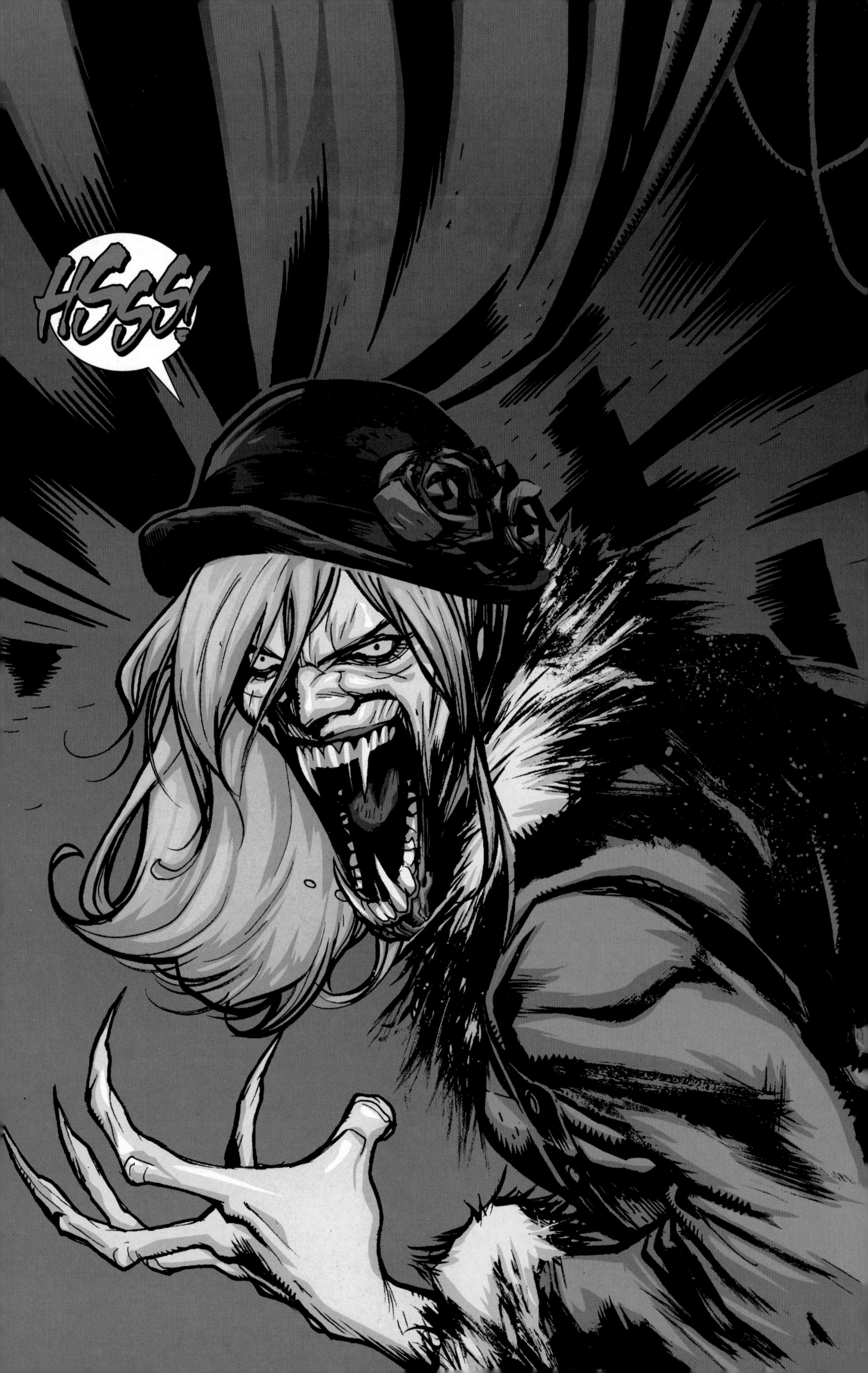
HSSS!

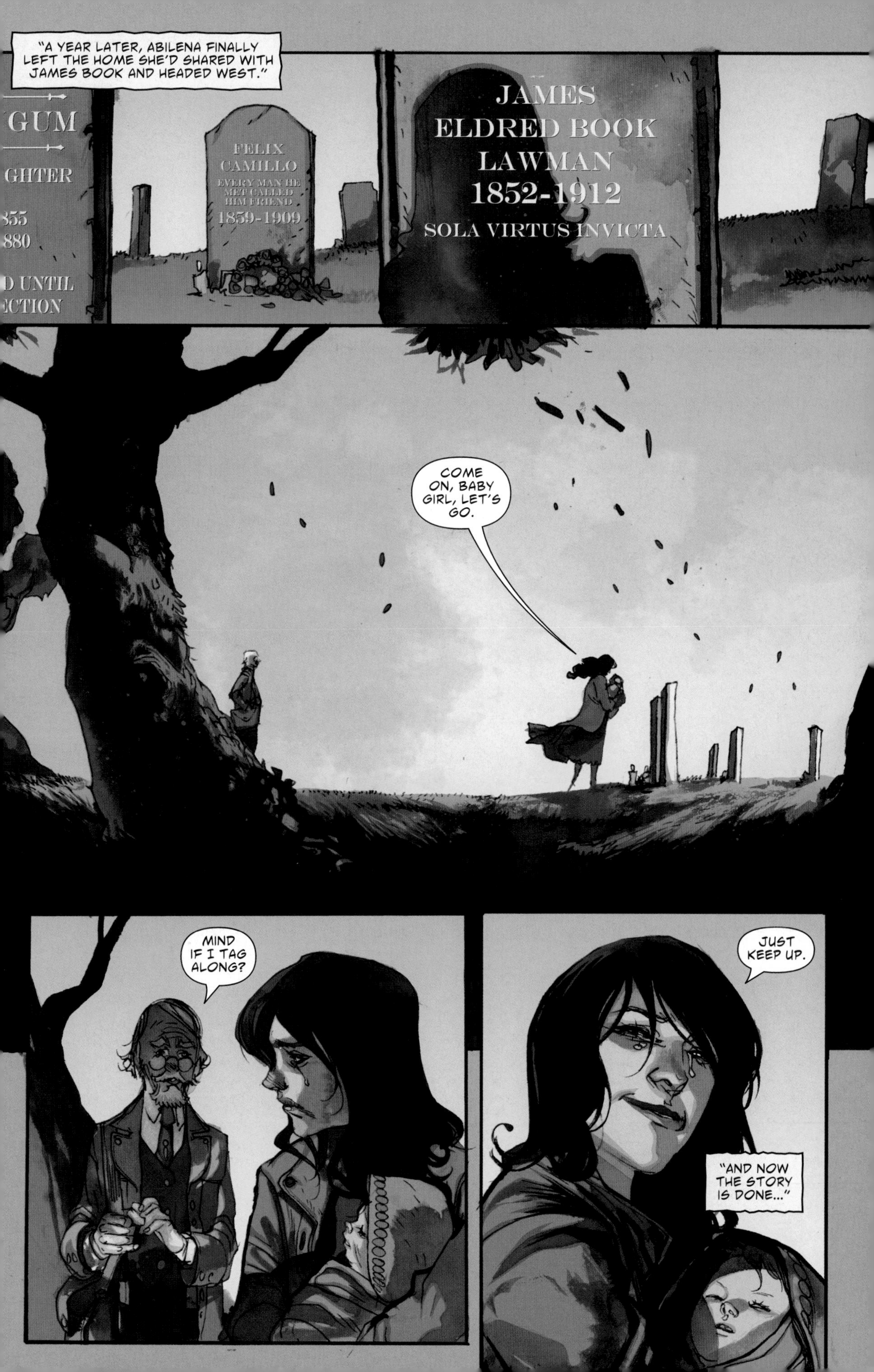
"A YEAR LATER, ABILENA FINALLY LEFT THE HOME SHE'D SHARED WITH JAMES BOOK AND HEADED WEST."
GUM
GHTER
355
880
D UNTIL
ECTION
FELIX CAMILLO
EVERY MAN HE MET CALLED HIM FRIEND
1859-1909
JAMES ELDRED BOOK
LAWMAN
1852-1912
SOLA VIRTUS INVICTA
COME ON, BABY GIRL, LET'S GO.
MIND IF I TAG ALONG?
JUST KEEP UP.
"AND NOW THE STORY IS DONE..."

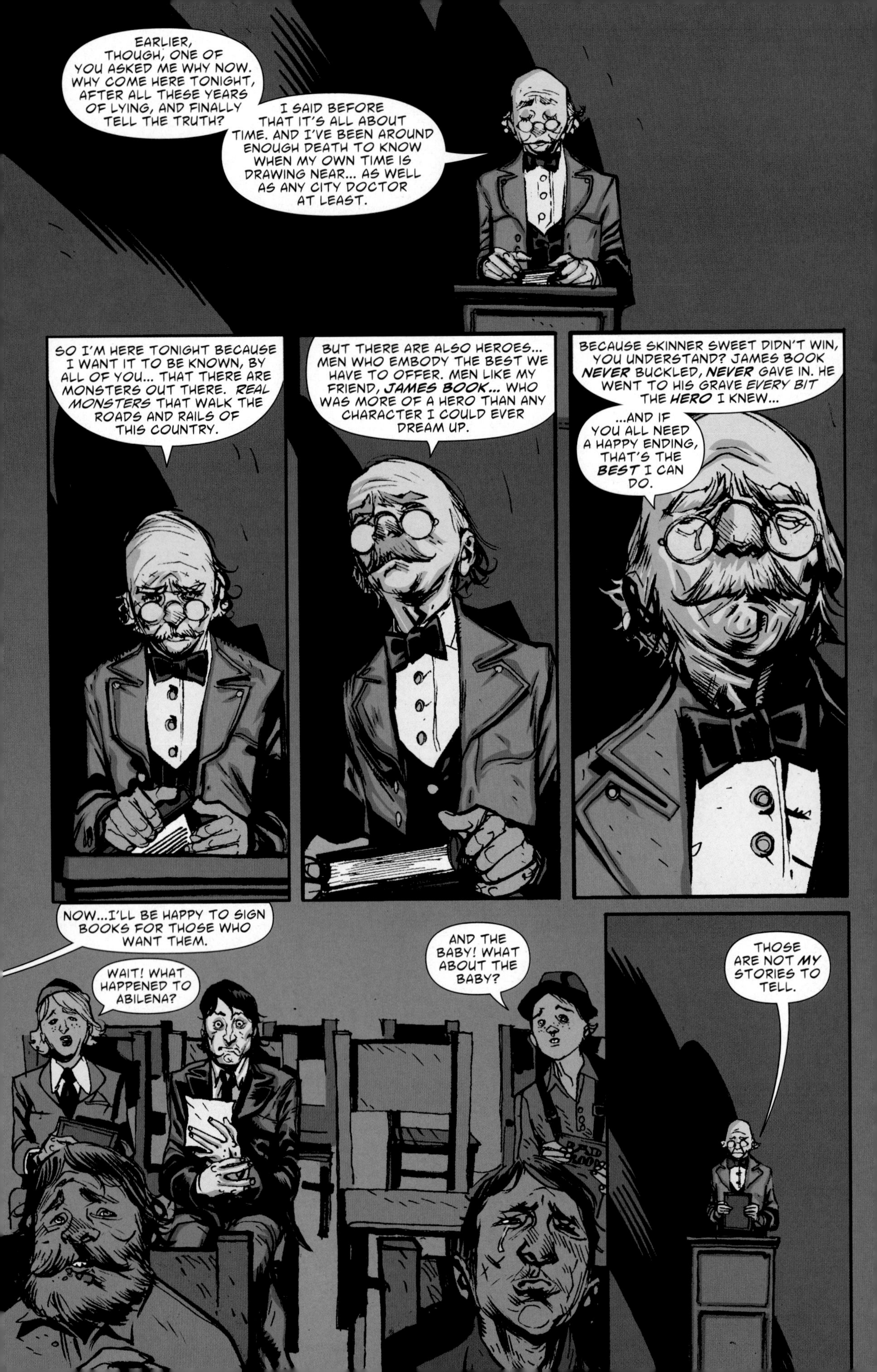
EARLIER, THOUGH, ONE OF YOU ASKED ME WHY NOW. WHY COME HERE TONIGHT, AFTER ALL THESE YEARS OF LYING, AND FINALLY TELL THE TRUTH?
I SAID BEFORE THAT IT'S ALL ABOUT TIME. AND I'VE BEEN AROUND ENOUGH DEATH TO KNOW WHEN MY OWN TIME IS DRAWING NEAR... AS WELL AS ANY CITY DOCTOR AT LEAST.
SO I'M HERE TONIGHT BECAUSE I WANT IT TO BE KNOWN, BY ALL OF YOU... THAT THERE ARE MONSTERS OUT THERE. *REAL MONSTERS* THAT WALK THE ROADS AND RAILS OF THIS COUNTRY.
BUT THERE ARE ALSO HEROES... MEN WHO EMBODY THE BEST WE HAVE TO OFFER. MEN LIKE MY FRIEND, ***JAMES BOOK...*** WHO WAS MORE OF A HERO THAN ANY CHARACTER I COULD EVER DREAM UP.
BECAUSE SKINNER SWEET DIDN'T WIN, YOU UNDERSTAND? JAMES BOOK ***NEVER*** BUCKLED, ***NEVER*** GAVE IN. HE WENT TO HIS GRAVE *EVERY BIT* THE ***HERO*** I KNEW...
...AND IF YOU ALL NEED A HAPPY ENDING, THAT'S THE ***BEST*** I CAN DO.
NOW...I'LL BE HAPPY TO SIGN BOOKS FOR THOSE WHO WANT THEM.
WAIT! WHAT HAPPENED TO ABILENA?
AND THE BABY! WHAT ABOUT THE BABY?
THOSE ARE NOT ***MY*** STORIES TO TELL.

END.

KING/ALBUQUERQUE

AFTERWORD
by Scott Snyder

On January 19th of this year, I got an email from Rafael Albuquerque that made me pause. The email had a page attached, but this was nothing new — we were neck-deep in issue two just then and Rafa had been mailing pages fast and furious all month. What made me hesitate was the subject line on the email:

"He's free!"

I didn't need to check the attachment to know what page had arrived. This would be page thirty-one, a splash that Rafa had been building toward for days: the splash page that shows Skinner busting out of that water-logged coffin, grinning in the watery darkness while that unfortunate diver recoils in terror. Skinner, unleashed, free and hungry and headed for the surface.

And so, yes, I'll admit I hesitated a minute before opening the page. More than anything I felt excited — I knew Rafa's page (like all his pages) would be better than anything I could have imagined. And even more than this, I was excited to see Skinner reborn as an American Vampire, to meet him all over again.

But part of me was afraid, too — afraid to open that page and see Skinner and look him straight in his yellow eyes.

Because the fact of the matter is that I'd come up with the idea for Skinner Sweet — this vampire outlaw with a new set of powers and weaknesses — a long time ago. Not just a year or two earlier, but several years. When I look through my notebooks from 2003, even 2002, I can find mentions of him: sketches, and dark, fun details. Most of the time, I'm good about putting pen to paper when I have an idea. I'm not a writer who lets an idea sit for a long time. When an idea excites me, I might spend a few weeks figuring it through a bit before diving in, but I'm talking a matter of weeks, not months, and certainly not years…

So yes, I felt a little afraid to face Skinner that day. Because I was the one who'd kept him locked up for so long. Sure, Book and Felix and the gang (and vampire Percy) might have laid him low, but if anyone was responsible for keeping him down there, in the dark murk where unrealized ideas live, it was me.

So why had I done it? Why hadn't I raised him from his watery grave earlier?

The honest-to-Elvis truth is that I tried. I thought of working up Skinner's story as a screenplay, and later as a novel. But nothing made sense… because his story was simply too big, too sprawling. And so Skinner stayed down there, waiting, waiting… Until one day in the late summer of 2008, after doing a few one-shots, I got the chance to pitch original project ideas to Mark Doyle at Vertigo… And when that happened, I could practically hear Skinner knocking around in his coffin, getting ready for the lid to open… Because I knew, sitting across from Mark in that pizzeria, that I finally had my venue: Skinner's was a story that could ONLY be a comic.

But I couldn't do it alone. Unleashing Skinner upon the world has been wholly a team effort — and so a huge thanks goes to my very own gang of monster outlaws: Rafael, Mark, and Steve. Mark, who believed in the series from day one. Rafael… what else is there to say about Rafa, except that he's the artist I've always dreamed of working with? He's brilliant, ferocious, and wholly invested in the series. The amazing Dave McCaig, who gives Rafa's art such striking color. Steve Wands, our great letterer. Will Dennis, the best "guy behind the guy" in comics. And our gang's wonderfully supportive and twisted den-mother, Karen Berger, who's encouraged us to do our best (and subsequently our worst) with these characters…

And Steve King… Right now, Steve's introduction to this edition is sitting on my desk. I haven't read it yet (would you read Stephen King's intro if you had to write the afterword?), but one thing I'm sure of is that it will be way, way too modest. Because the truth is that before Steve, Skinner was an idea in my head, a sketch, some notes on a pad; Steve is the one who brought him to vibrant, murderous life on the page. He's given so much to the character of Skinner — charisma and viciousness, a secret personal history. But he's also added a tremendous amount to Pearl's story, to the stories of characters to come, to the whole American Vampire mythology. This series — not just this cycle, but the whole series — is exponentially better for his involvement. So big thanks to Uncle Stevie for TCB.

Of course, I did eventually open page thirty-one. And yes, Skinner's cold, bright eyes did give me a bit of a chill. But I'm hoping there was at least a tiny flash of gratitude there, too. Because by waiting for the chance to do his story as a comic series — a series with Vertigo no less — I feel we've all done right by him.

Because while his is the story of the first American Vampire, it's a story about us, about Americans, about what makes us scary and admirable, monstrous and heroic. It's a giant story, bigger than just Skinner Sweet (sorry, Skinner), and the truth is that we're just getting warmed up. Next cycle we're off to Las Vegas of the 1930s. Then it's on to the turmoil of the 1940s and the great war… We'll explore the origins, too; we'll trace the history of human-vampire relations, as well as the history of vampire evolution itself; we'll discover new species, ancient and modern; learn about vicious interspecies conflict…

The bottom line is that this is the story I've always wanted to tell. And this is how it needs to be told.

So, as Skinner says: Off we go...

Scott Snyder
May, 2010

Issue # 1 Variant by Jim Lee

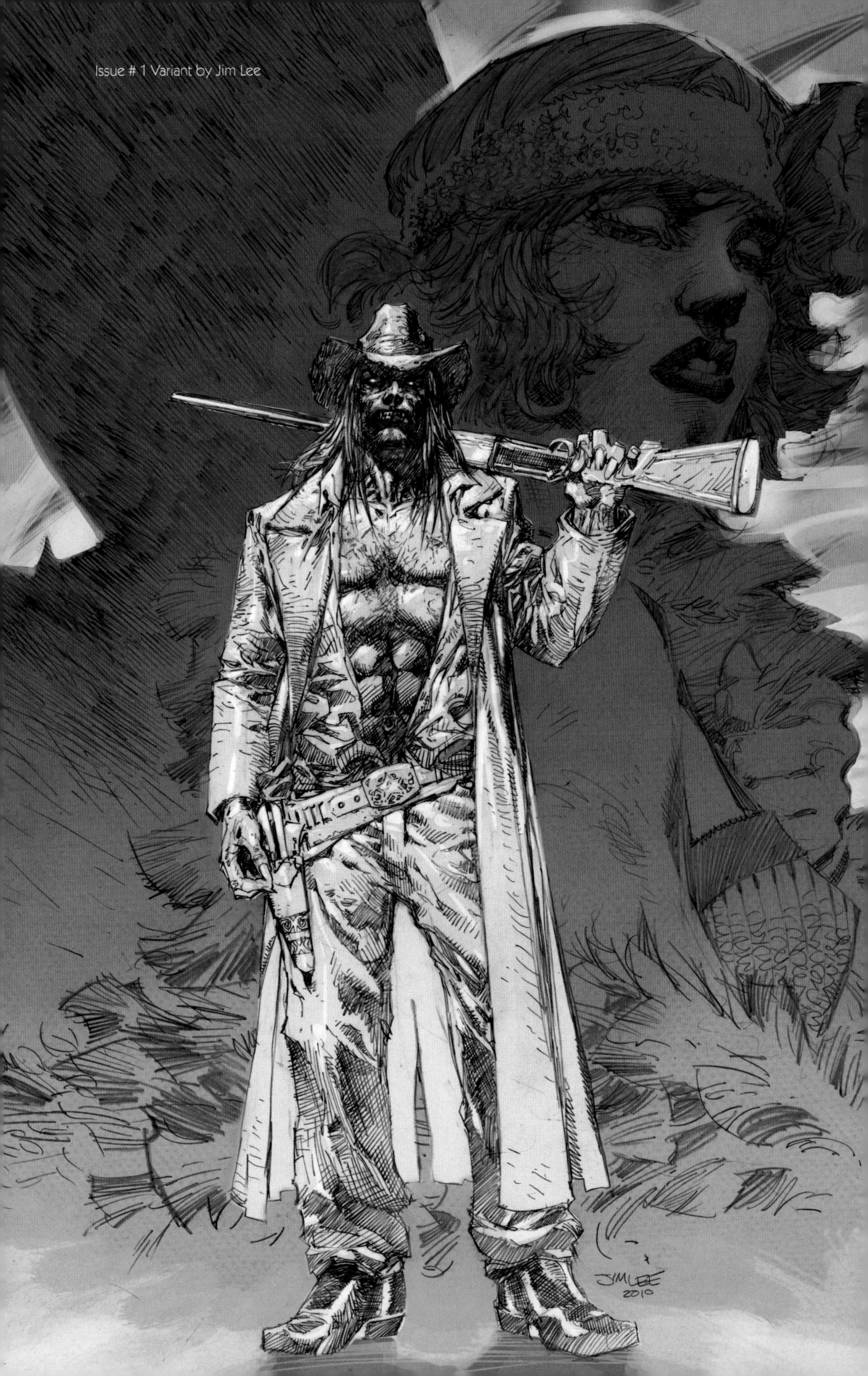

Issue # 2 Variant by Bernie Wrightson
Color by Dave McCaig

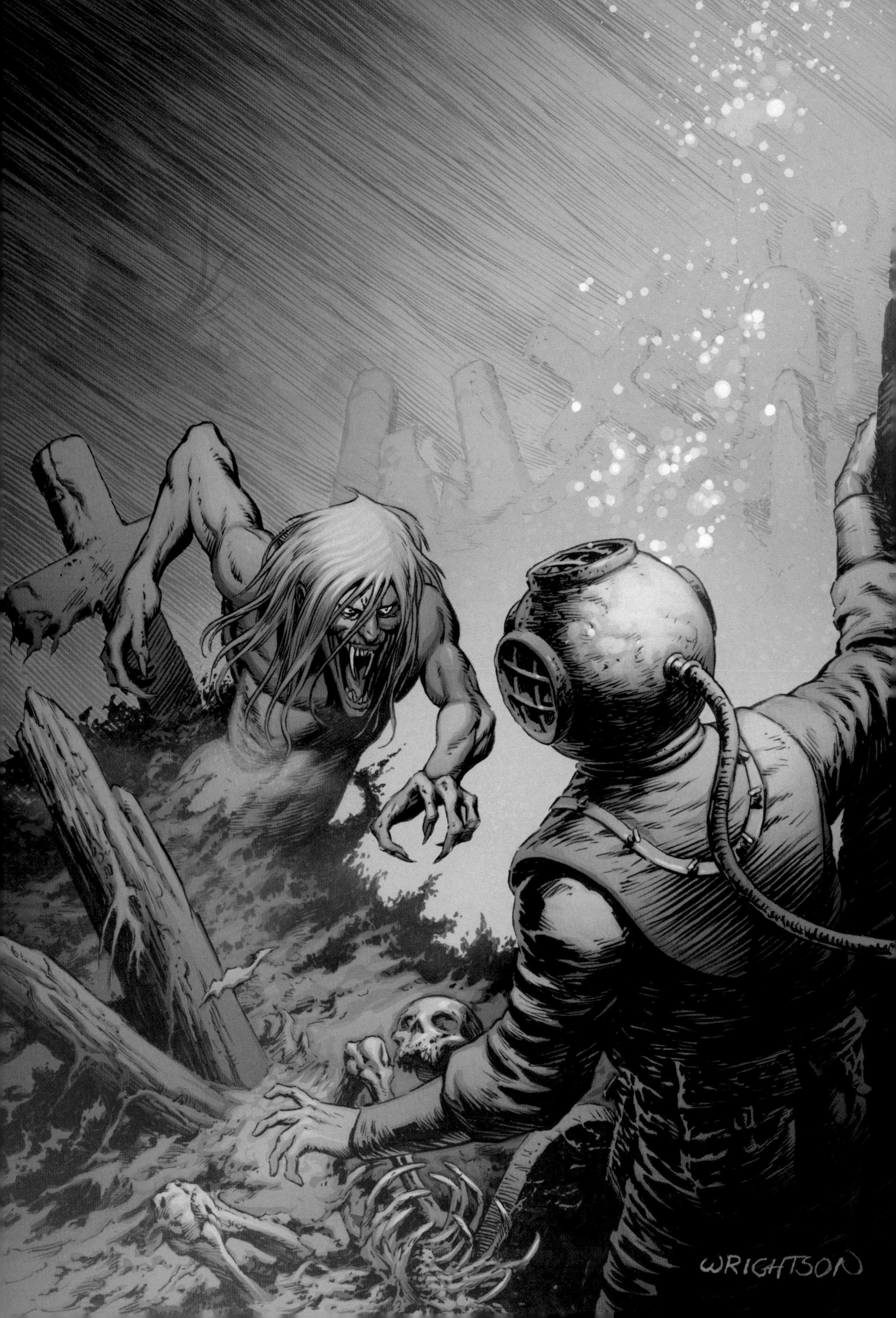
WRIGHTSON

Issue # 4 Variant by JH Williams III

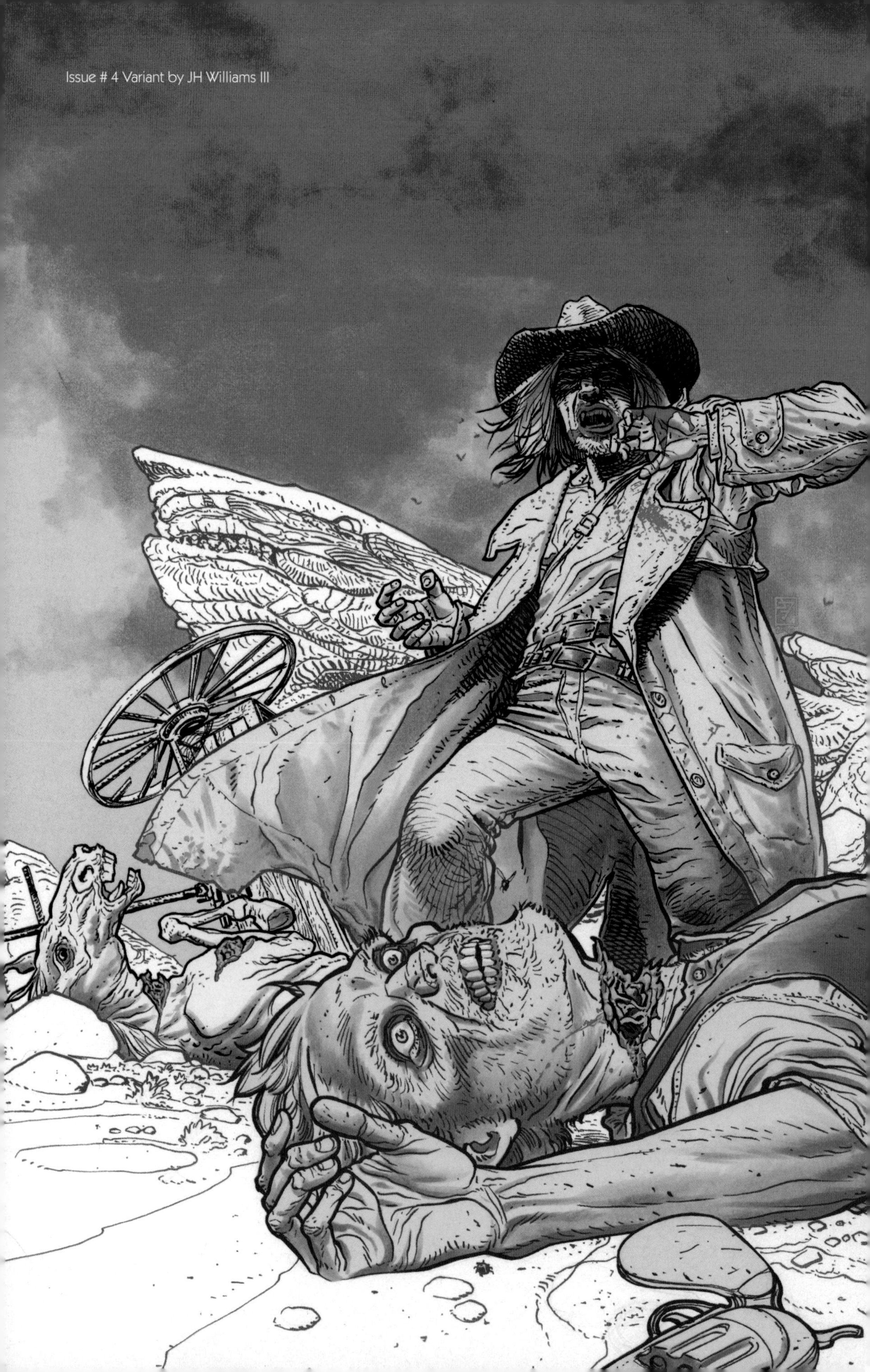

Issue # 5 Variant by Paul Pope
Color by José Villarrubia

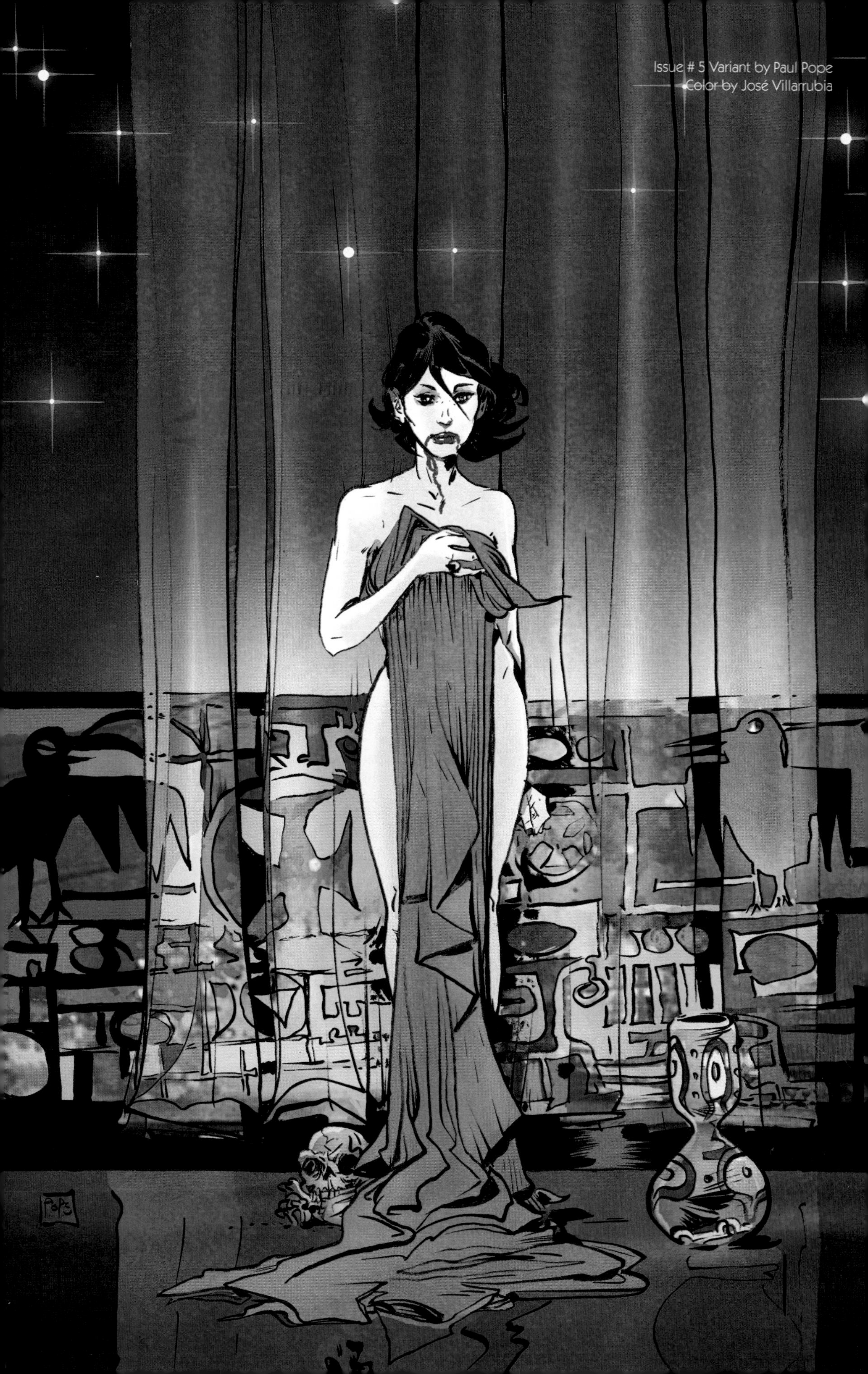

AMERICAN VAMPIRE #1, page 12
By Scott Snyder

PAGE 12:

12.1
Pearl, gathering herself. Skinner, sinking deeper into the chair.

PEARL: [to herself] God, why are the jerks always the cute ones?

PEARL: [to Skinner] Look. Just, don't be here tomorrow. Or I really will call someone.

SKINNER: The sheriff?

12.2
Skinner laughing.

PEARL: The sheriff, exactly. And she'll run you out of town before you know what hit you.

SKINNER: She'll run me out of town, ha ha! You know what? I like you, girlie. You got spunk. So I'll let you in on a little secret...

12.3
Skinner, pretending to whisper.

SKINNER: B.D. Bloch's parties? They ain't any fun at all. No, if I were you, I'd pass on his little jamboree tonight.

PEARL: Wow. And you eavesdrop, too... So I take it you and "B.D." are good friends?

12.4

SKINNER: More like old acquaintances. Actually, I'm just in town to finish a bit of business with the old coot.

SKINNER: And believe me, honey, his get-togethers — bunch of cheese-sniffing Eu-ro-peans drinking with their pinkies out. Why don't you stay here? I'll show you a real party.

12.5

PEARL: Thanks, but I happen to like drinking with my pinkie out.

Hattie appears behind her, surprised and smitten.

HATTIE: Okay, I'm ready to—Ooh. Hi.

12.6
Pearl pulling Hattie away.

PEARL: [to Skinner] Remember what I said about tomorrow.

SKINNER: Suit yourself....

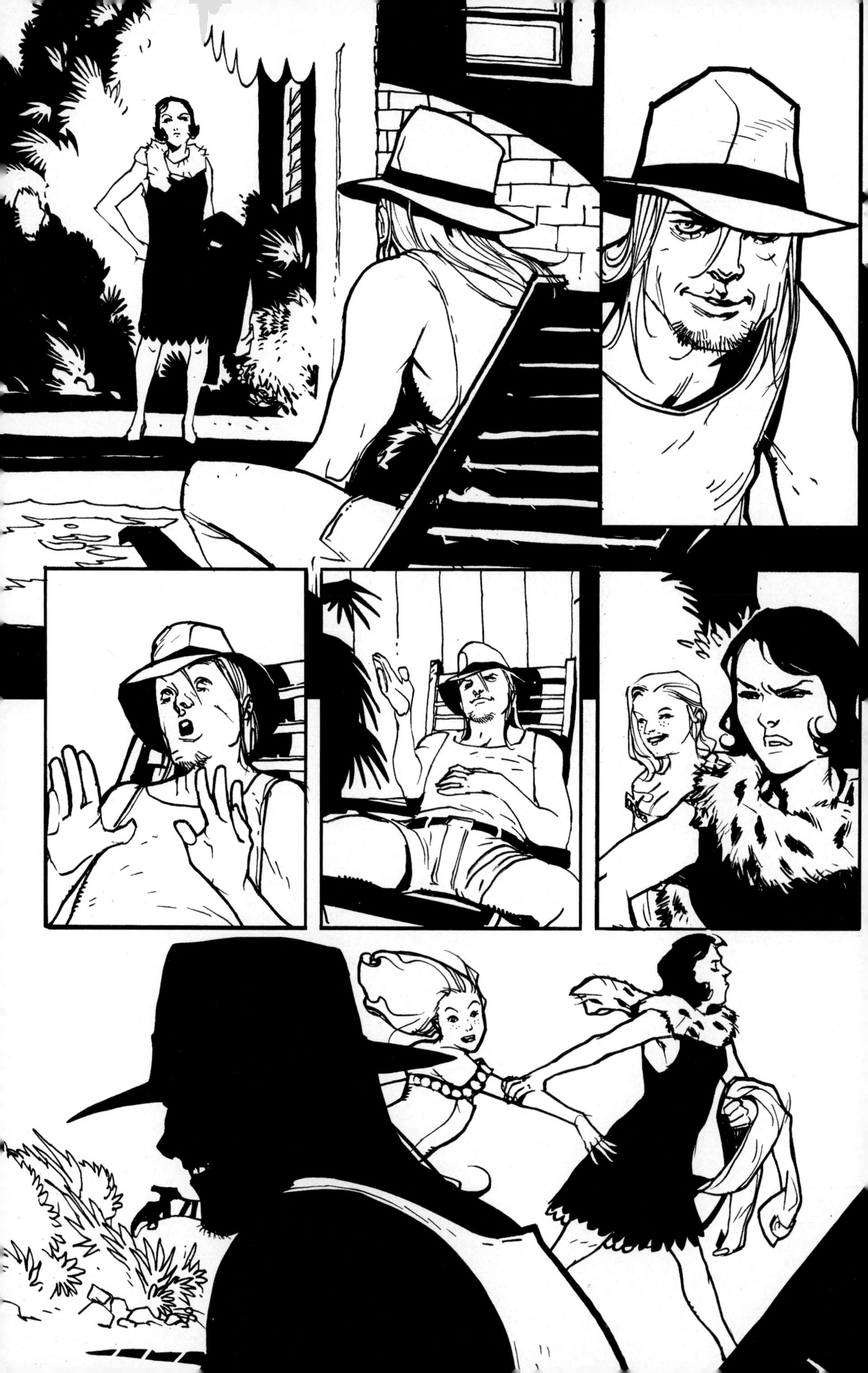

American Vampire #4, page 5
By Scott Snyder

PAGE 5:

5.1
And now Bloch's viciousness is apparent, his grinning, cruel, vampire face — hundreds of years of evil in his eyes.

BLOCH: And stab you with every god damned thing under the sun until we find what hurts you most.

5.2
Pearl, holding Hattie.

PEARL: Run, Hat...

5.3
To Hattie.

BLOCH: Ms. Hargrove, you wanted an audition?

5.4
Pearl, looking over her shoulder at Hattie.

PEARL: Hat? What is he —

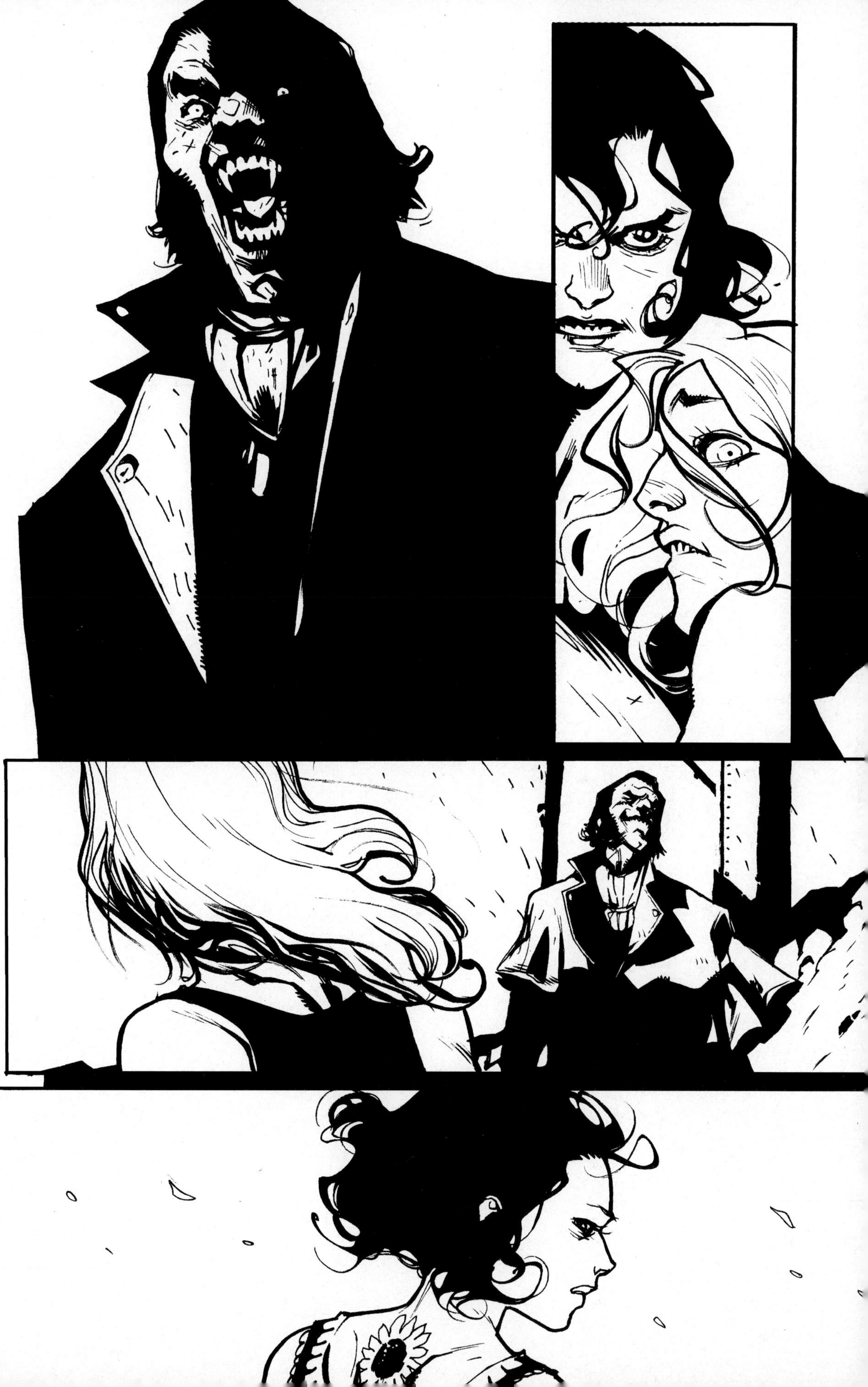

American Vampire #3 page 27
By Stephen King

PAGE TWENTY-SEVEN

Panel One

SKINNER (continues): . . . inside yonder warehouse.

This is a big panel. Behind SKINNER, the warehouse explodes in a gout of yellow-red flame. Bursts of wooden shrapnel rain down on the warehouse's side of the street. The roof, split into three or four large pieces, is lifting off like a bunch of 4th of July rockets. Townspeople flee from the explosion, screaming.

In the FG, the combined posse is shooting at SKINNER, giving him everything they've got, but SKINNER is unaffected. He pops a wooden match alight with a filthy fingernail.

[The following three panels are in a line across the bottom of the page, below the big panel.]

Panel Two

SKINNER [lighting his cigarillo]: Why, if it ain't Book's old boss. And I do mean old! Where is he, boss-man?

Panel Three

CU on FINCH, and he's scared to death.

FINCH: If I tell you, will you let me go?

Panel Four

SKINNER is holding a bundle of dynamite. He's got the burning tip of his cigarillo less than an inch from the fuse.

SKINNER: You bet, partner. C'mere. Let's palaver. Do I look dangerous?

(You bet he does.)

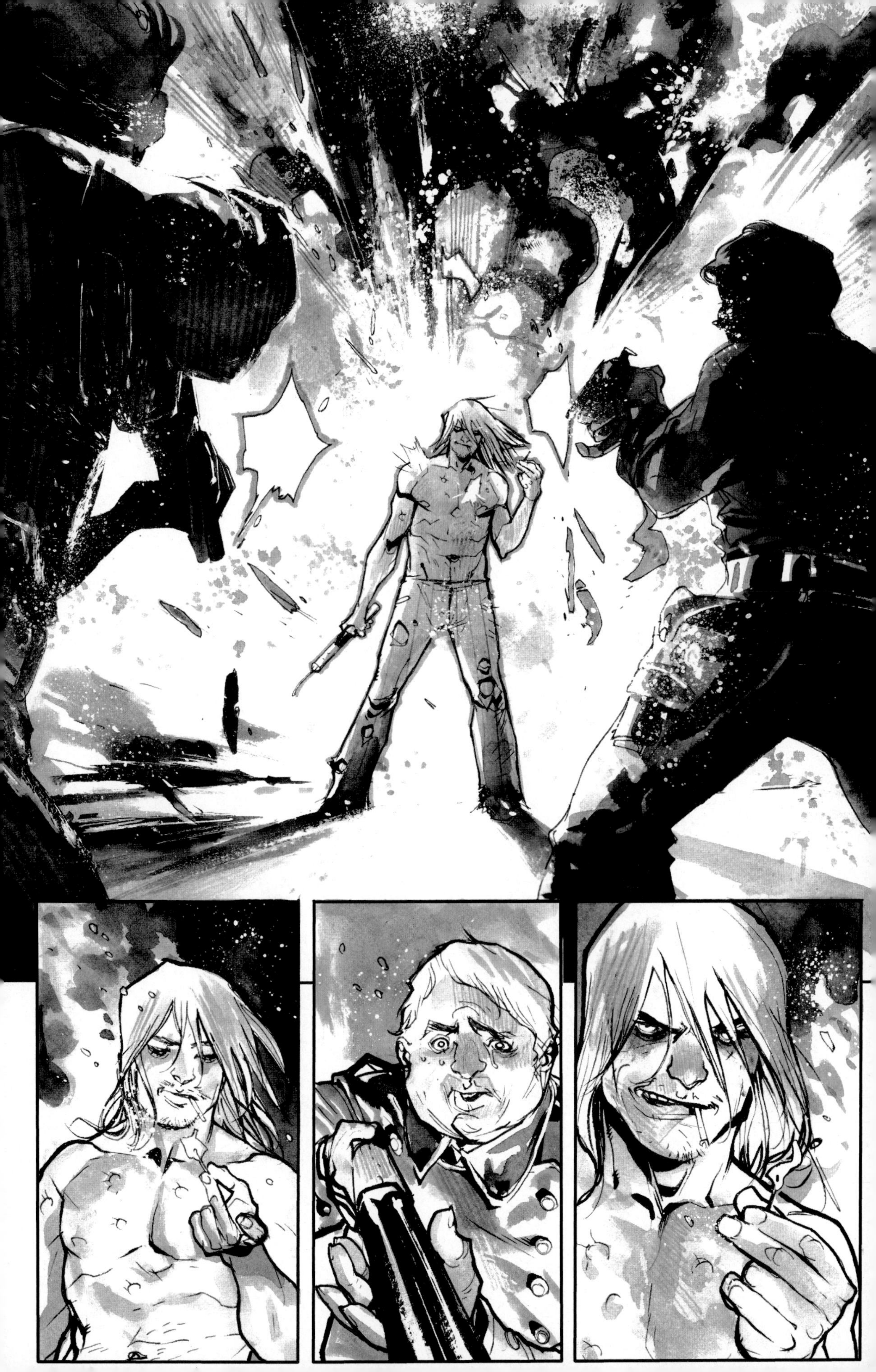

American Vampire #5, page 28

By Stephen King

Panel One

CLOSE on Will – We're back in SAGEBRUSH PAGES. OLD WILL'S head is lowered. He's lost in the past.

WILL: Does it matter how long they were together that night? To lovers, an hour can last a century. But even for lovers, every hour ends.

Panel Two

His audience is lost in his story (some may be in tears). Except…the FUSSY ACADEMIC looks dazed…hypnotized. And the seat next to him is empty. SKINNER'S gone.

VOICE-OVER BOX AT BOTTOM (BOOK): "Abi…I kept my end of the bargain. Now you keep yours."

Panel Three

BOOK'S bedroom. BOOK is holding the straight-razor. ABI (wearing a white shift) is looking at it with horror.

ABI: I…can't…with that.

Panel Four

BOOK (folds the razor shut): At the dark of the moon, I think it can be anything lethal. I was your godfather. I was your lover. Now be my friend.

Panel Five

Tears rolling down her cheeks, she reaches for the holstered .44 on the dresser. BOOK is lying back on his pillow, eyes shut.

BOOK: For the first time in three years, I feel like I can sleep.

Panel Six

The exterior of BOOK'S house, under all those amazing stars. From the window:

SFX: BLAMM!

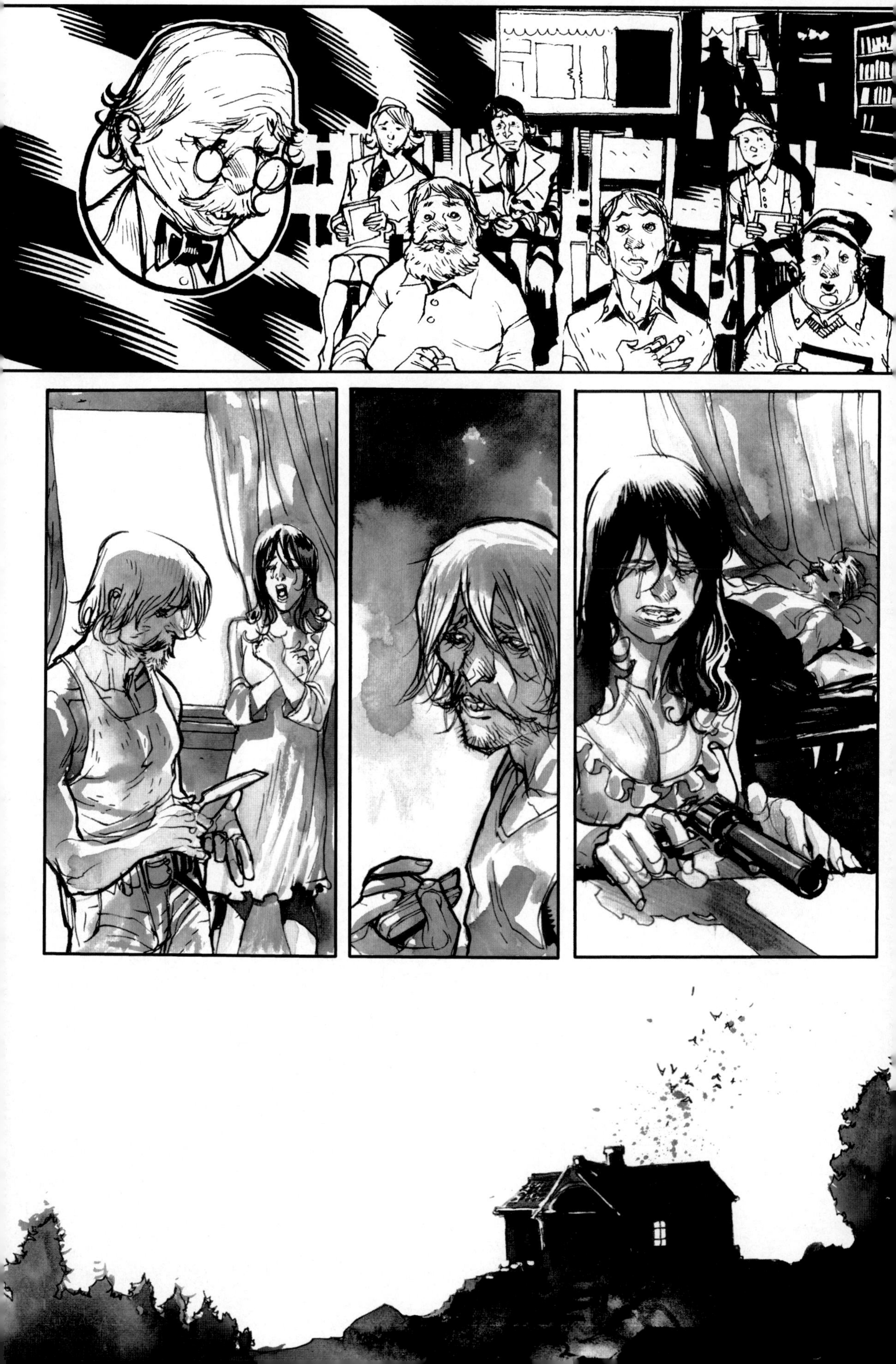

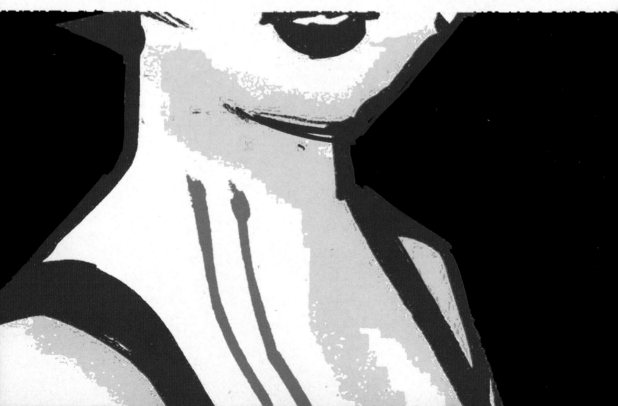

AMERICAN VAMPIRE

SCOTT SNYDER RAFAEL ALBUQUERQUE
AND STEPHEN KING

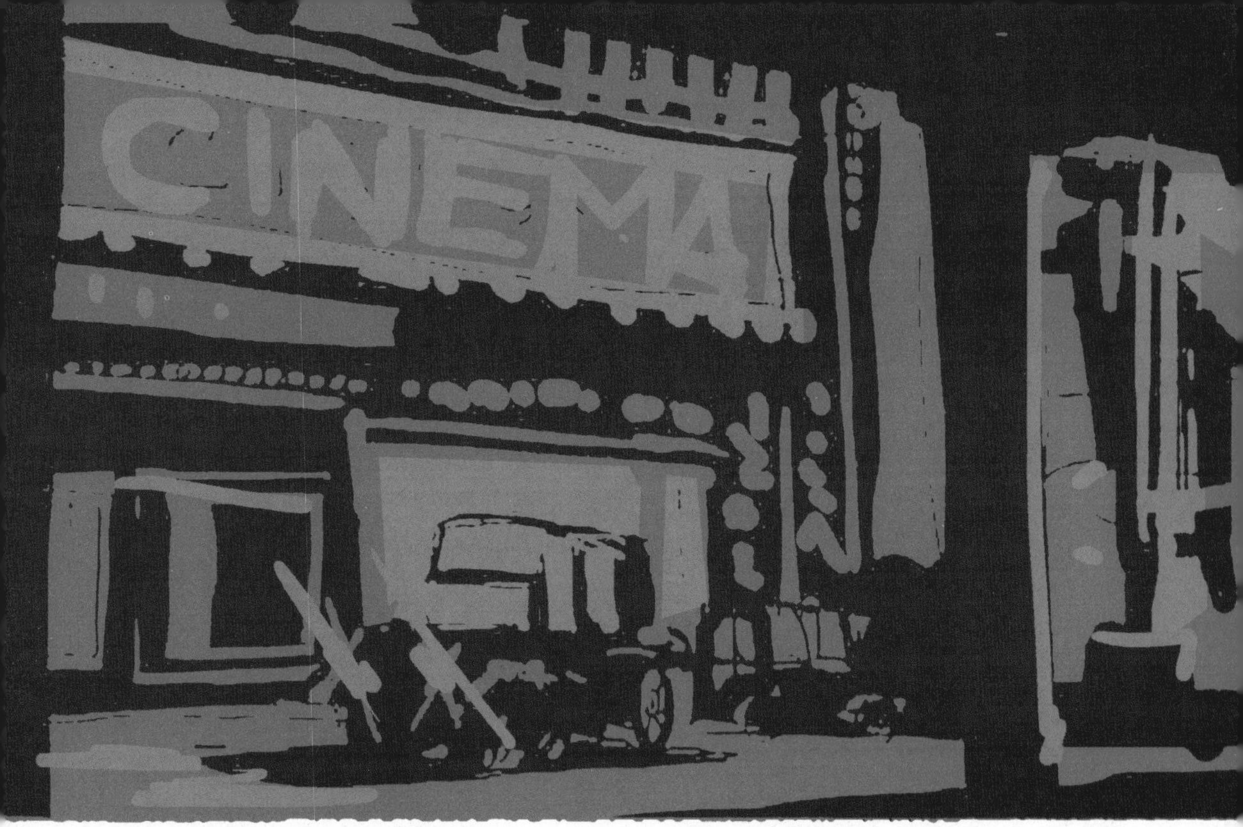
CINEMA

AMERICAN VAMPIRE

SCOTT SNYDER RAFAEL ALBUQUERQUE
AND STEPHEN KING

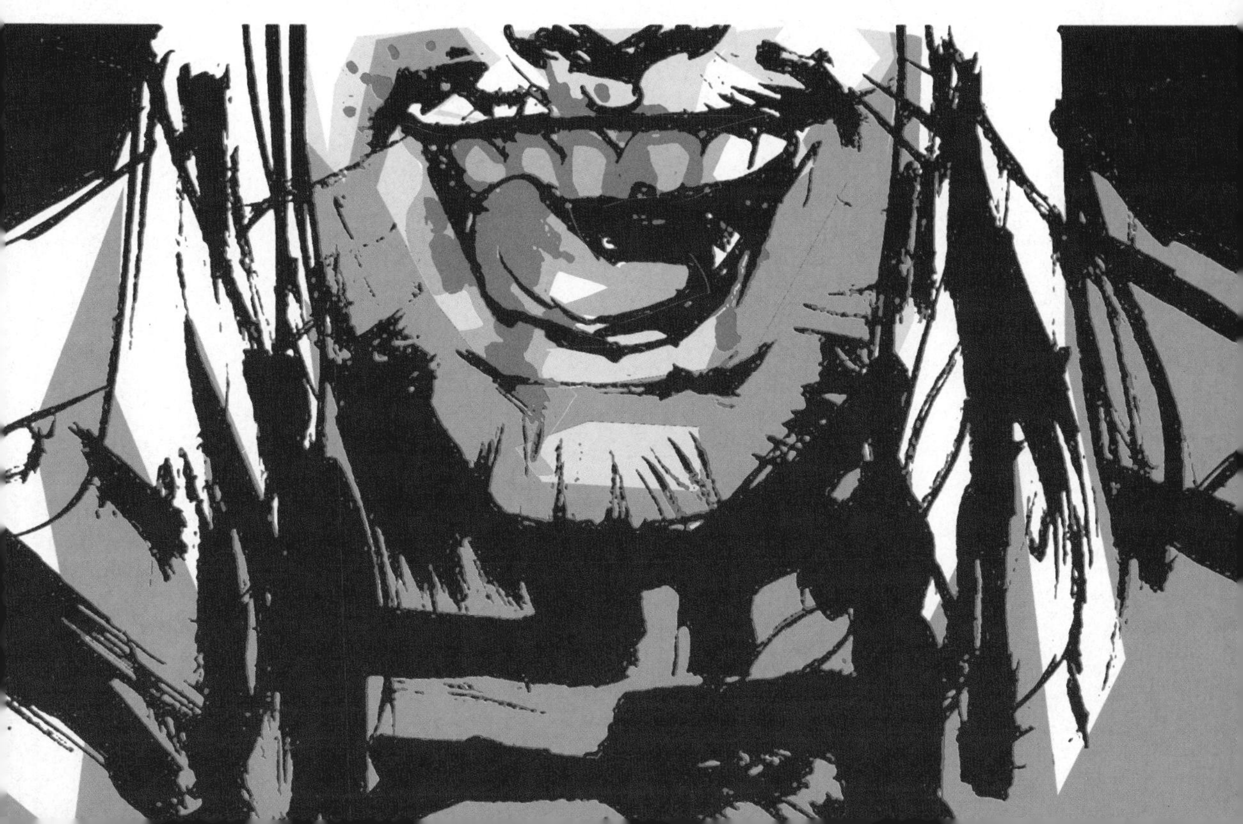

Original sketch of Skinner Sweet
1880s and 1920s version

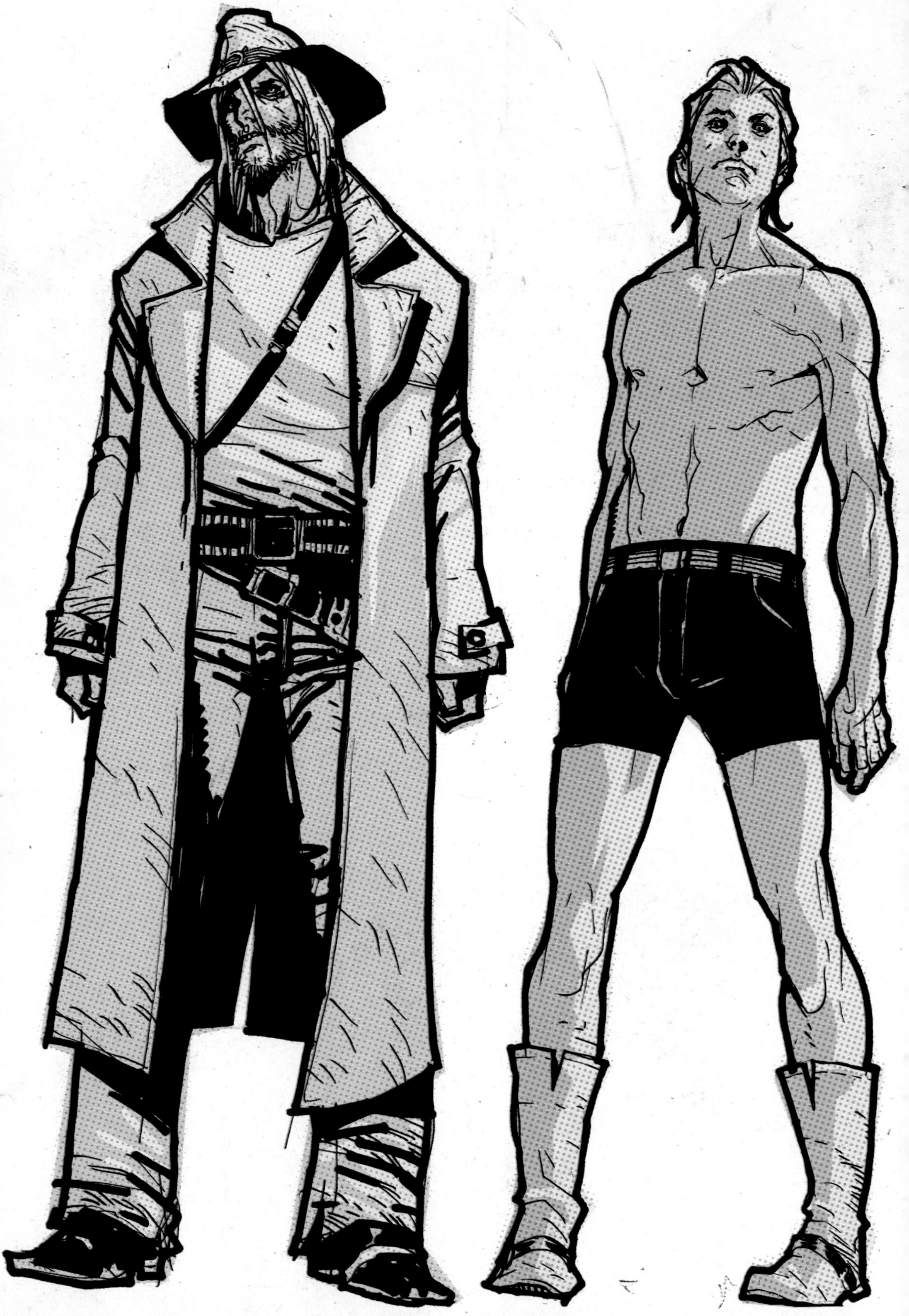

Conceptual Sketches of Skinner Sweet

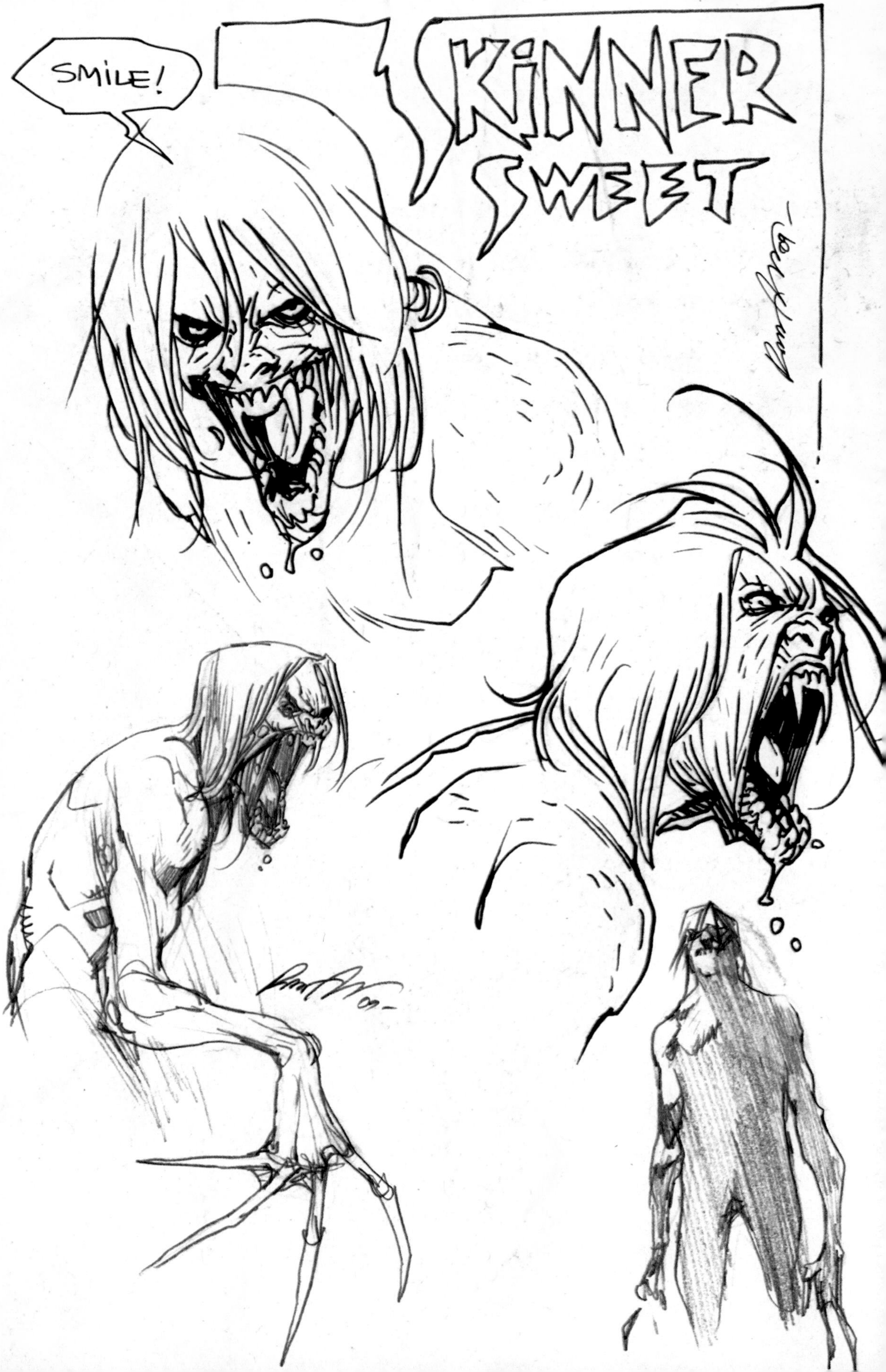
SMILE!
SKINNER SWEET

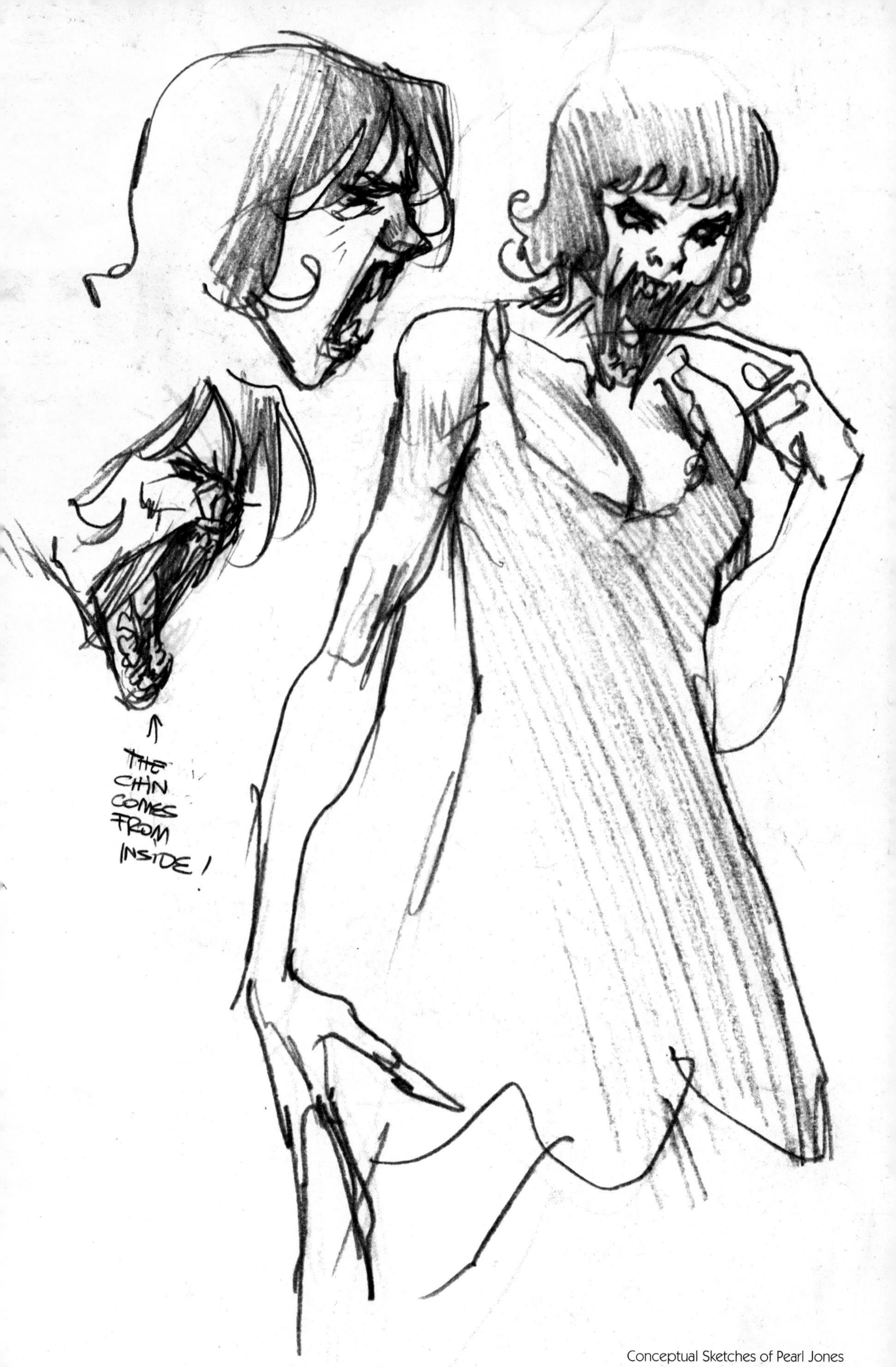
THE CHIN COMES FROM INSIDE!

Conceptual Sketches of Pearl Jones

Original sketch of James Book

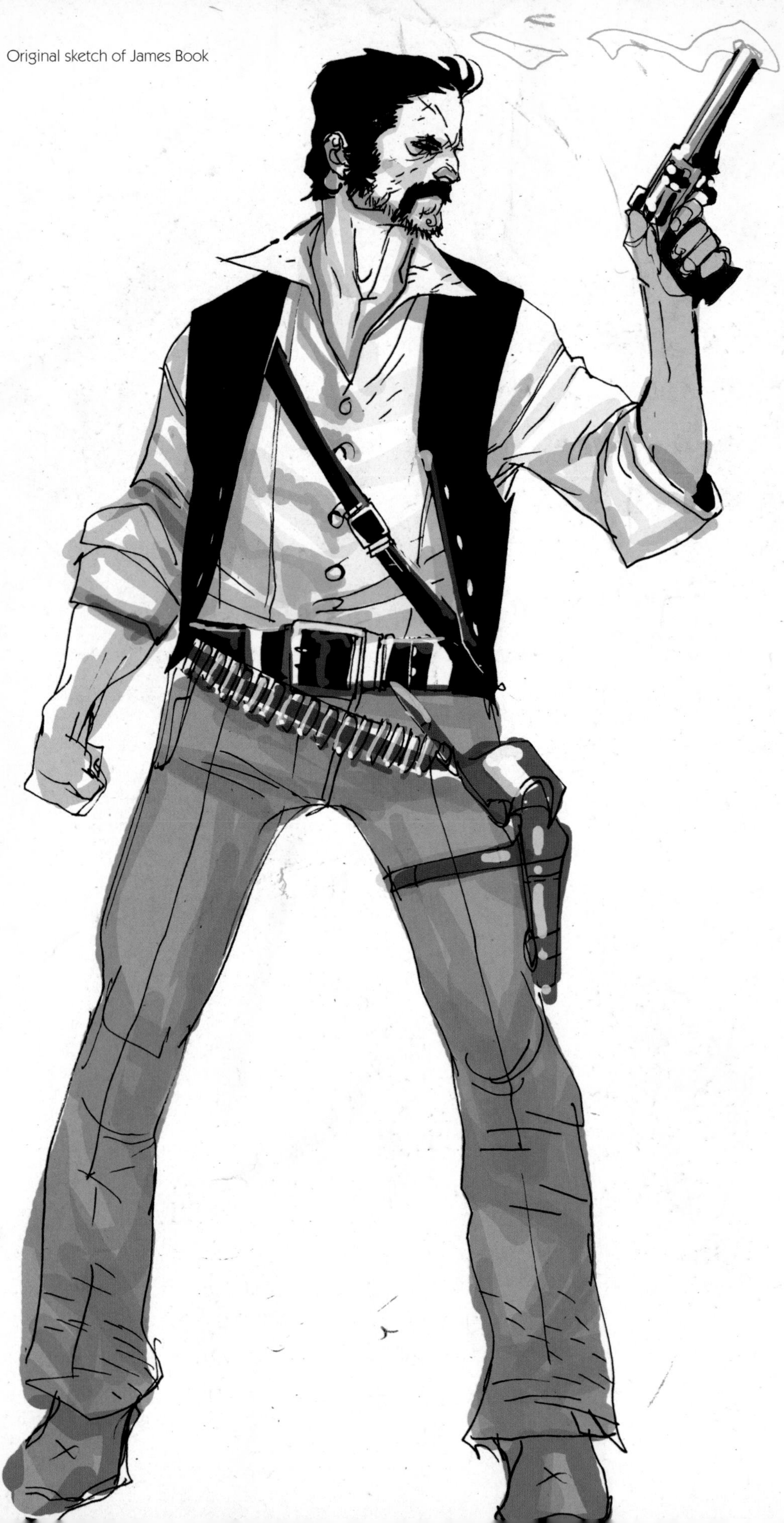

Original sketch of Henry Preston and Percy

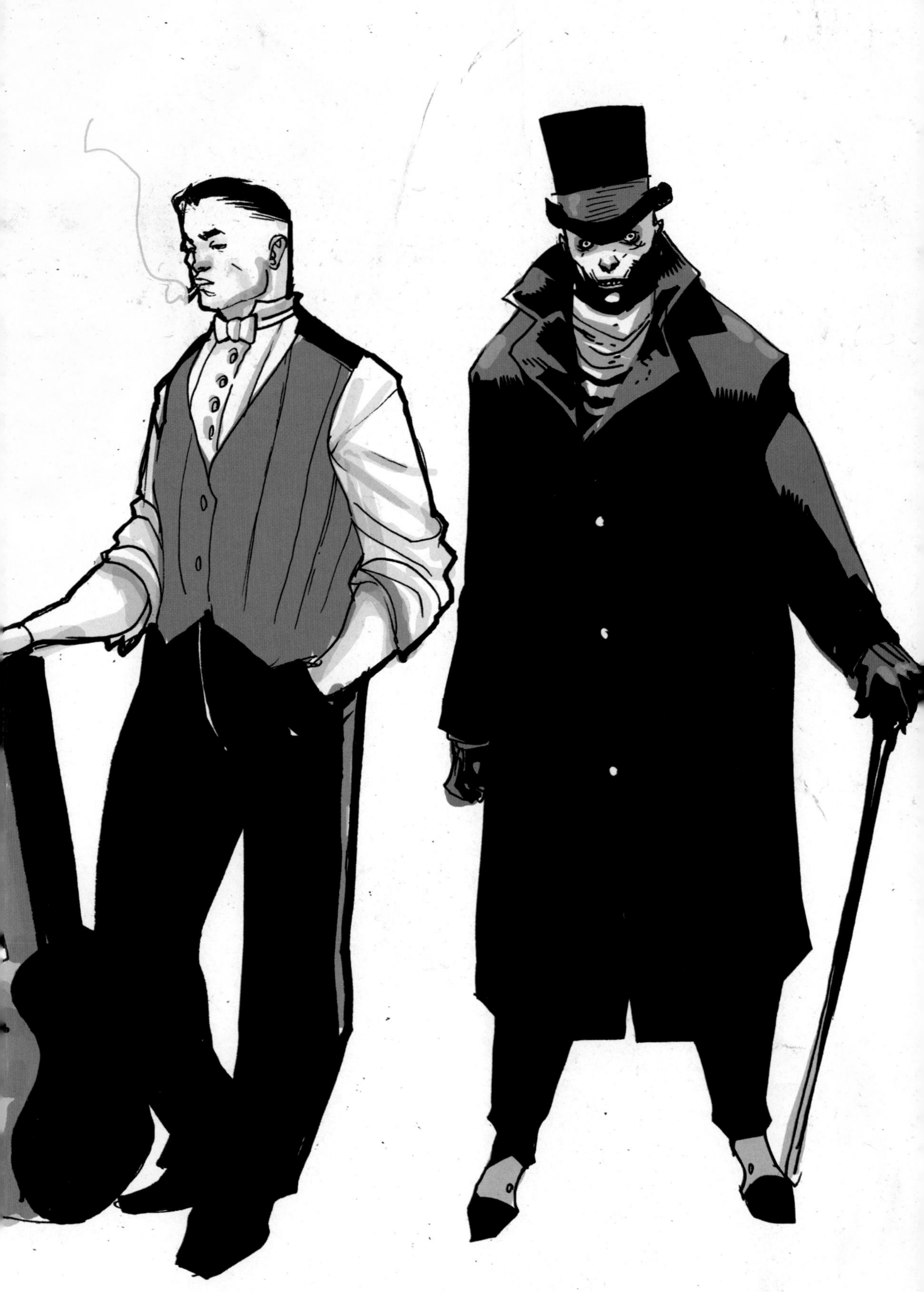

Scott Snyder's first collection of stories, *Voodoo Heart*, was published in 2006 by the Dial Press. He has written for both Marvel and DC, but AMERICAN VAMPIRE is his first creator-owned series. He lives on Long Island with his wife, Jeanie, his son, Jack Presley, and those chicken photos (originals and copies) in the event that Stephen ever acts up.

Rafael Albuquerque was born in Porto Alegre, Brazil. Rafael has been working in the American comic book industry since 2005. Best known for his work on the *Savage Brothers, Blue Beetle* and *Superman/Batman*, he has also worked on the creator-owned graphic novels *Crimeland* (2007) and *Mondo Urbano* (2010).

Stephen King lives in Maine with his wife, the novelist Tabitha King. He has written over 50 books. Although he has been adapted for comics before, AMERICAN VAMPIRE is the first time he's written one himself. He claims it's Scott Snyder's fault. Scott, he says, threatened to send pictures of Steve and the chickens to *The National Enquirer* if he didn't cooperate.